A Declaration of
Duties toward Humankind

A Declaration of
Duties toward Humankind

A Critical Companion to Simone Weil's
The Need for Roots

Edited by

Eric O. Springsted

Ronald K. L. Collins

CAROLINA ACADEMIC PRESS
Durham, North Carolina

LIBRARY OF CONGRESS CATALOGING-IN-PUBLICATION DATA

Names: Springsted, Eric O., editor. | Collins, Ronald K. L., editor.
Title: A declaration of duties toward humankind : a critical companion to Simone Weil's The Need for Roots / [edited by] Eric O. Springsted and Ronald K.L. Collins.
Description: Durham, North Carolina : Carolina Academic Press, LLC, [2023] | Includes bibliographical references and index.
Identifiers: LCCN 2023027758 | ISBN 9781531022020 (paperback) | ISBN 9781531022037 (ebook)
Subjects: LCSH: Weil, Simone, 1909-1943 | Philosophers--France--Biography. | Social ethics.
Classification: LCC B2430.W474 D435 2023 | DDC 194--dc23/eng/20230731
LC record available at https://lccn.loc.gov/2023027758

Carolina Academic Press
700 Kent Street
Durham, North Carolina 27701
(919) 489-7486
www.cap-press.com

Printed in the United States of America

In Memory of
Richard H. Bell
(1938–2016)

Contents

Chapter 9 · Work as the Spiritual Basis of Culture
SIMONE KOTVA · 245

The Critique of Working Conditions · 245
The Philosophy of Action · 251
A Changed System for the Concentration of Attention · 257
The Function of the Past · 262
Work as Daily Death · 267
Work and Obedience · 271

Appendix I · Study for a Declaration of Obligations towards
the Human Being · SIMONE WEIL · 275

Profession of Faith · 275
Statement of Obligations · 280
Practical Application · 282

Appendix II · The Legal and Moral Foundations of the
Resistance · ANDRÉ PHILIP · 285

Vichy · 286
The Spiritual Resistance · 286
The Sense of Risk · 288
Universal Values · 288
The Role of France · 289
A New Declaration of the Rights of Man · 290
Democracy · 291
The Present Situation · 293
The Function of the Free French · 293

Contributors · 297

Bibliography · 301

Index of Subjects · 311

Index of Names · 319

Preface

In a preface that was intended for, but never published with, *The Need for Roots*, Albert Camus spoke of that work as "a veritable treatise on civilization." Speaking of Simone Weil's mind, he added, "[s]he was biased against nothing, except cruelty and baseness, which are the same thing. She despised nothing except contempt itself, and reading her, one feels the one thing of which her surprising intelligence was incapable was frivolity."[1]

That says something important about *The Need for Roots*, something that is underlined by Weil's own title for the work: "A Declaration of Duties toward Humankind." She was writing about how a nation might be civilized; she was addressing herself to a deep spiritual concern of her time, and, as it turns out, ours as well. So, appropriately, Simone Weil's *The Need for Roots* has long been recognized as one of her most significant and important works. Yet, despite that recognition, and an admiring suspicion of many of her readers that it is one of the most significant and important works of our time for thinking about our communities, there has not been a lot of critical commentary on that work. It has received a great deal of notice, to be sure. But that notice has not been comprehensive with regard to the work as a whole. Much of the secondary literature has been rather piecemeal. Nor have a lot of connections been drawn between it and the numerous essays she wrote in London at the same time. And, finally, the context and her large aims in writing the work have been underplayed, and left in rather general terms, even to the point of treating it as if it were meant to be a blueprint, pretty much unasked for, for how France should reorganize itself after World War II.

---

1. *Quoted* in Desmond Avery, *Beyond Power: Simone Weil and the Notion of Authority*, (Lanham, MD: Lexington Books, 2008) 102, *citing* Albert Camus, *Essais* (Paris: Gallimard, Bibliothèque de la Pleiade, 1993), 1700–1702.

Largely due to the appearance of critical editions of *L'Enracinement* in the *Œuvres complètes* and in a second, competing critical edition, as well as the publication of her other London essays in the *Œuvres complètes*, much of that has changed. The context is clearer and the connections to the rest of her writings are more apparent. As such, we are in a much better position to appreciate the work in itself, and thus with respect to its continuing relevance.

The present volume is a critical commentary on *The Need for Roots*. Its chapters are taken from the outline of the book itself, with an eye on the topics of discussion that it has engendered since its first publication in 1948. We have been fortunate in having been able to put together a team of recognized, international Weil scholars. The group was not able to meet in person, largely due to the pandemic that continued through the time of its preparation. But we were able to discuss together drafts of all the chapters by electronic means, and everybody was able to make her or himself well acquainted with the work of the other authors. We have not aimed at a single viewpoint, even were such a thing possible. Each author speaks for him or herself, and each brings a distinctive point of view. But each chapter is very much enriched by the perspective of all the other contributors. This says something about the richness of Weil's thinking as it spawns so many interpretive possibilities. We thus hope we have served a valuable function of giving readers of *The Need for Roots* a new and deeper appreciation of Weil's work—and of the issues she sought to raise for our time.

We have used Arthur Wills' translation that appeared in 1952. The preparation of this critical commentary went on at the same time as a new translation was being prepared by Roz Schwartz, with a scholarly introduction by Professor Kate Kirkpatrick. Regrettably, this timing has meant that we were not able to consult or use the newer translation. Nonetheless, the reader should without a lot of difficulty be able to determine the locations of citations in the new translation.

Abbreviations for the
Works of Simone Weil

APP   *On the Abolition of All Political Parties*, trans. Simon Leys (New York: New York Review Books, 2013).

ENR   *L'Enracinement ou Prélude á* une *declaration des devoirs envers l'être humain*, ed. Florence de Lussy and Michel Narcy (Paris: Champs Classiques, 2014).

FLN   *First and Last Notebooks*, ed. and trans. Richard Rees (London: Oxford University Press, 1970; Eugene, OR: Wipf & Stock, 2015).

FW   *Formative Writings 1929–1941*, ed. and trans. Dorothy Tuck McFarland and Wilhelmina Van Ness (Amherst: University of Massachusetts Press, 1987).

GTG   *Gateway to God*, ed. David Raper (Glasgow: William Collins Sons, 1974; New York: Crossroad, 1982).

GG   *Gravity and Grace*, trans. Emma Craufurd (London: Routledge and Kegan Paul, 1952; additional chapter on "Israel" trans. Mario von der Ruhr, 2002).

I   *Simone Weil's The Iliad or the Poem of Force. A Critical Edition*, ed. and trans. James P. Holoka, (New York: Peter Lang, 2003).

IC   *Intimations of Christianity among the Ancient Greeks*, ed. and trans. Elisabeth Chase Geissbuhler (London: Routledge & Kegan Paul, 1957).

LPW   *Simone Weil: Late Philosophical Writings*, ed. and trans. Eric O. Springsted (Notre Dame, IN: Notre Dame University Press, 2015).

LPh   *Simone Weil: Lectures on Philosophy*, trans. Hugh Price with an introduction by Peter Winch (Cambridge: Cambridge University Press, 1978).

LP   *Letter to a Priest*, trans. Arthur F. Wills (London: Routledge, 2014; New York: Penguin, 2003).

NB   *The Notebooks of Simone Weil*, 2 vols., trans. Arthur Wills (London: Routledge & Kegan Paul, 1952).

NR   *The Need for Roots*, trans. Arthur Wills (New York: Harper & Row, 1971; London: Routledge & Kegan Paul, 1952, 1987).

OC   *Oeuvres complètes*, 7 vols. (Paris: Gallimard, 1988–). Citations are given in the format: tome.volume.page.

OL   *Oppression and Liberty*, trans. Arthur Wills and John Petrie (Amherst: University of Massachusetts Press, 1973).

SE   *Selected Essays 1934–43*, ed. and trans. Richard Rees (London: Oxford University Press, 1962; Eugene, OR: Wipf & Stock, 2015).

SL   *Seventy Letters*, ed. and trans. Richard Rees (London: Oxford University Press, 1965; Eugene, OR: Wipf & Stock, 2015).

SNL   *On Science, Necessity and the Love of God*, ed. and trans. Richard Rees (London: Oxford University Press, 1968).

SWA   *Simone Weil: An Anthology*, ed. Sian Miles (New York: Weidenfield and Nicolson, 1986).

SWR   *The Simone Weil Reader*, ed. George Panichas (New York: David McKay, 1977).

SWW   *Simone Weil: Writings*, ed. and trans. Eric O. Springsted (Maryknoll, NY: Orbis Books, 1998).

VS   *Venice Saved*, trans. Silvia Panizza and Phillip Wilson (London: Bloomsbury Academic, 2019).

WG   *Waiting for God*, trans. Emma Craufurd (New York: Harper & Row, 1973).

About the Back Cover

The photograph on the back cover of this book is a cropped version of a newly discovered photograph of Simone Weil, her brother André, and their colleague Claude Chevalley (a famous French mathematician). Presumably, it was taken during a meeting of the Bourbaki Group in Chançay, France, in September 1937. Simone served as a confrere and aide-de-camp at the event, which was originally scheduled for textbook preparation but which expanded to include innovations in set theory, abstract algebra, and other mathematical expressions. Simone attended at least one other Bourbaki meeting the following year, at Dieulefit.

The heretofore unpublished photograph was recently acquired from Chevalley's papers by an antiquarian bookdealer in Auray and is currently held in a private collection. Its imagery provides a unique perspective into Weil's leisure activities and reveals an intimate, almost wry persona not commonly observed in other photographs of her. Reproduced with kind permission of Lance D. Lovelette.

The front and back covers were designed by Alex Lubertozzi of Top Five Books.

A Declaration of
Duties toward Humankind

Introduction

Eric O. Springsted

The Need for Roots is an extraordinary book, written by an extraordinary woman in an extraordinary time. All that extraordinariness, however, may have the unwitting effect of keeping readers from fully appreciating how important the work is for social, moral, and political philosophy. On the one hand, there is often too little context when considering this book, especially about how Weil came to write it, and what she wrote. On the other hand, there is often too much context: one can easily lay too much emphasis on the differences that exist between our times and hers. The goal of this book is to deal with what her questions and insights were. This introduction seeks to give the general context of how Weil came to write this book, as well as a general consideration of how the contemporary reader might understand it.

First, we need to consider the context of how *The Need for Roots* came to be written. Its most striking points are often treated as oracular, without considering all that Weil meant by them. For example, one is usually struck by her very opening: it was a mistake to make rights the basis of society, as happened in the French Revolution. Instead, it ought to be obligations. There is something deeply intuitive about this insight, especially when she notes that "[r]ights are always mentioned in a tone of contention" (LPW 113). Living in a modern litigious society, it is very easy to say that she is on target, and then to put rights aside. But that is not quite right. She did not put rights aside, and obligations are not their opposite number and replacement. Obligations put rights within their proper *sphere* by elevating the agent's perspective.

It is, of course, tempting to take the book as something of an oracle simply because Weil herself is considered a mystic, and the book has a lot to it that can be seen as mystical. Weil describes a social organization that is ultimately religious, although without ecclesiastical authorities. It is "impregnated" with a spiritual inspiration, and much of what she writes about is how this can happen.

Undergirding this otherworldly quality is a sort of myth about how the book came to be. Like most myths, it has elements of truth to it, but it passes by a lot, too. According to the myth, Weil went to London in late 1942 from New York with a single goal in mind—to get back to France to carry out a dangerous mission she had concocted, namely, establishing a cadre of women who would serve as front-line nurses. While it was a plan that was meant to be useful, it also had its overtly sacrificial qualities and was meant to be symbolic of what the Allies stood for. What happened instead of being sent on this mission was that Weil only got as far as London, where she was stuck at a desk writing reports for the Free French. Her heart was broken when her mission was deemed ridiculous, and that she was, in any case, the wrong person for it. Her Jewish physical characteristics, it was believed, would have given her away the moment her parachute hit the ground. But she worked hard and was inspired. Despite the intense focus on getting her project put into operation, she managed to write in a period of five months an extraordinary amount of material—numerous essays such as "Are We Struggling for Justice?," "Is There a Marxist Doctrine?," "This War Is a War of Religions," "What Is Sacred in Every Human Being?," and "On the Abolition of All Political Parties," to name just a few. She also wrote a long work that came to be known as the book we now have, *The Need for Roots*, and did so virtually straight on.

To read her original manuscript, one is struck by the fact that there are few corrections or erasures; there are occasional half pages cut out, or whole ones inserted, but they are not many. The book has the appearance, so the myth stresses, of being born like Athena from the head of Zeus. The Free French expected reports from her. They got *this*, a proposal to say how France should be reconstituted after the Germans were chased out! It is often said that *The Need for Roots* was even meant to be a constitution for France when the Nazis were expelled. Then, in the end, because of overwork and tuberculosis, she collapsed, quit the Free French, and died a few weeks after.

Yet, there is much more than this story lets on. It glosses over the degree to which Weil and her projects had real context. While much of what she did was truly original, it had real connections with the projects of the Free French. There is no doubt that her main goal, even obsession when she went to London, was to get her nurses project approved, or, failing that, simply to be sent on a dangerous mission into occupied France. But she also knew what she was getting into, and what the Free French were up to in London. Her writings were not just a rather miraculous job on the side while pursuing a mission.

Weil in London[1]

When Weil left Marseille on May 14, 1942, for New York with her parents, she had consented to go with them only because she saw it as a way to return to occupied France. She was hopeful that it would be to lead her nurses' project, but ultimately she was also open to any dangerous mission that she might be sent on. When the Weils arrived in New York on July 6, Simone immediately set herself to the task of realizing her goal. She agonized over being in America so far away from the important action. She wrote little for the first three months, and in what comments we have from her, it is clear that she was frantic and depressed. To return to the action, she contacted personally, or by letter,

---

1. In recent years two important critical editions of *The Need for Roots* have appeared in French. The first is the OC version (OC V.2 *L'Enracinement Prélude à une déclaration des devoirs envers l'être humain*) published in 2013 with two introductory interpretive essays, critical footnotes, and the addition of various sketches, variants, and fragments. A second critical edition was published in 2014 as *L'Enracinement ou Prélude à une déclaration des devoirs envers l'être humain* (ENR) [ed. Florence de Lussy and Michel Narcy, Paris: Champs classiques, 2014]. This edition contains an introductory essay that deals with the history of Weil in New York and London, critical footnotes, fragments and variants, and André Phillip's New York lecture, as well as an essay by the personalist Jean Lacroix. Finally, OC V.1, which appeared in 2019, also contained an account of Weil's history in New York and London. I have drawn on all of these, as well as Pétrement, for this account, and for further details these sources should be the first to be consulted.

anybody she thought might be able to help—Jacques Maritain, Alexander Koyré, Admiral Leahy, even President Roosevelt, and numerous other French expatriates. She also reached out to former classmates from the École Normale who were working in London for the Free French, the government in exile under Charles de Gaulle. The reactions to her project were polite, but it would be an overstatement to say even that they were mixed. Nobody was as excited about her project as she was. However, she did manage to get the ear of her former classmate, Maurice Schumann, who was working with the Free French in London. He brought her name to the attention of André Philip, who was head of the Commissariat for the Interior. As Philip was going to the United States in the fall of 1942, he agreed to interview her. His interest in her was not in her project, which never got traction anywhere, but because the Free French were seeking to add staff, particularly those who had some intellectual weight. Part of this was because they were urged to do so by Churchill and the British Foreign Office who wanted to provide a counterweight to de Gaulle's leadership. So, Weil was interviewed by Philip when he was in New York and invited to come to London to serve on his staff. She sailed on November 10, arriving in Liverpool fifteen days later. She, however, did not make it to London until December 14, due to quarantine and interrogation. Once he finally had her, though, Philip was not quite sure what to do with her. Ultimately, she was given the job of an editor in the Commissariat for the Interior under Philip and Louis Closon. Her job was to receive reports from France, edit them and respond, and write studies on various issues, although it was never very clear which ones.

Weil and the Free French[2]

Weil's experience with the Free French has usually been described as an unhappy one as she never really connected well with them. In the end, she resigned from the organization. Her letters certainly reflect a lot of frustration. But it is probably more accurate to say that it was mixed. She was relieved to be in London, much happier than in New

---

2. After the defeat of French on June 11, 1940, the armistice led to the northern part of France being occupied and administered by the Germans. A puppet state known as

York. There were certainly points that she and her superiors had in common. Even if Weil and they did not see eye to eye on certain important philosophical principles, the work and the larger context in which that work was set were important for setting the stage for some of Weil's most important thinking. Her intense activity is that of a woman with serious purpose.

One aspect of the Free French's work was to think about some sort of larger picture about what had happened in the French collapse, and what should happen once the Germans had been defeated. The latter was something that was starting to become believable by the end of 1942, with Allied victories in North Africa. For the French, thinking about the causes of the collapse was not just about the pluses and minuses of military strategy. It was also a matter of moral reflection. Many people believed that France's defeat was because of a moral rot or weakness. Some of this was the usual conservative criticism that one finds in times of defeat. It was the excuse for Vichy. But many others took it seriously, including Weil herself.[3] It wasn't just the war; the problems of the Third Republic in the 1930s were well known. But now that the defeat had taken place, there was another reason to think about the moral state of the nation, namely, the craven capitulation, materially and morally, of Vichy to the Germans. Thus, when André Philip came to New York, he gave a lecture that briefly outlined the Free French reaction to all this, and above all called for a spiritual renewal of the nation.[4] The values that the Free French held, in contrast to those of Vichy, he said, were universal and were "centered on the fundamental idea of the sacred character of the human person."[5] Moreover, he called for a new declaration of human rights, a declaration that would be "a profession of faith."[6]

Vichy was established in the south under the leadership of World War I hero, Marshal Phillipe Petain. General Charles de Gaulle, refusing to accept the armistice, established a government in exile in London. This was first known as *France Libre* or Free France. On July 13, 1942, the name was changed to *France Combattante* or Fighting France. This would have been the name during the time Weil was in London. Following common usage, however, "Free French" will be used to refer to this organization, early and late.

3. See her essay, "The Responsibilities of Literature," LPW 151–154. Also of importance is the section on "Uprootedness and Nationhood," NR 98–182.

4. The full text is reproduced at ENR, 425–437; the translation of this lecture appears as Appendix II to this book.

5. ENR 429.

6. ENR 432.

Weil was likely present at the lecture, and from a letter that she wrote to Boris Souvarine the next day, if that is the lecture to which she referred, it is clear that she was impressed. So, she undoubtedly had some reason to be enthusiastic about going to London to work for the Free French. She had been thinking about this sort of thing since Marseille. Her own work in London in several places seems to bear the imprint of Philip's words: the center of *The Need for Roots* is about a spiritual renewal of the nation; her first thoughts about it were contained in a "profession of faith" that would be for all leaders.[7] There was also a working group in the Free French dedicated to these issues. Once she arrived in London, Weil sought inclusion in this sub-group of the Free French organization under the direction of Felix Gouin. This committee was tasked with dealing with problems for the nation after the war. Its discussions included ideas about a new constitution, with impetus from Philip. Weil may have been encouraged by Philip to work with this group. She was admitted to it (it was not in the department in which she was officially employed) and attended a couple of meetings. So, there were aspects of her relations with the Free French that were attractive to her, and even influential, as they in all likelihood spurred her thinking in the directions that would ultimately become *The Need for Roots*. Most of her writings in London are either directly or indirectly related to her concerns about a new constitution.

However, there was also a lot of failure to understand each other. We have a good sense of what the problems were from Weil's letter of resignation written to Closon at the end of July 1943.[8] (She had been in the hospital since April when she collapsed from exhaustion and was found by Simone Deitz on the floor of her apartment.) Not getting sent on a mission into France is not mentioned as the source of her frustration. Rather, it was the differences between Weil and her supervisors about her work; the greatest difference might be described as one of "altitude." She was intent upon looking at a very large picture from very high up, intensely interested in the spiritual renewal of the

---

7. However, as we shall see below, given Weil's opposition in principle to the personalism that Phillip was so clearly standing on, there may be a certain irony in these echoes. The "Profession" is found in translation below as Appendix I.

8. OC V.1 634–638. A translation of this letter can be found at Petrément, 529–31.

nation and what that might mean conceptually. For their part, they had in mind that she should be spending her time closer to the ground on particulars, such as giving a detailed plan for French trade unionism and doing a study of English trade unions. As she wrote to Closon, Philip's reactions to her big picture reports consisted in telling her that she needed to get all this off her chest (*"degorgez-vous"*), and asking "Why doesn't she tackle something concrete, such as trade union problems, instead of wallowing in generalities?"[9] As far as she was concerned, if that is what he wanted then he had the wrong woman. It would be much better if he were to find some people—there were lots of them—who could "write brilliantly on a subject of which they were ignorant."[10] She couldn't.

There was also a matter of a very deep philosophical difference on the issue of what the spiritual renewal of the nation should be, and what it means to talk about the sacred character of the human person. Not that she and Philip and Closon are known to have debated this directly, or if they did, what was said. It is likely, though, that this had something to do with the comments they wrote on her manuscripts, or made to her, which she found to be banal or failing to get what she was doing. She had to know from the beginning that they had differing views on what the spiritual renewal of the nation meant, and did not expect Philip and Closon to actually understand what hers were. The differences centered on one great issue, the one that was implicit in their admiration, and indeed the general admiration of the Free French, for Jacques Maritain. For them, he had the status of an intellectual hero and provided a philosophical framework for the moral aspects of their job. Weil, however, believed that Maritain had failed to capture what is really sacred in every human being.

There is no longer any guesswork about the issue, as we now know that Weil's target in the essay "La Personne et le sacré" ("What Is Sa-

---

9. Ibid.
10. Ibid.

cred in Every Human Being?"[11]) was Maritain.[12] Maritain's books were well known, but one in particular stands out for mention, *The Rights of Man and Natural Law*, which was first published in English and French in New York in 1942. In many ways, this little book was the philosophical blueprint for many in the Free French when they talked about a spiritual renewal of the nation and the sacred nature of the human being. What was sacred in the human being, according to Maritain, was the *personne*, the person or personality. This is something in each of us that allows "the expansiveness of being ... which in the depths of our ontological structure is a source of dynamic unity and of inner unification." Personality required freedom for expansion, but this was not individualism. This sacred center touched on the human relation to God and depended on it. Maritain's personalism was meant to highlight this sacred nature of the person and to argue for a social system that allowed its expansion and its protection by a system of rights. It is not hard to hear the echoes of this in Philip's address in New York. Indeed, it is more than an echo; he quotes Maritain directly and goes on to stress the idea of coming up with a new declaration of "the rights of man" that is taken from Maritain.

There is no doubt that Weil read Maritain's book, and perhaps had done so by the night of Philip's lecture; if so, she may well have bristled at his talking about the sacred character of the person. But there is also no doubt that she was responding to that book directly in the essay "La Personne et la sacré." This essay is one of the most important ones of all her writings. It is also likely the first, chronologically, of the essays written in London. It certainly provides the philosophical foundation for everything else that she writes in London, including *The Need for Roots*. Although it does not mention the distinction between "rights" and "ob-

---

11. In this book we use this title, which is the newer translation found at LPW 103–129. The older translation uses the title "Human Personality." Weil's own French title, after a number of different attempts at one, was ultimately "Collectivité—Personne—Impersonnel—Droit-Justice."

12. For a detailed examination of Weil's relation to Maritain see Eric O. Springsted, "Beyond the Personal: Weil's Critique of Maritain" in *Simone Weil for the Twenty-First Century* (Notre Dame, IN: University of Notre Dame Press, 2021). There is also a discussion in OC V.1, 205–211 and ENR 20–26.

ligations" that opens that book, her trenchant criticism of Maritain's personalism and the notion of rights undergirds that distinction, and that distinction is the proper bloom of her thinking. For rights, she argues, are fine in their place. But they only make sense within a limited *sphere* of social being. We do not want to get rid of them, but if there is going to be any sort of spiritual renewal of the nation, it is going to have to be by virtue of acknowledging a transcendent realm. This is a realm where our moral dealings with our neighbors are not limited by law or process, or centered in the expansion of personality, which she saw not as essential to the human being, but very much the result of adventitious social relations. We have, rather, she thought, as human beings with a spiritual destiny, permanent obligations to other human beings, and even to ourselves and the world of nature. There is nothing limited about it.

There is no need to spell out Weil's critique of Maritain and the development of her thinking any further in this introduction, as it has been treated elsewhere and will be treated in various ways throughout this book, especially in chapter two by Emmanuel Gabellieri, who notes that the differences Weil had with Maritain had begun already in Marseille. Suffice it to point out that Weil's disagreement with personalism is a central point in her thinking, one where she had serious differences with her supervisors, although it is not clear that they fully understood these differences or took great notice of them. Given Phillip's explicitly quoting Maritain and espousing the values of personalism in his New York lecture, Weil surely had from the very beginning of her history with the Free French important reservations. She and the Free French may have seen many of the same problems: the need to fight totalitarianism, the need for the spiritual renewal of the nation, and something to replace the 1789 Declaration of the Rights of Man. But she and they had very different versions of the principles by which they thought these problems should be tackled. They had rested on Maritain's personalism; Weil rested on a transcendent impersonalism. It is of great help to the reader of *The Need for Roots* to know at the outset her explicit, stated differences with Maritain and the Free French, and what Weil's central idea is in "What Is Sacred in Every Human Being?", as it runs throughout all of her writings while in London.

Weil's London Writings

It is worth considering for a moment just what these writings were.[13]
In a letter to her parents, written from the hospital and little more than
a month before her death, Weil says "I [...] have a sort of growing inner

---

13. These writings have not until recently all been published in one place, or given
any sort of reasoned ordering with respect to each other. The OC in French has remedied
that. Some have not appeared at all in English, and their locations are scattered. As an aid
to the reader, we reproduce the table of contents for the London writings of volume 5.1
of the Œuvres complètes (Écrits de New York et Londres), in their English translations and
their location, where there is such. The titles of untranslated essays are left in French.

Writings from London
I. Essays and Projects for Articles
The Person and the Sacred
What Is Sacred in Every Human Being? (LPW)/Human Personality (SE)
Reflections on the War
Are We Struggling for Justice? (SWW)
A War of Religions (SE)
Réflexions sur la revolte
The Colonial Problem
East and West: Thoughts on the Colonial Problem (SE)
Marx and Marxism
Is There a Marxist Doctrine? (OL)
Religion
Theory of the Sacraments (SWW), (GTG)
"Last Text" (GTG)
II. Political and Constitutional Questions
Politics
Légitimité du gouvernement provisoire
The Abolition of All Political Parties (AAPP)
On André Philip's "Project of a New Constitution"
Idées essentielles pour une nouvelle Constitution
Remarques sur le nouveau project de Constitution
On the Constitutional Projects of the Civil and Military Organization (OCM)
Les bases de la réforme constitutionelle
Structure du gouvernement et création d'un parti
Schéma de la Constitution hitlérienne francaise
Les responsabilités et les sanctions
On a Report of the OCM
Bases d'un statut des minorités françaises non chrétiennes et d'origine étrangère
On a "Report of X"
Rapport sur la situation actuelle
Besides these writings found in OC.V.1, in OC V.2, (L'Enracinement), is "Draft for A
Statement of Human Obligations" (appendix in this volume and SE, 219–227) and vari-
ous preliminary sketches for this this study. Weil also continued to write in her note-
books, although not nearly at the rate she had written at any point before then. She left a
notebook of a scant thirty pages.

certainty that there is within me a deposit of pure gold which must be handed on" (SL 196). She goes on to complain that, unfortunately, there is no one to receive it, and details this complaint by the banal, confusing, and contradictory comments that her boss, Philip, has made on her work: "'this is marvelous,' 'this is completely idiotic'" (SL 196–197). She thinks they haven't risked the fatigue of trying to understand it. It is something, she adds, that is indivisible and which, as it grows, becomes more and more solid. This is especially true of her writings in London; however, their solidity gives solidity to her work as a whole as they were truly their apex. There is, of course, a focus here that is due to the nature of her job. But, even so, those writings, written between December 1942 and April 1943 (it is not likely that she wrote much if anything while in the hospital) still cover a wide range of topics. Not only do they include studies having to do with the project of a new constitution and ultimately *The Need for Roots*, but they also include a personal confession, "Last Text," and an interesting study on the nature of the sacraments. A lot of what she wrote at this time is highly original, and, strictly speaking, many ideas in these writings appear only in them. They are also highly cohesive as a whole. The conceptual work of "What Is Sacred in Every Human Being?" is groundbreaking, and remains so, standing on its own two feet in social and moral philosophy. But it is not a stand-alone piece; it informs the other essays written at this time, and certainly *The Need for Roots*. As noted, it is the ground on which the distinction between rights and obligations, and hence Weil's distancing herself from classical liberalism, stands. It undergirds the important idea that there are such things as "needs of the soul," which *The Need for Roots* announces, and a rationale for why the state should care and do something about them. Above all, it gives a sense of what is really sacred, not just a social idol, and hence what would constitute a genuine spiritual reformation of the nation. It also allows Weil to think about in what sense a nation is religious as she does in the essay "A War of Religions" (SE 211–218).

If these writings were new and tightly intertwined, they also brought to a head many ideas that Weil had before London, especially as they envision an application for them. Her extensive argument on science in *The Need for Roots*, for example, draws on essays from the time she spent in Marseille, and it is helpful to go back to those essays to understand her argument. The notion of roots does not appear in her writings as such until *The Need for Roots*; yet the idea of a culture that transmits something like an original revelation was already broached in her essays on the medieval culture of Languedoc that she wrote in Marseille. She clearly was thinking of this culture as she set herself to the task of thinking about the spiritual renewal of France. So, to understand Weil's project in *The Need for Roots*, it is not just helpful to have some sense of her other writings; it is necessary.

With all this said, there is also a specific history of the writing of *The Need for Roots*. It does not appear that this ever-expanding study was requested as such by Philip, and was not therefore technically a report that she would have done in the course of her normal duties. It certainly is something, though, that grew out of her interest in the new constitution project he had started and was written in that context.

Weil described that lengthy essay/report/book in a letter to her parents as her "second *grand* œuvre," a description that should not be taken as meaning her "second masterpiece" but as her second "magnum opus," referring to its size and the effort she put into it. The first *grand* œuvre was her essay "Reflections concerning the Causes of Liberty and Social Oppression" in 1933. While it appears as an original work that Weil wrote in a rush, straight out of the gate, as Florence de Lussy puts it, *The Need for Roots* "obeys a law of constant amplification" (ENR 27). Preceding it, there are three versions of a text that we have in its final version as (in English) "Draft for A Statement of Human Obligations" (Appendix I; SE 219–227) (French: "Étude pour une déclaration des obligations envers l'être humain. OC V.2 91–106). The first draft is titled "Fundamental Declaration of Obligations towards All Human Beings," which is preceded by a "Preamble." In the second draft, the "Preamble" becomes a "Profession of Faith," which is something like a credo to which French leaders would be expected to adhere. It begins with the assertion that

> [t]here is a reality outside the world, that is to say, outside space and time, outside man's mental universe, outside any sphere whatsoever that is accessible to human faculties.
>
> Corresponding to this reality, at the centre of the human heart, is the longing for an absolute good, a longing which is always there and is never appeased by any object in this world.[14] (SE 219)

---

14. One could not give a better two sentence summary of what "What Is Sacred in Every Human Being?" is about.

The text as a whole, quite expanded, now is titled "Study for a Declaration of Obligations towards the Human Being," which is an expression used by Philip in his New York lecture. The final version includes the "Profession of Faith" followed by a "Statement of Obligations," which outlines the various needs of the soul that will be so important in the first part of *The Need for Roots*. It should be noted that the list of needs given in this Statement consists of strictly ordered pairs. In *The Need for Roots*, many of those pairs are kept, but some of them are now separated, and at least three items (the need for truth, the need for order, and the need for roots) do not have balancing opposite needs. This is worth noting since more than one reader, or even Weil scholar, has tried awkwardly to make the list of the needs of the soul in *The Need for Roots* come out as a matter of perfectly balanced pairs.

It is to Weil's philosophical credit that she recognizes that balanced lists have certain virtues, such as not allowing excessive weight on any one need, but lists and perfect symmetry should not rule one's thinking. Her last draft concludes with a statement of "Practical Application," which is that in order for "this Declaration to become the practical inspiration of the life of the country, the first condition is that it be adopted with just this intention by the people. The second condition is that those who wield or want to wield any kind of power ..., should pledge themselves to take it as the practical rule of their conduct" (Appendix I; SE 226–227).

On a final note: Weil's own title on her original manuscript was *Prelude to a Declaration of Duties towards the Human Being*. (Note the change from "obligations" in the preliminary study to "duties" in this manuscript, although this is where she treats obligations extensively.) The original division of the book into three parts—"The Needs of the Soul," "Uprootedness," and "The Growing of Roots"—is the work of the editors, Boris Souvarine (who brought the work to light) and Brice Parain, the editor at Gallimard who pushed for its publication. Weil herself had indicated some divisions which she added in the margin of the manuscript: "Uprooting of the Workers," "Uprooting of the Peasantry" and "Uprooting of the Nation," which name the three parts of the second division of the editors. The manuscript was transported from England to France after the war by André Weil along with many other of his sister's manuscripts and was then in the possession of Weil's parents. It was Souvarine, who, at the urging of Weil's parents, brought the manuscript to the attention of Parain at Gallimard, who got Albert Camus to include it, along with many of Weil's other writings, in the collection he was then editing under the collective title of *Espoir*. The editors decided to retitle it as *L'Enracinement*, which has been translated as *The Need for Roots*. The title has been kept in all subsequent editions. Its first publication was in October 1948.

The Need for Roots Today

What is the relevance of *The Need for Roots* today? Is it even applicable, and in what sense? These are not idle questions, and they have been raised consistently since its original publication three-quarters of a century ago. For some, its day may well be past. The sort of society that seemed to be envisioned in the book no longer exists. The France of 1943 to which Weil wanted to bring her ideas to bear was a nation that was relatively homogeneous. There is at least one document in which she clearly thought about the issue, and in it she does seem to assume some sort of spiritual homogeneity as a norm—in fact, as desirable. Responding to a report that suggests a statute suppressing certain rights of non-Christian foreigners and others (i.e., Jews), her comments tend toward a patient assimilationism that would come to a nation that was spiritually renewed, but in a moment of impatience, she also allows for unfortunate encouragements to hasten that end.[15] Now, given this homogeneity, the idea of reviving and living from common roots was not an impossible one. But that was before, for example, the wars of independence, such as in Algeria, where France either lost or shed its colonies, and immigration from them increased, resulting in a large non-native, non-Christian population. Weil herself had argued that forcing French traditions on colonials in the colonies was uprooting. The argument is easily extended to immigrant communities within the nation. In similar ways, the same problem exists in virtually every nation in the North Atlantic region where Weil is most likely to be read. More and

---

15. See "Bases d'un statut des minorités françaises non chrétiennes et d'origine étrangère" OC V.1 479–484. For a full discussion of this document and its implications see Robert Chenavier, *Simone Weil, une Juive antisémite?: Eteindre les Polémiques* (Paris: Gallimard, 2021).

more, we are living out a badly fractured politics of identity. It is not clear, at first, that *The Need for Roots* addresses this issue, and that as a consequence it may well appear that its search for roots is either forced to be exclusionary or assimilationist. To be sure, there is a very big difference between the two, but both options are rarely smiled upon now.

A second concern is whether *The Need for Roots* is genuinely political. It seems to ignore the push and pull of differing voices and options that are at the heart of the political process, at least within societies where something like Lockean liberalism is the dominant political philosophy. This is not just a general question, but one that is concerned with the fact that Weil is proposing a *spiritual* renewal of the French nation or any nation that might take her thinking seriously. She assumes a general Christian orientation. The book is a set of proposals rooted in her mystical thinking, and, by many definitions, mystical thinking cannot be political thinking. To wit, when she puts labor at the spiritual heart of a new society, she does so because she says that "physical labor is a daily death" (NR 297) and "[c]onsent to suffer death, when death is there and seen in all its nakedness, constitutes a final, sudden wrenching away for what each one calls 'I'" (NR 297). She does not use the term "decreation" in *The Need for Roots*, but what it means is certainly implied in some sense in her consideration of labor as the spiritual heart of "a well-ordered social life" (NR 298). This certainly reflects her mystical thinking. So that is the question: is what she is proposing anything that involves genuine *political* options or is this a bit of wishful spiritual hegemony?

Both these questions help get at what Weil's project really is in *The Need for Roots* and what sort of important contribution it has to make to political and social thinking today. What they force us to consider is the question of "altitude." Both questions arise from a concern with current, concrete conditions and the sorts of solutions that are considered possible in that context. They are asked from within that context. As such, they assume no very deep revisioning of our political and social thinking. They are asked from an abiding context of classical liberal politics, one where the individual and the individual's choices about the good reign. Weil's thinking challenges that assumption of classical liberalism directly and does so from a deliberately different plane.

There is a sense in which, even in its original context, *The Need for Roots* does not engage concrete politics. Weil does not lay out what the contemporary options were among the Free French, or within France itself. She does not choose sides. Indeed, in discussing what the role of the Free French ought to be, and de Gaulle's role in particular, she argues that if they are to have real credibility they need to stand above the concrete political battles of *who* will be in charge and with what policies. They need to propose a social order *without considering their own advantage or their own roles*. That alone, she thinks, will give what they say genuine authenticity. While that can be a highly unrealistic expectation of political actors, Weil did believe that France had a unique opportunity. There was a clean slate, and it was possible to begin anew in a way that few nations ever could. Her proposal is meant to go this far and to take advantage of this opportunity.

For all these reasons, *The Need for Roots* is not a reformist document. It is not meant to fix standing problems or to tailor solutions to what is possible, outlining a distant goal and figuring out how to affect a transition from here to there. She is not interested in fine-tuning the technical choices of politics, which is what political philosophy usually does. That has its place, but it isn't one she is trying to occupy. Her book is far better described as a utopian critique. This suggestion was first made by David McClellan, who states that she is still interested in the political questions of how power is wielded, of centralized state power, and of the liberty of individual choice.[16] But, she is concerned above all to outline what kind of culture all these particular matters might occur in—so that as power is wielded and choices are made, the human *soul* might actually be nourished. What she is interested in is describing what a healthy *milieu* is, one that is made up of different, but mutually supporting institutions and communities, and that have some kind of connection to a larger eternal purpose.

Using a method that is typical of her thinking, Weil draws out what the perfect is, and then uses it to critique the actual. Thus, as she makes clear, the harmony of the universe as a whole is an example of how many worlds can cohere. It gives souls a vision of purpose, and of a balance that is justice. She wants to expand the horizons of our political and social thinking at a time when they are being shrunk and flattened. That

---

16. See David McClellan, *Simone Weil: Utopian Pessimist*. London: Macmillan, 1989. Commenting on his suggestion, see Eric O. Springsted "The Need for Order and the Need for Roots," in *Simone Weil for the Twenty-First Century*. Notre Dame, IN: University of Notre Dame Press, 2021.

is not a blueprint, at least not one for immediate change. She recognizes that a spiritual renewal would take time, a lot of it. Thus, as Robert Chenavier suggests, there is something eschatological about her ambitions in this book; what she envisions will come about only when the society has been spiritually impregnated by a real sense of the good.[17] At this point, then, the book means to provide a new *orientation*. She is calling for what we now call a paradigm shift. As she notes at the end of the "Study for A Declaration ...," it will take generations to develop the institutions and morals necessary to implement the renewal she envisions.

So, it is in this way that her thinking *is* religious. There is no getting around this. From the very beginning when she heard Philip's lecture in New York, and even before that, she was interested in the spiritual renewal of the nation. For her, it was the only alternative in the modern world to totalitarianism. Having a high sense of what spirituality is and a low opinion of Maritain's liberal accommodations that paid lip service to the eternal, but which made present options the real horizon, Weil set out to say something about how that affected political thinking. While the various chapters in the present book provide in-depth discussion of this issue, it is worth noting the sort of big choices that she thought political and social thinking had to deal with if they took into consideration a much larger horizon.

Simone Weil's thinking is religious, but that is because she thought the problems that France faced were ones that demanded religious thinking. In the essay "A War of Religions," she notes that human beings cannot avoid the "religious problem." This is because one finds that "the opposition of good and evil [is] an intolerable burden" (SE 211). There are three ways, she says, of dealing with the problem. First, one can deny the reality of the opposition, which is moral relativism in its various forms. Or, second, one can evade it by idolatry, which "consists in delimiting a social area into which the pair of contradictories, good and evil, may not enter" (SE 212). This is to say, one treats an area as sacrosanct, beyond good and evil, although the area is, in fact, very much part of this world. Nationalism is such a choice, and in *The Need for Roots* she blames the ascendance of nationalism, wherein the nation became an idol, for the uprooting of the nation (NR 98–182). Science is another example, she says—and she deals with this explicitly in *The Need for Roots* (e.g.,

---

17. See Chenavier, *Simone Weil, une Juive antisémite?*, 182–201.

NR 239–244) for it does its work without consideration for good and evil as if it were above the problem, and then delivers its results and opinions. Or, third, and finally, one can employ the "mystical way," which "means passing beyond the sphere where good and evil are in opposition, and this is achieved by the union of the soul with the absolute good"(SE 214). Her point is that dealing with good and evil is inescapable, and there are a limited number of ways of dealing with it. At a point of crisis, such as is the case when one is at war, which way one uses to deal with it is an important matter and not idle metaphysics. How one has dealt with it in the past should be examined, and the way one will deal with it in the future is a big choice that has to be made. It is a choice that goes well beyond questions of policy, and reform of policy. Those questions will only start to fall in place once the bigger picture is determined.

If then, *The Need for Roots* is a "mystical" document, it is deliberately and very consciously one because it is at this level, as Weil saw it, that the problems at the end of the Second World War needed to be solved. The real questions that needed to be solved were not at the level of new policy, or who or what party was going to wield power. Rather, they were ones that needed a much greater consideration of the nature of force itself, and of how human beings need to interact. Additionally, there was the question of what kind of communities were needed for people to flourish in every way and of what those communities needed to be rooted in—hence, where they would ultimately draw their moral and spiritual nourishment from.

If *The Need for Roots* has genuine and lasting relevance, it is at this level. One can mine it for various practical insights, but in the end, one has to see it as changing the level of conceptuality. This does not mean moving to a higher level of abstraction, which is more inclusive because it is less particular. The difference in altitude is not a matter of "higher" but of deeper. The inclusivity here is more generous because it tries to take in things that are important to the human being because they are things of depth, and take in things of the community, such as the needs of the soul, that had been put to the side before. The level Weil seeks is one of personal engagement and intimacy that is too often left to the private realm.

Thus the needed level is necessarily religious, as it requires contemplation and touching things at a depth that is different than that required by problems at technical levels. When dealing with these questions we cannot remain "buffered selves," as Charles Taylor has named it.[18] So, it should also be evident that when Weil wanted to make sure that "religious" was understood not to be a matter of privileging the Church as a political authority she did so for this reason. For all these reasons, then, it is not really a damaging criticism to say that the book's proposals depend on a kind of mysticism or that she is looking for a religious or spiritual renewal of our communities. That is exactly what Weil was doing. Such criticism if it thinks that it has disqualified her position by saying that it is "mystical," has only begged the question of level.

Weil thinks that the questions that are important are at a different level. This was true of her day. There is good reason to think that it is true of our day, even if our particular situations are very different than those during the time in which Weil wrote. Our concerns with our communities—e.g., continuing racial injustice, divisive politics, authoritarianism and totalitarianism, and the demands of identity politics—may well signal the need to think out these issues at a greater depth and with respect to much larger concerns than we have allowed ourselves to consider them. Their present insolubility may be the result of being stuck at an old level.

Perhaps, in the end, Weil was not entirely right; perhaps, what she is proposing is not readily applicable to modern regimes. But, even if that were true, to take Weil seriously is to learn something of great importance in challenging the limitations of reductiveness, party politics, identity politics, and possessive individualism—the very impediments that dog the way we presently struggle to realize our political options.

---

18. Charles Taylor, *A Secular Age* (Cambridge, MA: Harvard University Press, 2007) 339.

CHAPTER 1

Simone Weil on Rights and Obligations*

Mario von der Ruhr

Focusing on Simone Weil's discussion of the relation between rights and obligations in *The Need for Roots*, this paper explores some of the philosophical issues surrounding her distinction between the two, including the similarities and differences between Weil's and Kant's views on the foundation of moral value. A recent controversy in Germany concerning the nature of rights and the state's obligations to its citizens illustrates the continuing relevance of Weil's thought for our own times.

The Need for Roots and the Language of Rights

Simone Weil's *Need for Roots* (*l'Enracinement*) was written during the last months of her life, sometime between her arrival in London on December 14, 1941, and her death at Ashford Sanatorium on August 24, 1943. As the assigned title of the book suggests, its subject matter is the question of rootedness, understood both literally and metaphorically: What does it mean to be grounded in, and sustained or nourished by, the place and community in which one finds oneself? What are the condi-

---

* I am grateful to John Kinsey, Andrew Lugg, Eric Springsted, Ronald Collins, and Emmanuel Gabellieri for their helpful comments on an earlier draft of this essay.

tions under which the citizens of a country can truly flourish, both physically and spiritually, and feel genuinely *at home*? The inquiry with which
these questions are associated is not so much concerned with Aristotelian "external goods" and their role in the attainment of individual *eudaimonia* (happiness), however, but with the principal *values* that ought
to inform the framework of a *polis*.

At the very least, this normative aspect makes *l'Enracinement* a work
of lasting significance, though it is, of course, also a personal response to
particular historical circumstances, including the efforts of the French
résistance during the Second World War, the *Comité National de la
France Libre*'s interest in proposals for the legal, educational, administrative and constitutional reorganization of post-war France, and the political status of women at the time. With respect to the latter, Patricia Little
reminds us that "[in] France at this time women had no political rights;
they were enfranchised only in 1944, had no right to property, [and]
required the permission of their husband to run a business, or obtain a
passport."[1] In the sphere of education, too, women "had been admitted
to the Lycée Henri-IV only a year before Simone entered, and at the
École Normale [Weil] found herself in an all-male class."[2] Such treatment
was clearly as unjust as the fact that when, in 1934, Weil was working as
a packer in Boulogne-Billancourt and in the Renault and Alsthom factories in Paris, women were always the first to get fired, and so were
forced to be even more competitive than men.[3] It is not surprising, therefore, that reflections on the notion of *rights* and its relation to that of
justice should also figure prominently in *l'Enracinement*. As we shall see
below, Weil's critical observations on that relation are just as relevant
now as they were in the early 1940s, not only because of the ubiquity and
proliferation of rights-talk in our own political culture, but because the
questions she raises about the nature of such talk, its meaning and ultimate ground, go right to the heart of our spiritual predicament and its
effects on communal living.

---

1. J. P. Little, *Simone Weil* (New York: St Martin's Press, 1988), 12.

2. *Ibid.*

3. See Mario von der Ruhr, *Simone Weil—An Apprenticeship in Attention* (London:
Continuum, 2006), 12. What angered Weil was that, even though there was already a
great deal of soul-destroying competition among workers, this particular injustice put
even more pressure on women—not only in regard to their male "comrades" but in relation to each other.

Dignity, Rights, and God—The Case of the German *Grundgesetz*

In the spring of 2017, Elisabeth Scharfenberg (a member of the German Green Party) proposed that the state should pay for "Sex Carers" or "Sex Assistants" catering to the needs of elderly and (mentally or physically) disabled citizens who were confined to care homes.[4] Not surprisingly, the suggestion was met with a mixture of applause and outrage, depending on which side of the ideological fence observers found themselves. There were those on one side who commended Scharfenberg for addressing a long-held taboo about the sexual needs of the old and disabled, and for highlighting Articles 2 and 3 of the German *Grundgesetz* (the nation's "Basic Law"), which are concerned with personal freedoms and equality before the law, respectively. According to the former article, "every person shall have the right to free development of his personality insofar as he does not violate the rights of others or offend against the constitutional order or the moral law," while the latter article (3.3) stipulates that "[n]o person shall be disfavoured because of disability."[5]

Sexual gratification, so defenders of Scharfenberg's proposal reasoned, was clearly integral to the free development of one's "personality," and since that development was just as much enshrined in the *Grundgesetz* as a (positive) fundamental right as the (negative) right to non-discrimination, it followed that, if care home patients required the help of a "Sex Carer" to exercise these rights, then justice demanded that they be given that help.[6] The only question was: who would pay for the service when the rights holders themselves were unable to? Would financial

---

4. "Debatte über Sexualbegleitung—Sex auf Rezept," in *Der Spiegel Online* (Oct. 1, 2017): https://www.bundestag.de/resource/blob/425096/ecc17a8eebd0b36bc9313d057f5 32136/wd-3-067-16-pd-data.pdf.

5. *Basic Law for the Federal Republic of Germany* (2019), trans. Christian Tomuschat, David P. Currie, Donald P. Kommers, and Raymond Kerr, in cooperation with the Language Service of the German Bundestag: https://www.gesetze-im-internet.de/englisc_ gg/, 15.

6. The sentiment is also shared by citizens of Germany's neighbouring country, the Netherlands, where sex care is an established and loudly applauded practice: "You are a human being just like everyone else, and it is your right to live your life to the fullest—disabled or not!" cf. Chuka Nwanazia, "Sex Care in the Netherlands: Helping the disabled find intimacy," *Dutch Review* (Oct. 22, 2018) in https://dutchreview.com/ culture/relationships/sex-care-in-the-netherlands-helping-the-disabled-find-intimacy/.

support come out of the federal budget? Should municipalities set aside a special fund for sex assistance? Might local councils carry the financial burden? Underlying these questions was the recognition that rights, especially when codified in law, entail duties, and that claims of the form "I have a right to x" mean little without a specification of the agent or institution whose duty it is to provide the claimant with x. Hence Scharfenberg's suggestion that, in this case, the duties associated with Articles 2 and 3 of Germany's *Grundgesetz* should be placed on the respective municipalities.

The public controversy over "Sex Carers" was by no means confined to issues of financial liability, however. On the contrary, even parliamentarians on the liberal side of the political spectrum thought Scharfenberg's proposal "bizarre" and instead joined the Social Democratic Party (SPD) Vice Chair Karl Lauterbach's protest, "We don't need paid-for prostitution in retirement homes, least of all on prescription."[7] While advocates of state-subsidized "Sex Carers" were quick to point out that the "care" in question might involve no more than regular conversations and emotional support, a sympathetic pat on the shoulder, or an empathetic cuddle,[8] their critics objected that the boundaries between these kinds of attention and the granting of sexual favors was too fluid to allay any concerns about state-funded prostitution. Presumably, these critics were not only worried that state-subsidized institutions might be seen to

---

7. "Debatte über Sexualbegeitung."

8. In a similar vein, Dutch defenders of sex care have insisted that "[i]n the Netherlands, sex care does not only consist of having sex with a client: sometimes clients ... just need attention and someone to show genuine interest in them." In Chuka Nwanazia, "Sex Care in the Netherlands," *op. cit.* The claim that sex carers show "genuine interest" in their "clients" raises problems of its own, however. One of these concerns the language used in social care contexts more generally. As D. Z. Phillips rightly observes: "Is it not said that a social worker must show an interest in the client? But what of what the client *says*? How is one to show an interest in what is said, if what is said does not interest one? One may *appear* to show interest for all sorts of reasons connected with the policies of the profession, but whatever these appearances amount to, they cannot be the real thing—a natural show of interest." In D. Z. Phillips, "Can You Be a Professional Friend?", in *The Gadfly* vol. 5 (1983) 41. In the present case, the difficulty is compounded by the fact that the carer's "attention" and "interest" come at a financial cost of $100 an hour. The debate about sex carers thus betrays a conflation of categories in which unwitting or deliberate equivocation on the meaning of terms like "care" and "interest" plays a major role. Here, it helps to be reminded of familiar yet important distinctions: "The old person is one of the social worker's cases. The social worker has the old person on the books. Our friends are not cases, and we do not have them on our books" (Phillips, 37).

support a "trade" that many women still regarded as demeaning and exploitative. In addition, they may have felt that dispatching "Erotic Care Providers" to the physically frail and mentally infirm would be undignified and, at any rate, far exceeding the state's duty of care towards its citizens.

It is tempting to think that this—seemingly intractable—controversy over "Sex Carers" might be resolved by invoking the *Grundgesetz*'s most fundamental postulate (Art. 1.1) *viz.*, that "human dignity shall be inviolable" and that "to respect and protect it shall be the duty of all state authority,"[9] but this would be merely postponing the problem. Apart from the fact that Article 1.1 leaves the notion of dignity wholly unexplained—because the *Grundgesetz* is essentially a consensus-driven catalogue of rights rather than a contribution to the philosophy of law—both parties to the debate might justify their views in terms of what that dignity requires, with one insisting on state-funded "Sex Carers" and the other claiming that the original framers of the *Grundgesetz* would hardly have envisaged, let alone endorsed, a right to such services. The latter conjecture is worth pondering further.

In the 1949 Preamble to the *Grundgesetz*, the Parliamentary Council note that the German people have adopted it because they are "conscious of their responsibility before God and man."[10] Curiously, the reference to God—as the ultimate ground of human dignity and its derivative rights and duties—was retained even in the revised 2019 edition of the *Grundgesetz*. Given the German state's self-professed ideological neutrality, the inclusion is puzzling. Indeed, the Preamble elicited so many complaints that the parliament's "academic services" were prompted to draft a response to the most common objection against it, which was that its mention of God was clearly incompatible with Article 4.1 of the very same document, according to which citizens have the right to adopt and express religious and secular world views alike.[11] How, so the complainants argued, could the *Grundgesetz* be associated with a divine creator when a crucial component of that law explicitly took *all*

---

9. Article 1.1

10. *Basic Law for the Federal Republic of Germany* (2019), 15.

11. Wissenschaftliche Dienste/Deutscher Bundestag, *Zum Gottesbezug in der Präambel des Grundgesetzes*, https://www.bundestag.de/resource/blob/425096/ecc17a8eebd0b36bc9313d057f532136/wd-3-067-16-pdf-data.pdf, 3.

world views to be of equal (epistemic, if not ethical) standing? In their response, the lawmakers argued that this reading was both hasty and a misrepresentation of the Preamble's intended meaning.

First, and in agreement with its critics, the parliamentary office explicitly confirmed that "in order for the citizens to exercise these freedoms effectively, it is necessary that the state take a neutral stance with respect to the various expressions of belief."[12] Second, it pointed out that "the Preamble is a preliminary remark, informing the reader of the lawgiver's reasons, his motives and goals, as well as of the political circumstances under which the constitutional text was drafted."[13] However, the Preamble "does not formulate an aim of the state, nor can the individual deduce any rights therefrom."[14] Why a reference to God, then? Here, the exponents of the constitution draw a distinction between mentioning God (*nominatio dei*) and invoking Him (*invocatio dei*). "While, in the latter case, the legitimacy of the constitution is thought to derive from God as its source ('In the name of God'), the Preamble to the *Grundgesetz* merely contains a mention of God."[15] But this seems to be begging the initial question, for why refer to God at all? For clarification, the reader was told:

> It is true that, in referring to God, the fathers and mothers of the *Basic Law* were thinking of the Christian God of the Old and New Testaments. However, this does not contradict the state's religious/ideological neutrality. For while the lawgivers were conscious of their responsibilities toward God, they also envisaged a religiously and ideologically neutral state when they formulated Article 4, Sect. 1 and 2.[16]

In other words: the Christian world view of the original lawgivers was *incidental* to both the framework and the contents of the 1949 *Grundgesetz*, as these do not *depend* upon belief in God.[17] But, so the legal commentary continues, there were nevertheless good reasons for including

---

12. *Zum Gottesbezug*, 3.
13. *Ibid.*, 4
14. *Ibid.*
15. *Ibid.*
16. *Ibid.*
17. *Ibid.*

a *nominatio Dei* in the *Grundgesetz*'s Preamble: as the document was drawn up in the immediate aftermath of the National Socialist régime, the parliamentary council thought it important to "emphasize the rejection of totalitarian forms of government, which regarded state power as 'absolute' and saw it as an end in itself," and felt the need to refer to "something that is above the state and the people."[18]

More specifically, the use of "God" should be taken as "a kind of proxy" or "example," a reminder of human limitations and the imperfections attaching to man-made institutions like the state.[19] Thus, the initial puzzle over God's mention in the Preamble is now solved: "For the most part, the reference to God is interpreted as an expression of humility."[20] Does this mean that "something that is above the state and the people" is elliptical for "an ideal of which the state and the people are bound to fall short"? Would the latter capture the original lawgivers' awareness of their "responsibility toward God"? If not, then would this matter for the *result* of their deliberations, *viz.*, the individual rights postulated in the *Grundgesetz*? The legal commentators do not shed any light on these questions, nor are the readers of the document likely to lose any sleep over such quandaries so long as the document contains the *rights* safeguarding their particular interests.

In what follows, I will not be concerned with the interpretative issues surrounding Germany's *Grundgesetz* or with the scope of human rights more generally, but rather with the difficulties it raises—as an exemplar of modern political constitutions, so to speak—about the nature and legitimacy of rights talk, the notion of dignity, and the role of the transcendent in thinking about human obligations.

More concretely, I shall take a closer look at what Simone Weil has to say about this conceptual triptych (rights/dignity/the transcendent)—most notably in *The Need for Roots*—and at the implications of her thought for our understanding of contemporary political constitutions. As Weil scholar Patrice Rolland rightly notes in his preface to Gallimard's new and annotated edition of *L'Enracinement*, Weil's critical

---

18. Christian apologists would no doubt argue that while morally virtuous action does not require *belief* in God, there can be no absolute and unconditional value without God. But I will not pursue this matter here.

19. *Zum Gottesbezug.*, 5.

20. *Ibid.*

comments on the language of rights, in particular, present a "radical attack on political modernity and democracy," not least because the latter has "set itself the task of guaranteeing human rights in terms of concepts inherited from the Enlightenment,"[21] and it is well worth exploring the reasons for Weil's sceptical stance on the subject.

As to the last point, I shall revisit Immanuel Kant's construal of moral obligation. Apart from its lasting influence on public discourse about human dignity, and Weil's admiration for his work, Kant's notion of duty appears to come closest to the kind of transcendentalism Weil espoused.

The Language of Rights and "Supernatural" Obligations

The opening sentence of *The Need for Roots* reads:

> The notion of obligations comes before that of rights, which is subordinate and relative to the former. A right is not effectual by itself, but only in relation to the obligation to which it corresponds, the effective exercise of a right springing not from the individual who possesses it, but from other men who consider themselves as being under a certain obligation towards him. (NR 3)

At first sight, Weil's claim that the notion of obligation is logically prior to that of rights sounds strange. For isn't the former simply a (logical) correlate of the latter, such that "X has a right to a" implies "Y has an obligation to provide a" or "Y has an obligation not to interfere with X in obtaining a"?[22] For example, if students pay the university $30,000 in annual tuition, they have a right to attend lectures and seminars, and to be given a degree certificate on successful completion of their studies. Conversely, the university has a duty to provide them with qualified teachers, lecture rooms, diplomas, etc. But what would it mean for the university's obligations to come *before* the students' rights? This is the

---

21. *Ibid.*

22. Patrice Rolland, "Avant Propos", OC 5, 20. He speaks of "un soupçon d'atteinte radicale à la modernité politique et à la démocratie, elle qui se donne pour mission de garantir des droits de l'homme dans la conception reçue des Lumiéres."

wrong question. It misses the point of Weil's remark. She is not denying that rights are (logically) correlated with duties, but pointing out that (i) the meaningful invocation of a right is always contingent upon its public recognition and the particular context in which that invocation takes place;[23] (ii) our moral duties include obligations whose existence is entirely independent of interpersonal or public agreement, and which belong to a realm that is "situated above this world" (NR 4); and (iii) an undue emphasis on rights impoverishes our critical moral vocabulary, falsely suggesting that justice is essentially transactional and distributive, and vainly seeks to anchor our highest moral values in the "middle" realm of social institutions and conventions.[24]

In connection with (i), the contextual and conditional nature of rights claims, Weil uses the following example: "A peasant, whom a buyer in the market puts undue pressure on to get him to sell his eggs cheaply, can very well answer: 'I have the right to keep my eggs if no one offers me a good enough price'" (LPW 115). The farmer's liberty to determine the price of his eggs is clearly part of a network of social conventions surrounding the acquisition and disposal of private property, safeguarded by a legal code stipulating the rights and duties of buyers and sellers. Since the buyer, too, acknowledges these background conditions of public trading, the farmer's retort is an intelligible reminder of his—and indeed every seller's—*rights*. Conversely, a buyer who obtusely insisted on paying merely a fraction of the asking price and refused to let the matter rest, would be thought to be either deaf or unhinged. On the other hand—and this is what Weil is driving at—the farmer's response would be laughable if the "buyer" were a member of the mafia, threatening violent "punishment" in case of non-compliance. Another way of putting the point would be to say that the reference to rights only makes sense in contexts where the mutual agreement on which they are based has not been unilaterally suspended: "But a young girl who is in the midst of being forced into a brothel," so Weil rightly observes in an even

---

23. See John Searle, *Making the Social World: The Structure of Human Civilization* (Oxford: Oxford University Press, 2010), 177.

24. "The notion of rights, being of an objective order, is inseparable from the notions of existence and reality.... Rights are always found to be related to certain conditions" (NR 4).

more striking example, "will not speak of her rights. In such a situation, the words would seem ridiculously inadequate" (LPW 115). [25]

The reason why "I have a right to my passport!" would be in the wrong (linguistic) key here is not only that the request would leave the girl's oppressors stone cold and elicit at best a condescending chuckle. That choice of words would also misrepresent the girl's predicament and the nature of the harm done to her, which goes well beyond whatever physical harm and psychological agony she may be going through: she is also suffering from the *injustice* that has been done her—a separate and quite distinctive harm, which has the potential to pierce her soul in ways that other kinds of affliction would not. As Weil observes in her reflection on this case, it takes a certain sensitivity and moral sensibility to respond to such harm: "If you say to someone who has ears to hear: 'What you are doing to me is not just', you may touch and awaken at its source the spirit of attention and love" (SE 21). Where no such response can reasonably be expected, ordinary invocations of rights must necessarily ring hollow.

It is tempting to think that this is merely stating a truism about human conduct, *viz.*, that the appeal to moral propriety may either bear fruit or fall on deaf ears. But we have already seen that Weil's reservations about the language of rights are far more substantial than that. What primarily concerns her is whether that language can adequately capture the fact that an encounter with another human being is *ipso facto* an encounter with a *soul* whose sufferings must be accorded a certain kind of *meaning* and *significance*. Weil's worry is that overreliance on "rights," no matter how well-intentioned, may redirect our—including the speaker's own—attention to a mediocre sense of (distributive) justice, one whose currency is chiefly that of external goods, even if broadly construed. So, her skeptical conclusions on this issue are neither trivial, nor do they lack argumentative support. On the contrary, her reasoning involves important conceptual distinctions—e.g., between rights and obligations (or better: certain *kinds* of obligation); conditional

---

25. "Putting words in the mouth of the afflicted, words that belong to the middle region of values, such as democracy, rights, or person, is to give them a present that is not open to leading them to any good, and that inevitably makes for much harm. These notions do not have their place in heaven, but are suspended in mid-air, and for this reason they cannot get any sort of bite on the ground" (LPW 118).

and unconditional duties; lower and "higher" realms of value, and such salient examples as those of the farmer and the girl in the brothel.

(ii) To further highlight the limitations of rights talk and the associated contrast between context-dependent and unconditional obligations, Weil imagines "a man considered in isolation" (NR 3) or "a man left alone in the universe" (NR 4). Such a person, she argues, "would have no rights whatever, but he would have obligations" (NR 4), including "certain duties towards himself" (NR 3). While many, including moral philosophers of a consequentialist stripe, would readily assent to the former, the latter may seem more controversial. Given that rights are typically claimed *against* someone—an individual, an institution, or even the state—it would certainly be absurd for Weil's Robinson Crusoe to invoke the right to such things as a Social Security number, decent housing, or the timely delivery of his mail.[26] Since, *ex hypothesi*, there are no individuals or institutions against whom these rights could be claimed, their invocation would be meaningless. Even so, Weil wants to insist, our isolated man would, at a minimum, have certain obligations or duties "towards himself."[27] Her point, I take it, is the Kantian one that if human beings are thought of as ends-in-themselves and thus as beings with inherent dignity—a notion that still needs to be fleshed out, of course, and to which I will return below—then the recognition of that fact generates special obligations, not only towards others but towards oneself. As Kant writes in his *Groundwork for the Metaphysics of Morals*:

> I cannot dispose of man in my own person by mutilating, damaging, or killing him. (A more exact determination of this principle, so as to avoid all misunderstanding, e.g., regarding the amputation of limbs in order to save oneself, or the expo-

---

26. Ronald Collins has pointed out to me that the wider Western legal context—e.g., constitutional law, precedent-based common law, etc.—may well affect the character of what we would say about the victim's response. In *NR*, I take Weil to be primarily interested in what the rights/obligations contrast shows about the "supernatural" and "transcendent" roots of our duties towards our fellow men, but see Ronald K. L. Collins and Finn E. Nielsen, "The Spirit of Simone Weil's Law, in Richard H. Bell (Ed.), *Simone Weil's Philosophy of Culture* (Cambridge: Cambridge University Press, 1993), 235–259, for a detailed and helpful discussion of Weil's conception of law.

27. Some constitutions do, in fact, protect the right to decent housing. See Eric Tars, "Housing as a Human Right," National Low Income Housing Coalition (2018), 1, https ://nlihc.org/sites/default/files/AG-2018/Ch01-S06_Housing-Human-Right_2018.pdf. (I am grateful to Ronald Collins for bringing this to my attention.)

sure of one's life to danger in order to save it, and so on, must here be omitted.)[28]

Unlike those who would defend the moral permissibility of such acts on the grounds that they do not harm *others*, that they are sanctioned by the demands of freedom, or that the corresponding prohibitions are malleable social conventions in which morally neutral *facts* have come to be invested with (negative) *values*—e.g., Hume's description of suicide as "turning a few ounces of blood from their natural channel"[29]—Weil agrees with Kant that human beings have duties towards themselves that are just as *unconditional* as the obligations they have to their fellow men. For her, these are also "situated above this world," in the sense that they are both *absolute* and independent of the individuating contingencies that mark out one human being from another. Their ground, in other words, is *impersonal*: "What is sacred in a human being is that which is, far from the personal, the impersonal" (LPW 107).

As Eric Springsted has rightly pointed out, this does not mean that Weil is trying to anchor our moral obligations in an abstract notion of the self.[30] Nor is she saying—surface grammar to the contrary notwithstanding—that what is sacred "in" a human being is an immaterial substance stripped of its bodily manifestations, a Kantian *noumenon*, or some other "I-know-not-what" (Locke).[31] This kind of impersonalism would lend human interrelations a transcendental aspect, to be sure, but would it also deepen our understanding of the kind of limit other human beings place on our will, or of what a victim of violence and injustice—like the young girl in Weil's example—is going through? Mindful

---

28. More precisely, Weil says that such a man would have *only* duties, "amongst which are certain duties towards himself" (NR 3). Unfortunately, she does not indicate what duties he would have *apart* from those towards himself—as suggested by the phrase "amongst which"—and it is not clear what these would be. Duties towards animals, perhaps, or, if our man had an environment-friendly orientation, towards the surrounding ecosphere?

29. Immanuel Kant, *Grounding for the Metaphysics of Morals*, James W. Ellington trans. (Indianapolis, IN: Hackett, 1981) (All references are to the standard Prussian Academy pagination: Gr. 430.)

30. "Essays on Suicide, and the Immortality of the Soul. Ascribed to the Late David Hume, Esq." (anonymous), *The Monthly Review*, vol. 70 (1784) reprinted in Stanley Tweyman, ed., *Hume on Natural Religion* (Bristol. Eng: Thoemmes Press, 1996), 285.

31. Eric Springsted, *Simone Weil for the Twenty-First Century* (Notre Dame, IN: University of Notre Dame Press, 2021), 130.

of the fact that "whenever there is a grave error in vocabulary, it is hard to avoid grave errors in thought" (LPW 104), Weil is just as wary of postulating unhelpful metaphysical "explanations" as she is of condoning the language of rights and the problematic personalism with which it is typically associated.[32] As she writes:

> The cry of sorrowful surprise that rises up from the bottom of the soul upon the infliction of evil is not something personal. A blow to the person and his desires is not enough to make it burst forth. It always bursts forth by the sensation of some contact with injustice through pain. It is always, just as in the case of Christ, [and] in the case of the least of men, an impersonal protest. (LPW 107)

In other words, an adequate account of the evil done to an innocent victim of grievous bodily harm, for example, is one in which the (personal) experience of pain *also* appears under the aspect of (impersonal) injustice. Once again, it is important to be clear about what Weil is *not* saying here, *viz.*, that the sacred dimension of human beings simply stems from their reverence for such ideals as perfect justice, truth, and beauty. Indeed, it is difficult to see how the love of an *ideal* could provide the kind of spiritual rootedness, sustenance, and hope that Weil is after. Even Socrates' pursuit of truth and his insistence that it was better to suffer evil than to do it were ultimately grounded in beliefs about a cosmic order involving, not only the Form of the Good, but a prophetic narrative about the souls of the departed and their final resting places on the *Isles of the Blessed* or in *Tartarus*.[33] It would be easy to construe such narratives as metaphorical affirmations of value, but Weil would surely think such reductivism just as hasty as a merely figurative interpretation of Christian beliefs in the Incarnation, the Resurrection, and the Holy Trinity. Indeed, it seems to me that she would reject the underlying distinction between the metaphorical and the factual as a false dichotomy, and point at Plato for clarification. For example, it is not accidental that when Socrates says in the *Phaedo* that "those who have purified them-

---

32. John Locke, *Essay Concerning Human Understanding*, II, XIII, 15.

33. For an excellent discussion of Weil's criticism of Maritain's personalism, see Eric Springsted, "Beyond the Personal: Weil's Critique of Maritain," in *Simone Weil for the Twenty-First Century, op. cit.*, 121–132.

selves sufficiently by philosophy [will] … make their way to even more beautiful dwelling places which it is hard to describe clearly, nor do we now have the time to do so,"[34] his interlocutors do not press him further. Plato was well aware that responses like "You are being evasive, Socrates," or "If there isn't enough time now, when *could* you tell us more about those dwelling places?", would have betrayed a serious misunderstanding of his central concern, which is that human actions fall under a moral judgment whose measure is itself part of an impersonal order. Weil, in whose thinking Platonic and Christian influences frequently merge, makes the same point in her remark that "[t]his impersonal and divine order of the universe has its images among us: justice, truth, and beauty" (LPW 128) and, even more strikingly, in a reference to Matthew 5:45, when she writes:

> [When Christ talks about the kind of perfection men ought to strive for, he uses not only the image of a person but also, above all, that of an impersonal order:] "Become children of your Father who is in heaven, and who makes his sun shine on the evil as well as the good, and who makes the rain fall on both the just and unjust." (LPW 128)

(iii) One can see more clearly now why, from the perspective of this impersonal order and the "higher" tier of values with which it is associated, the language of rights—with its undue focus on the interests of socially and institutionally defined "persons"—must appear flat and reductive, incapable of deepening our understanding of others as well as of ourselves. Weil puts it well when she says that "[the] notion of rights is linked with the notion of sharing out, of exchange, of measured quantity," that "[it] has a commercial flavour, essentially evocative of legal claims and arguments," that rights are "always asserted in a tone of contention," and that "when this tone is adopted, it must rely upon force in the background, or else it will be laughed at" (SE 18). Now, the public controversy over "erotic services" with which my paper began largely revolved around the question whether the right to the free development of one's personality and the right to non-discrimination *also* entailed the right to state-funded sexual gratification. Its promoters no doubt saw their predicament—the chronic absence of physical intimacy and lack

---

34. Plato, *Gorgias* 524 a–b.

of sexual fulfilment—as a serious affliction, nor should their plight be trivialized on the grounds that their outrage over the lack of state-funded "Sex Carers" belongs in a different category from that of a sex-trafficked teenager's cries "from the depth of the soul." On the other hand, the meanings of "rights violation," "injustice," and "affliction" are by no means coextensive, nor do the underlying *motives* of the protagonists have to be homogeneous. But they become problematic when they arise from "a much more superficial level of the soul," and are of the kind that "prompts a little boy to watch jealously to see if his brother has a slightly larger piece of cake" (SE 10), culminating in the lament, "Why has somebody else got more than I have?" (SE 30). When such lower-order motives come to dominate public discourse about rights, they also loosen "the chain of eternal obligations which bind every human being to every other" (NR 21), and so hollow out the meaning of expressions like "human dignity," "our common humanity," and "the sanctity of life." On the other hand, it is doubtful whether even the presence of higher-order motives could plausibly yield a (moral or legal) right to the fulfilment of our emotional needs or sexual desires, especially if the satisfaction of those needs required third parties to act as *means* to these ends. The fact that "Erotic Care Providers" might be prepared to offer hugs, kisses, and other "services" at the rate of $100 an hour hardly provides a remedy here. On the contrary, the practice trivializes the nature of human needs, confuses genuine attention to our fellow men with counterfeit forms of it,[35] and highlights the precariousness of rights whose practical implementation depends exclusively on paid *volunteers*. Moreover, the conceptual and ethical issues in question are frequently concealed by the use of language that, though seemingly innocuous, seriously distorts the realities it ostensibly describes. Thus, defenders of "sex care" in the Netherlands, for example, have argued that social stigma attaches neither to the nature of the activities in question, nor to those who perform them:

> In the Netherlands, sex care workers aren't regarded as prostitutes. They are seen as professionals who care for the disabled. According to the World Health Organisation, every human being has the right to the highest attainable level of sexual

---

35. Plato, *Phaedo*, 114 c in Plato, *Complete Works*, John M. Cooper, ed., G.M.A. Grube trans. (Indianapolis, IN: Hackett Publishing Co., 1997) 97.

health, including access to sexological and reproductive health.
It is the duty of these sex care professionals to cater to the sexual needs of the disabled members of the Dutch community.[36]

In short: the moral opprobrium associated with prostitution does not
taint "Erotic Care Providers" because its practitioners are, in fact, no
different from other "workers" and "professionals" whose "duty" it is to
attend to the rights-based "health" needs of their disabled fellow citizens. However, a social evil cannot be turned into a public good except
by stipulative redefinition, and Weil would condemn such linguistic
sleights of hand just as strongly as she opposes the practice of prostitution itself. While she sympathizes with the plight of women who have
been forced into it, and even thinks that there is a sense in which "the
vilest prostitute in the streets is better than a self-righteous woman born
in a rich family" (SL 104), she is also clear that prostitution is "an institution which is a disgrace to France" (NR 85),[37] that "the condition of
professional prostitute constitutes the extreme degree of uprootedness"
(NR 86), and that "prostitution … is to real marriage what almsgiving
and punishment without charity are to almsgiving and punishment
which are just" (WG 156).[38] In thus contributing to uprootedness and
self-degradation, "Erotic Care Providers" are getting more than
they—literally—bargained for.

Now, the contrast between institutionally decreed rights and eternal
obligations becomes particularly vivid when one thinks of a saint's relation to his fellow men. "One cannot imagine St. Francis of Assisi talking
about rights" (SE 20–21), Weil says, and the reference is illuminating. If,
like the Good Samaritan in Luke (10:29–37), St. Francis passed by a man
in a ditch, he would come to his aid without either hesitation or deliberation, acting simply out of compassion for his plight—just as the evan-
gelist portrays him.[39] Indeed, the Samaritan acts from a certain kind of

---

36. See D. Z. Phillips's observations on this subject in footnote 5 above.

37. Chuka Nwanazia, "Sex Care in the Netherlands, *op. cit.*

38. "It may be mentioned, by the way, that we have paid dearly for this disgrace.
Turning prostitution into an official institution, in the way this has been done in France,
largely contributed towards demoralizing the army, and completely demoralized the po-
lice, which was bound to bring about the ruin of democracy" (NR 85).

39. In connection with the history of Israel, Weil notes: "Abraham visited Egypt—where
he prostituted his wife to Pharaoh—and had Ishmael from an Egyptian slave before becoming circumcised. The history of Israel begins with a prostitution" (NB, vol 2, 574).

necessity, one that, elsewhere in her work, prompts Weil to compare the moral integrity of a good man to the "fidelity" of a geometrical relation:

> There is an analogy between the fidelity of the right-angled triangle to the relationship which forbids it to emerge from the circle of which its hypotenuse is the diameter, and that of a man who, for example, abstains from the acquisition of power or of money at the price of fraud. The first may be regarded as a perfect example of the second. (IC 189)

For the good man, certain courses of action are simply ruled out and so have no deliberative voice. This does not mean, however, that St. Francis would rush to help his neighbor *because* he has an "eternal obligation" towards him. As far as moral integrity is concerned, the corresponding thought—"I have an eternal obligation to come to his aid"—would already be one thought too many, and no more commendable than "It is my duty to help, so I will." Such self-conscious prescriptions might still prompt the Samaritan to do the right thing, but they would hardly make him a model of spontaneous and perfect obedience to God's will, let alone a saint. The same holds—*a fortiori*—for the invocation of *rights* on both sides of the human encounter. Imagine a victim who appealed to various (unconcerned) passers-by with "I have a *right* to be helped!" In the state of Ohio, a legally savvy pedestrian could legitimately brush off that request with the retort, "No, you don't. If the ditch were located in Minnesota, Louisiana, Rhode Island, or Vermont, you would have a case, as these states have so-called 'failure-to-act' laws requiring bystanders to offer emergency assistance. Indeed, in Minnesota the corresponding omission could incur a misdemeanor charge and a fine of up to $300. But I'm sorry. You don't have the right to my help here in Ohio." [40] The imaginary exchange has a grotesque ring to it, and that is the point. The problem is not just that the rights associated with "failure-to-act" laws are geographically restricted—as if lying in a ditch in Ohio weren't quite so bad as lying in one in Minnesota. Even if these laws were ubiquitous and non-compliance was appropriately sanctioned, the result would still be a codified response to human suffering in terms of rights

---

40. "But a Samaritan, as he journeyed, came to where he was; and when he saw him, he had compassion, and went to him and bound up his wounds, pouring on oil and wine; then he set him on his own beast and brought him to an inn, and took care of him."

backed by force, rather than an acknowledgment of "eternal obligations" honoured out of love for our fellow men.

It might be objected that it is not the state's responsibility to lead its citizens towards the kind of moral *aggiornamento* that would obviate the need for a formal stipulation of rights and duties. Indeed, aren't the latter needed precisely because people do *not* always act as they ought, and doesn't the law provide at least prudential incentives for morally responsible conduct when "higher" motives are lacking? Weil's response to the objection has at least four aspects. One is the recognition that morality and law are by no means coextensive, and that they may engender different kinds of obligation. Another is that the language of rights *does* have a place in public political discourse, as Weil herself acknowledges when she talks about the workers' rights to aid from a relief fund (FW 110), the absence of rights in a factory setting (FW 211), territorial rights (FW 264), the rights of African or Asian people (FW 265), or citizens' rights (LP 160). Indeed, there is no reason why she should disagree with Stanley Hauerwas' observation that "[f]or many, claims to 'rights' express the hope that something like a human community exists, making possible declarations that all people deserve to have their dignity recognized," and that "[f]rom a theological perspective, rights so understood can be regarded as an expression of the Christian eschatological hope that all people are to be ultimately united in common worship of God." [41] On the other hand, even the strictest observance of rights does not necessarily result in justice—e.g., when defendants' rights allow a guilty party to evade conviction on a technicality—and, as Peter Winch rightly observes, "there is the danger that a concern for rights will take one farther and farther away from justice; or that the quest for justice will be entirely submerged." [42] Lastly, Weil would plausibly question whether the citizens' hope for genuine human community, one in which they could also feel spiritually rooted and at home, could be realized unless the state created a climate in which their longing for justice and truth, for example, was properly nourished. [43] The language of rights, though not without merit and justification, clearly falls short of what would be required to provide that nourishment.

---

41. For a detailed description of Good Samaritan Laws by state, see https://world populationreview.com/state-rankings/good-samaritan-law-states.

42. Stanley Hauerwas, "How to Think Theologically About Rights," in *Journal of Law and Religion*, vol. 30, no. 3 (Oct 2015), 402.

43. Peter Winch, *Simone Weil, op.cit.*, 187.

Kant and the "Men of 1789"

I already noted above that Weil's reflections on the notion of obligation contain interesting allusions to the work of Immanuel Kant (1724–1804), and readers familiar with her philosophical training will not find this surprising. [44] Having been introduced to Kant by her teachers Alain (1868–1951) and Jules Lagneau (1851–1894), Weil continued to be impressed with his writings. They struck her as "philosophical doctrines impregnated with Christianity" (NR 92), and even prompted the claim that "Kant leads to grace" (NB, vol.1, 202). While she was also familiar with *The Critique of Pure Reason* and repeatedly commented on various aspects of Kant's *transcendental aesthetic*—e.g., in an essay she wrote for Alain in 1926,[45] the 1933–34 *Lectures on Philosophy*,[46] and her *Notebooks*[47]—she was primarily interested in Kant's moral philosophy, on which she also taught a course while at the girl's lycée at Roanne. I think that what attracted her to the *Groundwork of the Metaphysics of Morals*, in particular, was: (a) its anti-consequentialist orientation, and (b) a transcendental foundation of moral obligation that, even though not overtly religious, strongly resonated with her own (Christian) conception of value. In what follows, I shall briefly comment on each of these features and ask whether, unlike "the men of 1789," who first promulgated rights and then tried to postulate absolute principles detached from a normative realm "situated above this world," Kant is *not* guilty of "a confusion of language and ideas" (NR 4).

---

44. In discussion, Eric Springsted has rightly noted that even if we agree that a *polis* in which citizens can feel properly rooted must be one in which *obligations* are placed in the foreground, it is not (yet) clear how this *desideratum* would be translated into *praxis*. The observation that the language of rights "falls short of what would be required," though true, is still entirely negative. For explorations of more positive responses, see Ronald K. L. Collins's "What Is Greatness—On Reading the Past" (Ch. 7) and Eric Springsted's "The Spirit of Truth: Science and Providence" (Ch. 9). For a critical and insightful examination of Weil's claim that there is a method for instilling in citizens the proper kind of moral and spiritual "inspiration," see Robert Chenavier's "A Unique and Universal Method for Multiple Domains."

45. Given that the Kantian project also inspired writers like Rawls, Habermas, and other promoters of an "impersonal" discourse ethic, it is a pity that commentaries on Weil usually give short shrift to Kant's influence on her ethical outlook.

46. Cf. OC1 60–73. In assessment of Kant's transcendental aesthetic, for example, Weil claims here that "one must affirm in the first place that this analysis of Kant's is true, like the rest of his work."

47. LPh 88.

(a) Implicit in what has been said above about the "lower" motivations associated with the language of rights is the rejection of merely prudential reasoning in favor of a certain kind of attention to our neighbor, one that sees the other as a soul in need, rather than as an occasion for promoting the general welfare or some other earthly goal. Consonant with this, Weil dismisses utilitarianism as a "philosophical fraud" and notes: "One can always ask oneself, when dealing with a moral question, how a utilitarian would tackle the question. Example: punishment is something bad because it harms the culprit; it is good because it prevents crimes. One simply makes an arithmetical calculation" (LPh 166). In the same context, she says: "Pleasure is, by definition, an end in itself, but the pleasure of one's neighbour is not an end in itself. Once it is a question of my neighbour's pleasure, it is no longer an end for me" (LPh 166). Weil's criticism of utilitarianism may be broad and sketchy, but this does not mitigate the force of her central observation, *viz.*, that unconditional obligations cannot be grounded in such (empirical) properties as the capacity for human flourishing or the susceptibility to pain and pleasure. Quite apart from the fact that not all human beings are (constitutionally) capable of flourishing in Aristotle's sense of *eudaimonia*, even the claim that pleasure is an end in itself or that pain is intrinsically bad loses its normative force when agents shift their perspectives from themselves to others. For unless they invest their neighbor's pleasures and pains with a certain kind of meaning, the corresponding obligations—to increase their pleasures and minimize their pains—are likely to remain motivationally impotent. As for the (hopefully redundant) question, "What *kind* of meaning do these agents have to accord their fellow men?" the answer would be: "The kind that shows itself, for example, in the Good Samaritan's act of love and selfless attention to the victim in the ditch."

(b) In contrast to utilitarian conceptions of morality, Kant's notion of obligation involves duties towards others that are at once unconditional and independent of any shared physical or psychological properties of moral agents, because "[man] ... exists as an end in himself and not merely as a means to be arbitrarily used by this or that will."[48] To see our fellow men as ends in themselves involves a perspectival shift—away from the ego and *its* interests towards a self that now appears as a dis-

---

48. NB, vol 1, 163.

tinctive obstacle to our will, and whose concerns—including the need for truthfulness—acquire overriding normative significance. Suppose, so Kant hypothesizes, that

> when I believe myself to be in need of money, I will borrow money and promise to pay it back, although I know that I can never do so. This principle of self-love or personal advantage may perhaps be quite compatible with one's entire future welfare, but the question is now whether it is right. [49]

For Kant, truthfulness in our interaction with others is a strict obligation, not merely because lying undermines the "collective intentionality" and the "deontic powers" associated with speech-acts like "I promise" or "I will," [50] but because treating others as ends in themselves goes hand in hand with a respect for (their legitimate expectation of) the truth. In her *Lectures on Philosophy*, Weil elaborates on Kant's central idea as follows:

> For example, it is not forbidden to allow men to work for us, but we should treat these workers as thinking beings. Every time you speak to someone who serves you only as someone who is your servant, you think of him only as a means. Kant's formula is like what we find in the Gospel: "Love your neighbor as yourself." (LPh 174)

In the light of the above, it is not surprising that Kant's list of obligations towards others also includes the duty to promote their happiness, broadly construed. While that duty allows some latitude—e.g., I do not have to promote the happiness of *everyone* I encounter, am not required to fulfil that duty *all the time*, and should not promote my neighbors' (individual) well-being in the *same* (general or mechanical) manner, e.g., by giving them $5 without paying attention to their particular circumstances or needs, etc.—it is nevertheless obligatory for all morally responsible agents. In the context of Weil's critique of utilitarianism, this means that my (general) duty to increase the pleasurable experiences of others is not rooted in the idea of pleasure as an intrinsic good, but rather in unconditional respect for those whose pleasure it is.

---

49. Kant, *Groundwork*, 428/35.
50. Kant, *Groundwork*, 422.

At this point, it might be objected that, in spite of the (surface) similarities between Kant's deontology and the Gospel's exhortation to love one's neighbor as oneself, the metaphysical framework of the *Groundwork* could not be more different from the Christocentric world view that underlies much of Weil's own thinking. For Kant, so the objection goes, the *ultimate* ground of our moral obligations is an abstract, transcendentalized notion of autonomous rational agency—"transcendentalized" because the idea of freedom that necessarily underpins human action cannot be (empirically or logically) *proven*. Indeed, Kantian impersonalism goes so far as to transcend even *human* rationality. Moral obligations, he insists, "should not be made to depend on the particular nature of human reason ... [but] should be derived from the universal concept of *a rational being in general*, since moral laws should hold for every rational being as such."[51] The primary intention behind Kant's *Groundwork*, so critics might continue, is laudable enough, *viz.*, to preserve the idea of an (objective) moral order that, in his view, *already* informs common ways of talking about moral duty and justice, including the notion of international law and universal declarations of the rights of men. And since Kant's moral values are part of a normative realm "situated above this world," his account of moral obligation is also immune to the criticism Weil levelled against "the men of 1789" earlier, *viz.*, that their naturalist construals of absolute value were the product of conceptual confusion.

Even so, Kant's critical friends might argue, the normative realm from which his ethical values are derived is at once *too* high "above this world" and *not high enough*. The former charge relates, not only to Kant's abstract "rational being in general," but to the linguistic register of his *Groundwork* as a whole, which, on the face of it, seems to be woefully inadequate in capturing what is involved in feeling remorse for a serious crime like murder, for example. As Raimond Gaita puts it: "In remorse he is not haunted by everyman; he is not haunted by his principles; he is not haunted by the moral law; he is not haunted by the fact that he did what he ought not to have done: he is haunted by the particular human

---

51. cf. John Searle, *Making the Social World: The Structure of Human Civilization* (Oxford: Oxford University Press), 8. Weil herself would, of course, not express her thoughts in these terms. On the contrary, Searle's references to "collective intentionality" and "deontic powers" only illustrate the contrast between such ways of talking and Weil's own.

being he murdered." [52] For similar reasons, Cora Diamond is skeptical about how much readers of the *Groundwork* can actually *learn* from Kant, when his philosophical system—replete as it is with abstract terminology like "synthetic a priori," "categorical imperative," "heteronomous principles," "universalizable maxims," etc.—seemingly "allows no place for an active moral self to come to a deeper, or even just a different, understanding by the insightful turning of words." [53] Gaita's and Diamond's complaint is not merely that Kant's work betrays an unfortunate choice of words. It is rather that the language in which his thought about moral relations is couched seriously distorts rather than deepens our understanding of these relations—as if the terribleness of murder, say, consisted in the violation of an abstract idea of "rational being in general" and the individuality of the victim could simply be absorbed into that idea.

I have previously tried to defend Kant against these charges and argued that his third-person philosophical perspective on moral agency should be distinguished from the kind of description that would be appropriate—indeed required—for a first-person point of view, and that the respective (philosophical and ordinary) vocabularies are not incompatible. [54] In this context, I also acknowledged that "[a] murderer who merely regretted killing a member of the species homo sapiens would be a different murderer from one who was haunted by the death of a precious individual," and suggested that Kant would surely concur. [55] The problem—and the reason why I am no longer as confident about my then *apologia* of Kant—is that it is difficult to see how the more natural and richer conception of that death could be distilled from the abstract terminology of the *Groundwork*. The "preciousness" of a human being easily evaporates when viewed as "an instance of humanity or rational nature." One might just as well say that what makes us irreplaceable is

---

52. Kant, *Groundwork*, *op. cit.*, 412 (emphasis added). See also Gr. 408, where Kant says: "We cannot but admit that the moral law is of such widespread significance that it must hold not merely for men but for all rational beings generally."

53. Raimond Gaita, *Good and Evil—An Absolute Conception* (London: Macmillan, 1991), 48.

54. Cora Diamond, *The Realistic Spirit* (London: MIT Press, 1991), 25–6.

55. Mario von der Ruhr, "Kant and the Language of Reason," in *Commonality and Particularity in Ethics*, Lilli Alanen, Sarah Heinämaa, Thomas Wallgren, eds. (Berlin: Springer, 1997), 384–400.

the fact that our bodies trace unique spatio-temporal paths through time, in which case our uniqueness would be no different from the numerical identity of tables and chairs. Here, the Christian understanding of individuals as children of God, *willed* and *chosen* to play a particular role in the divine dramaturgy, sounds much closer to the mark than the "Gradgrind rationalism"[56] tainting Kant's description of our moral phenomenology, including our use of such terms as "dignity," "respect," and "justice." In this regard, the foundations of the *Groundwork* are not placed high enough "above this world."

And Simone Weil? Fortunately—and despite her lasting admiration for Kant—she realized that an adequate account of our relation to other men requires both a certain kind of impersonalism *and* a notion of the sacred that fully preserves their *reality*. That is why she wrote, in her essay "What Is Sacred in Every Human Being?," that "[it] is neither his person nor his personality that is sacred to me. It is him. Him as a whole. Arms, eyes, thoughts, everything. I would not violate any of this without infinite scruples" (LPW 104). What is sacred in one's neighbor is "him, this man, wholly and simply" (LPW 104), even though that sanctity is not rooted in any of his character traits or features of his personality or physical appearance. Kant's declaration that human beings are ends in themselves and "do not have a price"[57] certainly gestures in the right direction, but does it properly circumscribe Weil's use of the term "sacred"? In this context, she also writes:

> There is at the bottom of every human heart something that goes on expecting, from infancy to the grave, that good and not evil will be done to us, despite the experience of crimes committed, suffered, and observed. This above all else is what is sacred in every human being. (LPW 105)

It is not clear exactly how one is to take this remark. Is it an *empirical* observation about a general feature of human psychology? A *personal* perspective on life? In the former case, Weil's remark might also have been made by an atheist like Albert Camus or a Schopenhauerian pessimist propagating an ethic of compassion. The respective *Weltanschau-*

---

56. Mario von der Ruhr, "Kant and the Language of Reason," 390.

57. Cora Diamond, "Martha Nussbaum and the Need for Novels," in *Philosophical Investigations*, vol. 16, no 2, 141.

ung would, however, be radically different, not least with regard to the idea of *justice*. Consider, for example, this remark by Pope Emeritus Benedict XVI:

> This innocent sufferer has attained the certitude of hope: there is a God, and God can create justice in a way that we cannot conceive, yet we can begin to grasp it through faith. Yes, there is a resurrection of the flesh. There is justice. There is an 'undoing' of past suffering, a reparation that sets things aright. For this reason, faith in the Last Judgment is first and foremost hope. [58]

Indeed, so Benedict XVI continues:

> Grace does not cancel out justice. It does not make wrong into right. It is not a sponge which wipes everything away, so that whatever someone has done on earth ends up being of equal value.... Evildoers, in the end, do not sit at table at the eternal banquet beside their victims without distinction, as though nothing had happened. [59]

These last comments allude to an idea of justice that would resonate with Socrates and Plato as strongly as it does with most modern-day Christians, but they would certainly be rejected by thinkers like Camus and Schopenhauer. [60] And Weil? I suspect that, in spite of her deeply Christian orientation, she would take Benedict XVI's comments with more than a pinch of *eschatological* salt, not least because of their retributive resonances. As for her attempt to spell out more fully what is sacred in human beings, it seems to me that Socrates' rejoinder—"it is hard to describe clearly, nor do we now have the time to do so" (*Phaedo,* 114c)—would, on this occasion, have been better than an "explanation" in terms of (subconscious?) hopes and expectations.

---

58. Kant, *Groundwork*, op. cit., 434.

59. Benedict XVI, *Saved in Hope* (San Francisco: Ignatius Press, 2008), 90.

60. *Ibid.*, 92.

Weil, Religion, and the Public Sphere

Given what has been said above about Weil's criticism of rights, her conception of moral obligation, and the sanctity of human life, one would think that her views on the role of religion in the public sphere are clear enough, *viz.*, that its voice should be heard just as loudly as that of any other *Weltanschauung*. Indeed, doesn't *L'Enracinement* insist that "there is no true dignity without a spiritual root and consequently one of a supernatural order" (NR 94), or that "[c]ontact with the beauty of Christianity ... would imperceptibly imbue the mass of the population with spirituality, if it is still capable of being so imbued, far more effectively than any amount of dogmatic teaching of religious beliefs" (NR 93)?

Even so, Weil is aware that this spiritual *desideratum* also raises the question whether the values connected with a distinctly Christian world view *can* be couched in a language common to believers, atheists, and agnostics alike. Her answer, perhaps somewhat surprisingly, is affirmative: "One must try to define them [Christian values] in terms with which an atheist can fully agree, and without removing from them anything that is specific to them. This is possible" (OC 5, 380). Even more succinctly, "It is necessary that one propose something that is precise, specific, and acceptable to Catholics, Protestants and atheists," and yet "not as a compromise" (OC5, 380). It would be going too far to say, as Patrice Rolland does in his preface to *L'Enracinement*, that what Weil is advocating here is a proto-Rawlsian "political liberalism,"[61] but what she says *is* strikingly reminiscent of Charles Taylor's claim that "we are condemned to live an overlapping consensus" because "a really diverse democracy can't revert to a civil religion, or antireligion, however comforting this might be, without betraying its own principles."[62] Somewhat analogously to Weil's distinction between "the language of the market place" and that of "the nuptial chamber" (WG 79), Taylor suggests that "there are zones of a secular state in which the language used has to be neutral," including that of legislation, administrative decrees, and court

---

61. These might embrace a secular analogue of this conception of justice, e.g., in terms of obligations dictated by reason or primitive reactions towards the suffering of our fellow men, but not the metaphysical framework within which this religious conception of justice is set.

62. OC 5, 44.

judgments.[63] Thus, a law passed by parliament could not contain justifying clauses like, "Whereas the Bible tells us that ...", "Whereas Marx has
shown that religion is the opium of the people ...", or "Whereas Kant has
shown that the only thing good without qualification is a good will...."[64]
This does not mean that Christians or Marxists cannot articulate their
values in another zone of the predominantly secular or religious state, or
that the choir of ideologically different voices should not result in common agreement about the significance of such things as the right to life.
On the contrary:

> A Kantian will justify the rights to life and freedom by point-
> ing to the dignity of rational agency; a utilitarian will speak
> of the necessity to treat beings who can experience joy and
> suffering in such a way as to maximize the first and minimize
> the second. A Christian will speak of humans as made in the
> image of God. They concur on the principles, but differ on
> the deeper reasons for holding to this ethic. The state must
> uphold the ethic, but must refrain from favoring any of the
> deeper reasons.[65]

It looks, then, as if Weil would agree with Taylor that it *is* possible even
for the advocates of otherwise radically different world views to concur on
the principles of a common ethic while disagreeing over the "deeper reasons" for holding that ethic. On the face of it, this seems plausible enough,
especially when one thinks of "citizen deliberation"[66] about certain kinds
of rights, including pension rights, residency rights, rights to freedom of
speech and assembly, etc.

Then again, even agreement on general ethical principles such as the
right to life may result in legislative deadlock precisely because the
"deeper reasons" underlying the interlocutors' ethical views may prevent agreement on how that principle is to be applied. For orthodox
Christians, for instance, the right to life also holds for the lives of the
unborn, and so abortion is condemned along with prostitution, assisted

---

63. Charles Taylor, "Why We Need a Radical Redefinition of Secularism," in Edwardo
Mendieta and Jonathan Van Antwerpen, eds., *The Power of Religion in the Public Sphere*
(New York: Columbia University Press 2011), 48.

64. *Ibid.*, 50.

65. *Ibid.*, 37.

66. *Ibid.*, 50.

suicide, premarital sex, same-sex unions, and the ordination of women. Conversely, most atheists would find such prohibitions tyrannical and freedom-denying. In the absence of an Archimedean vantage point from which such diverse *Weltanschauungen* could be reconciled, it is unclear just how far Weil's proposed "translation" of Christian values into a more commonly accepted idiom could go. If, as we have seen, even Kant's "language of reason" is not quite in the right key, then what language *would* preserve the meaning of such values and ideals *salva veritate*? While *The Need for Roots* does not provide a clear answer to this (difficult) question, its critical reflection on the language of rights already tells us much about what that answer would have to look like. It is only when we redirect our attention away from values hanging "in the middle air" and turn towards unconditional obligations "situated above this world" (NR 4) that the ideas of dignity, justice, and the sanctity of human life can properly "root themselves in earth" (SE 23) and continue to nourish our spirits.

CHAPTER 2

The Needs of the Soul as a
Basis for a New Civilization?

Emmanuel Gabellieri

A hurried reading of *The Need for Roots*, especially by someone who takes the word "rootedness" in a conservative sense, can raise, quite spontaneously, two objections with respect to the section that theorizes on the "Needs of the Soul" and that constitutes the first part of the book. First, doesn't speaking of the "needs of the soul" reflect a vague spiritual nostalgia, one that is analogous to that with which the French philosopher Henri Bergson was reproached in talking talked about "nourishing the soul" when faced with the rise of modern technology? Second, to speak of needs "of the soul and of the body," as Weil does in the beginning of the text, seems to be a sign of a soul/body dualism rooted in a Platonic or Cartesian "essentialism" that modern critiques of metaphysics and "philosophies of suspicion" no longer allow us to assume. What new thing could such a return to ancient metaphysics or to modern philosophies of the subject possibly raise? Or is it a question of introducing something of the "spiritual" into politics in a sense analogous to what Wassily Kandinsky proposed as "something spiritual in art"? But what exactly does that mean?

One can respond to these questions and objections in several ways. First, recall that for Weil talk about the soul is not principally an ontological issue, but a practical one: genuine philosophy envisions a "transformation of the soul." The notion of a soul therefore invites a movement, an aspiration of the subject to "fullness" or "plenitude," an experience of transformation of the self. This parts ways with classical philosophies of the subject. This is because for her it is not a question purely and simply of thinking about what transcends the body, nor even of a transcendence that goes beyond subjectivity; it is a question of being *indwelt* by what is bigger than the self. Whence arises the very important theme of the "impersonal," for what counts is not subjectivity insofar as it is subjectivity, but the *universality* to which subjectivity *opens itself.*

At the same time, there isn't here a perspective of a salvation of the soul that lets it be separated from the truth of the world, for the soul is revealed and realized by the simultaneity of its earthly, social, and spiritual needs. At the same time that the expression "needs of the soul" looks back at a metaphysics of desire, from the "hunger" calling for "nourishment" (which opens up the classical theme of the "passions of the soul"), it also roots the soul in the *metaxu*, those things between heaven and earth, our heavenly country and our terrestrial country. In London, Weil thought about rewriting Plato's *Republic* in a contemporary context, with its overarching theme of the likeness of the soul and the city now taking the form of a theory of the "needs of the soul." Here Weil would try a novel transposition, according to a principle of "the union of contraries," which she took from the teachings of the Pythagoreans.[1] This would require a new anthropology, more profound than the one underlying the modern declarations of "the rights of man" that came from the thinkers of the French Revolution (whence her debate with Jacques Maritain—see Introduction) This would then lead to a meta-politics that would (a) rehabilitate the "social" and "collectivities" as places of nourishment for the soul and (b) articulate in a new way both the secular and the spiritual via a universal relation, mediated by the *metaxu*, of all human beings to a Good that transcends politics.

---

1. See on this point the clarifying study of de Francesca Simoni, "Qu'en est-il de Platon à Londres? Traces platoniciennes dans la psychagogie politique de l'impersonnel," *Cahiers Simone Weil* XLIV n°2, juin 2021, p. 129–55, which expands her thesis submitted jointly to Internationale Universita LUMSA de Rome/Institut Catholique de Paris in 2021 under the title *Custodire nella Trascendenza. Platone e l'impersonnel nel pensiero di Simone Weil.* Part of the following analyses follows those of this work.

Context: The Debate with
Jacques Maritain over the "Rights of Man"

More than twenty years ago, I argued that Weil's debate with Jacques Maritain had actually begun in her Marseille period, as can be seen in the way in which Maritain's name comes up in a decided way in the successive drafts of her May 26, 1942, letter to Father Perrin[2] (WG 88–101). If, as she says there, the sort of new saintliness that Maritain tried to define in the context of the present age appeared insufficient to her, it was because he didn't root it deeply enough in a love coming "from God himself."[3] This was so in Weil's eyes because neo-Thomism didn't think deeply enough about the link between human nature and the "supernatural." This was confirmed for her by reading Maritain's book, *The Rights of Man and the Natural Law* (1942), in New York.[4] It is here that the text of St. Thomas Aquinas on friendship is "quoted by Maritain," and then noted by Weil in her London writings, which were published in *La Connaissance surnaturelle*[5] (FLN), as well as in her text on the notion of "rights" found in *The Need for Roots*.[6] Her critique of Aristotle and Mar-

---

2. See E. Gabellieri, *Etre et Don. S. Weil et la philosophie*, Louvain, Paris: Bibliothèque philosophique de Louvain, Peeters, 2003, first, the section «S.Weil et J. Maritain. Une clef des Ecrits de Londres?, 451–62, then the «Annexes» I, 1, 2, and 3 with a *facimilé*, analyzing the successive drafts of the unpublished *Lettre* inédite to P. Perrin of May 14, 1942, which prepared for the *Lettre VI* published in *Attente de Dieu* (*Etre et don ... op.cit.*, p. 533–542). A very good understanding of Weil's critique of Maritain has also been given by E. O. Springsted in *Simone Weil for the Twenty-First Century*, Notre Dame: University of Notre-Dame Press, 2021, «Beyond the Personal: Weil's Critique of Maritain», 121–31 and 138–41.

3. On the occurrence of this expression and its variants see Gabellieri, *Etre et Don*, 536–37.

4. See on this point my «De la lecture des *Droits de l'homme et la loi naturelle* à l'enjeu des *Ecrits de Londres*», in Gabellieri, *Etre et Don* 458–62. The first one to have noted this work was Simone Fraisse, «Simone Weil, la personne et les droits de l'homme,» *CSW* VII-2, juin 1984. 120–32.

5. This passage is from the *Commentaire sur l'Ethique à Nicomaque* d'Aristote, where Weil denounces a concept of his conception of friendship as radically "contrary to Christianity" (FLN 355) is cited by Maritain at 53–54 *Les Droits de l'homme et la loi naturelle* which appeared in English in New York in 1942, by Editions de la Maison Française, in the collection "Civilisation" that Maritain had just created. This was the edition that Weil used.

6. The "Roman conception of God" which "still subsists today, especially in minds such as Maritain's" (NR 274) is a citation of Maritain, *Les Droits de l'homme* 85.

itain comes up again overtly in "What Is Sacred in Every Human Being?"[7] where the references to Maritain are not hidden but fully transparent, and to which there are several links to her "Fragments de
Londres" and to the essay "Is There a Marxist Doctrine?" (OL 169–195).[8]

Her repeated references to a single work, and to a work which had
just appeared, is without doubt unique in Weil's writings, and should
alert us to the weight she laid on her reading of it. What is clearly at
stake, in Weil's mind, is to oppose to Maritain's thinking—a philosophy
of "natural law" and "rights," a way of thinking wherein all reality needs
to be related to the "supernatural." Maritain's philosophy appeared to her
to be too dependent on the continuity between an Aristotelianism,
which she judged "naturalistic," and modern humanism. And this is all
the more obvious since Weil opposed the insufficiency of Maritain's
thinking and its influence in the Gaullist milieux. She was visibly trying
to put together structurally, *but in her own way*, something along the
same lines that Maritain had proposed. Where she parted ways with
Maritain was primarily over his defining a "personalist" philosophy as
being capable of opposing totalitarianism. She also took exception to his
objective of developing a diverse and robust philosophy of natural law
that mainly depended, ontologically, on a descending movement of
"natural law" into positive human law,[9] and then on to the social plane
with respect to the diversity of rights by defining them according to their
social situatedness.[10] The appendix of his book, which was comprised of
the text of "The 1929 International Declaration of the Rights of Man,"
symbolized to her the attempt to find a universal norm capable of being
a regulative ideal for political action, while at the same time a common
spiritual ideal for a society divided in its beliefs. One is struck, nonethe-

---

7. "It is by a singular confusion that one could assimilate the unwritten law of An-
tigone to natural right" (LPW 114), is a quotation in which Weil is refers to Maritain, *Les
Droits de l'homme* 78–80. Weil goes on: "Supernatural good is not a sort of supplement
to natural good, as certain people would like, with Aristotle's help, to persuade us of to
our great comfort" (LPW 117). This is confirmation of the debate over the relation of
nature and supernature.

8. The critique of this essay applies to Maritain as well as to Marx, since in both the
order of nature would be thought without any relation to the supernatural.

9. See Maritain, *Les Droits de l'Homme* 67–103.

10. See Maritain, *Les Droits de l'Homme* "Les Droits de la personne civique" (104–
113), "Les droits de la personne ouvrière" (114–134), and then "Résumé des Droits
énumérés" (135–138).

less, by the formal parallel with what Weil herself developed out of this reading in London. It is that parallel that we need to consider.

The text that has come down to us as *The Need for Roots*, we know ought to be introduced by Weil's "Study for a Declaration of Obligations towards the Human Being" (Appendix II). Fortunately, this text has now been put in the beginning of the recent French critical editions of *L'Enracinement*.[11] If one looks closely, this "Prelude" plays the same role in it as chapter one and the appendix of Maritain's book does in that work, but with this difference: in Weil's eyes, the sacred for Maritain is "the person" insofar as the person is the individual, rather than the "human being,"[12] or the "impersonal" part of the soul.[13] We need to draw out this parallel structure a bit, for it is obviously the diversification of the rights of the person (Maritain's chapter two) that she wants to directly oppose with her own diverse "needs of the soul," the first part of *The Need for Roots*. With respect to the second part on the different types of uprootedness—those of the worker, the peasant, and the nation—Weil develops it as a parallel to Maritain's second chapter, which tried for a description of the concrete modalities of rights in modern societies. The third part, which we know under the title of "The Growing of Roots," demands a more detailed analysis, but, even without it, it is clear that the structural parallels continue. Consider, for example, Weil's critique of false greatness in the West's philosophical, religious, and political realms (see Chapter 7). It is similarly Weil's reply to all those for whom the history of Christianity or of humanism and modern personalism is a set of figures that she thinks we need to substitute for with a new vision.

Nevertheless, in all this there still does not appear the most original theme of *The Need for Roots*, as well that of other texts from London (and probably the most problematic theme in the eyes of many), namely, that

---

11. See OC V.2 96–101. In a second critical edition of *L'Enracinement* (ENR) the editors have put in the appendix two versions of "Study for a Declaration of Obligations towards the Human Being." The "Profession of Faith" is found at 403–409.

12. See: "The object of any obligation, in the realm of human affairs, is always the human being as such" (NR 5). Beyond the rejection of the classical terms of "person" or "individual" the use of the term "human being" expresses, it seems to me, a desire to replace the "human" in the field of universal being: "the human being," "human things" being a domain of the universal, and not the universal in itself, as modern anthropocentrism tends to think.

13. This is the essential point of "What Is Sacred in Every Human Being?" as well as of "The Study for a Declaration of Obligations."

of what it takes to *grow* roots in all the human and social dimensions that are put in play in any reference to the desire of "a pure Good present in all human beings." It is therefore necessary to take up the suggestion that *The Need for Roots* ultimately played for Weil's thinking an equivalent role to the one that *The Theologico-Political Treatise* did for Spinoza.[14] But given that the "theological" pole here does not refer us back to any classical theological figures, its principle is, then, for Weil, the determination of what she called in Marseille, "the forms of the implicit love of God." And, that is while understanding that it is a question in *The Need for Roots* of starting with the opening of the human to a pure and transcendent Good and then moving to seeking the possible ways of this Good finding its way into the entirety of social and political reality.[15] However, what this perspective involves is only clarified by looking at its relation to her writings in Marseille, which then ought also to clarify what she means by "the needs of the soul." For if the notions of "soul," "sacred," "impersonal," and the "desire for the Good" express the search for a human political principle deeper than the modern concept of "person," which is too often identified with the "individual," it is so in its being a furthering of a metaphysics of mediation—in Marseille Weil had profoundly reworked classical anthropological and ontological notions in a way in that was necessary to rethink certain basic features of the human.

The Needs of the Soul and Collectivities

Attempting a comprehensive overview of Weil's philosophy of the human soul undoubtedly means going back to her earliest, youthful texts. Thus if one refers to her commentary on "The Six Swans of Grimm," which she wrote when she was sixteen years old in Alain's class, something appears there which will not cease to deepen in the following

---

14. See Gabellieri, *Etre et don*, «*L'Enracinement* ou le *Traité théologico-politique* de S.Weil», 462–474.

15. Whence formulas of this type, expressing the universalization with which Weil thought to be Christian truth: "The Gospel contains a conception *of human life* not a theology" (FLN148), and "I believe that the mysteries of the Catholic religion are an inexhaustible source of truth concerning the *human condition*" (OC VI. 266) (emphasis added).

years. As the example of the younger sister sewing in silence six shirts of anemones for six years in order to save her six brothers shows, the truth of human action is "to establish *in the body* a truth which is in the soul" (OC I 59). By developing in this way her first example of the truth of "work as mediation," which will come to be one of the keys to her life and thought (see Chapter 9), Weil also forges an anti-dualistic vision of the relation of the body to the soul. For "the drama of the tale only happens in the soul of the heroine," but we are only pointed to it by "the expression *in our body* of what only the naked and dead judges of Plato can see in the depth of our souls" (OC I.59).[16]

This early text precociously affirms that the soul is at one and the same time a principle of transcendence and of incarnation, in such a way that its first job is to act out "a pact between the mind and the body." The "soul" should not be reduced to either thought or intelligence; it appears both below and above the intelligence, a view inspired notably by the Platonic tripartite soul in the *Republic* (Bk. 4: 439–443).[17] As a principle of mediation, it appears to go even beyond the principle of action that Alain impressed upon his students,[18] that it is above all the power of unification and "transformation of the being" by which Weil defined philosophy in her Marseille *Notebooks*, and where she linked this definition to the famous Platonic philosophical saying: "To go towards the truth with all one's soul."[19] This is confirmed in the essay "Some Reflections on the Concept of Value" where she says that "philosophy does not consist in accumulating knowledge, as science does, but in changing the whole soul" (LPW 33). Beyond the intelligence or the will, the idea that the soul is an "orientation towards value," is thus confirmed as "a relation not only to knowledge but to the sensibility and action" (LPW 33).

To recognize the soul fully in this way then leads us also to leave behind a Cartesian sort of philosophy of consciousness, for we do not have a complete consciousness of our soul, which is the secret focus of our

---

16. Emphasis added.

17. See Simoni, *Custodire nella Trascendenza. Platone e l'imperonnel nel pensiero di Simone Weil* (*op.cit* note 1).

18. See the formula of Alain: «There is no vile soul; but only a lack of soul. This beautiful saying is not a being but an action.» (Alain, *Les Arts et les Dieux*, Bibliothèque de La Pléiade, Paris, 1979.1031).

19. See, for example, OC VI.1 174 which cites the *Republic* (Book VII 518c). "If one goes to the truth with all one's soul, it is a matter of the whole person" (OC IV.1 67).

aspirations and orientations of which we know neither the principle nor the end: "the soul can only be unified with the truth in the night, in the unconscious" (OC VI.3 46). To define the soul as "a self-sculpture," as has been constantly done from the Stoics to Foucault, can still have a limit here, namely, that of the "relation to the self" which belongs to the Greek idea of autarchy, or self-sufficiency. For if the soul is plastic and malleable, it is because it takes the form of what it is open to, from what it orients itself towards, and it doesn't know ahead of time what is going to follow from that. The science of the soul is this "psychagogy" linking the soul to a Good that is at both transcendent and capable of descending into it, but without dominating it in the process.

If this Good can descend into the human being, it needs to do so into both body and soul[20] for the "fullness of reality" for the human being "exists here below"(OC VI.3 51).[21] Metaphysically, the soul is "desire for the Good," but it cannot be united with it immediately and directly. Because it is in the flesh, it can only be oriented to the Good by a ladder of particular goods which are so many *metaxu*, or intermediaries. This is why the "respect" due to the desire for the Good exceeds the respect due to the different needs of the soul and body. And, phenomenologically, that which needs to be developed also needs a "milieu," or environment. This notion of a "milieu" does not appear explicitly when Weil defines "rootedness" as the most fundamental of the soul's needs at the end of the opening section of *The Need for Roots* (NR 38, OC V.2 142–143). But she implies it, since from the beginning of the text, the needs of the soul

---

20. It is necessary here to point out all the fragments in the *Notebooks* where the union of the body and soul is insistently underlined, a union thanks to which one can, "with all the soul" be "united with the whole universe." See, for example, OC V.1 172, 290, 295; VI. 2 337, 353). Many of these passages seem to be forerunners to the theory of "the needs of soul and body."

21. See also this well-known passage "The whole soul needs to be detached from this world, but it is only the supernatural part that comes into relation with the other world… The natural part of the soul, detached from one world, while attaining another that is beyond it, is in the void during the operations of deliverance. It is necessary to put it in contact with this world that belongs to it, [emphasis added], but the right kind of contact, one that is not an attachment." [¶] "To sum up, after having torn the soul from the body, having traversed death to go to God, the saint needs in some way to incarnate himself in his own body, so that he might shed upon this world, upon this earthly life and this world a reality, for until then it is only dreams. It is incumbent upon him thus to achieve creation. The perfect imitator of God first of all disincarnates himself, then incarnates himself." (LPW 69).

are defined as vital needs, "analogous to bodily hunger" (NR 7; OC V.2 114). Thus the fundamental need of the soul as well as of the body is to be "nourished," implying, in effect, the existence of this other: "we owe our respect to a collectivity, of whatever kind—country, family or any other—not for itself, but because it is food for a certain number of human souls" (NR8, OC V.2 115).

The insistence here on the notion of the "collectivity,"[22] in contrast to her rejection of the "collective" and the "social" that characterizes her texts during the 1930s, goes back to the idea that "certain collectivities, which instead of serving as food, do just the opposite: they devour souls" (NR 9, OC V.2 116).[23] However, to speak of a "milieu" implies a *plurality* of the needs of the soul, for the soul, like the body, is constituted by a set of vital relations. No need is absolute by itself and cannot satisfy the desire for the Good. Every need is limited, and an unlimited need is an impossibility. Therefore, all the needs ought to be put into some kind of equilibrium, complementing each other in opposite pairs that correspond to immediate needs, but which also ought to permit them to be oriented toward that which transcends their reciprocal limits. Whence arises the proper structure of the theory of needs, which it is now necessary to consider in detail.

The Polar Structure and the Unity of the Needs of the Soul

Once the distinction between "need" and "desire" is made, the second characteristic of the needs to be noted is that they are "arranged in antithetical pairs and have to combine together to form a balance"[24] (NR 12, OC V.2 119). It is striking to note that the principle of "a union between

---

22. The term "collectivity" taken in the sense of a nourishing milieu shows up a dozen times in two pages (NR 8–9) which immediately precede the discussion of the needs of the soul. One concludes from this the importance of this insistence.

23. Weil distinguished four types of collectivity: (1) those which are truly nourishment for a succession of generations; (2) those which "eat souls"; (3) those which furnish to souls insufficient nourishment; (4) the collectivities which, without devouring souls, no longer nourish them.

24. There is the same formula in another fragment: "The needs of the soul can for the most part be listed in opposed pairs which balance and complement each other" (OC V.2 370).

contraries," which was at the heart of the Pythagorean-and-Platonic-in-spired metaphysics of Weil's Marseille writings, serves once more as a principle for the doctrine of the needs of the soul in the London writings.[25] But in considering the list of the six pairs of contraries found in the text of *The Need for Roots* we are obliged to note two further points at the outset. The first is that this list, if one also consults various fragments and related texts from this time, is undoubtedly not exhaustive, and can be expanded, as we are going to argue below.[26] But the second, and the more striking comment, is that two of the needs of the soul that Weil puts forth, the "most essential ones" do *not* seem to have a place on the list of contrary needs. The first of them, that is, order, seems to have its role as linking the set of needs and obligations (NR 10, OC V.2 117–118). With respect to the second unpaired need, namely, "the need for roots," "the most important and least recognized need of the human soul," (NR 43; OC V.2 142–3) it is the one that is hardest to define precisely because of the intersection of "roots" and the "vital *milieux*" that are so necessary to the human soul. How does one understand the concurrence between these two needs, which both seem to be uncategorizable and all embracing, and their relation to the other needs of the soul that have been organized into contrary pairs?

Recently, Eric O. Springsted has looked carefully at Weil's notion of "order" and has raised the question of a possible tension between these two needs. On the one hand, "order" appears above all to refer to a principle of unity, whereas, on the other hand, "rootedness" always means for Weil having multiple roots. This suggests that the difference can come down to one where the idea of order, a major source for which in Weil's thinking was the ancient idea of an "order of the world" (of which the human world is a microcosm), is ahistorical, whereas Weil's analyses of rootedness are always historically determined.[27] This remark, from

---

25. Recall the formula of "The Romanesque Renaissance" ("*L'inspiration occitanienne*") that I put as a chapter in *Etre et Don* (462), which can be seen as a prelude to the theory of needs of the soul: "Liberty was loved. Obedience was loved no less. The unity of these two contraries is the Pythagorean harmony in society" (SE 51;OC IV.2 422).

26. The remark that the needs of the soul "are much more difficult to recognize and to enumerate than are the needs of the body" (NR7; OC V.2 115) clarifies why Weil considered the list of needs incomplete.

27. Springsted, *Simone Weil for the Twenty-First Century*, chapter 11, especially 160–165.

Springsted's point of view, goes to underline just how important but how misunderstood concrete history is in Weil.[28] For him, the two concepts are linked and complementary (see Chapter 8). However, I would like to underline this in such a way as to stress their linkage such that at a certain level, it seems to me, they are circular.

In effect, as order is "above all needs properly so-called" (NR 12, OC V.2 118), "rootedness" is also, but from a different point of view. Both are supra-categorial. But whereas order seems above all to be perceived as a principle of unity that is transcendent and harmonizing the contrary needs,[29] rootedness appears first as a immanent and vital result of the satisfaction of needs. It is by rootedness that the soul receives "wellnigh the whole of its moral, intellectual and spiritual life by way of the environment (*milieux*) of which he forms a natural part" (NR 44, OC V.2 143). As a result of the interweaving of all the needs, rootedness expresses their unity and harmony, but less from the point of view of the notion of obligation and more from the point of view of a vital principal that animates these obligations and which nourishes the soul by the web of relations that gives it life in the heart of a community. On this this plane, Weil, it seems to me, is therefore fully faithful to the Pythagorean and Platonic inspiration acceding to which the union of contraries is only possible by their mutual relation to a principle of unity, *transcendent* in its origin and *immanent* in its destination. Order and rootedness thus express the relation and the solidarity amongst the other needs. One thus finds, as Springsted has indeed stressed, the articulation between an idea of order which, on the metaphysical plane looks back at the micro/macrocosm scheme of the ancients, and the idea of rootedness which, more visibly, sinks its roots, so to say, into the concrete particularities that belong to the history of cultures.[30] But this does not

---

28. This is in debate with other commentators such as David McClellan and Peter Winch, concerning what has sometimes been called Weil's "utopian" dimension.

29. Order expresses in effect "a texture of social relationship such that no one is compelled to violate imperative obligations in order to carry out other ones" (NR 10; OC V.2.117).

30. See, for example: "If the need for order suggested a need to instantiate the order of Being itself, or to link social order to the order of the universe, the idea of rootedness would appear to run in the opposite direction; rather than supporting any suggestion that there is a single order to be instantiated, it suggest that our particular and distinctive histories are what are most important." Springsted, *Simone Weil for the Twenty First Century*, 164.

mean that there is an opposition or tension between the two planes. The tension is not between these two planes, but is at the interior of each of them, between the principle of harmony and the plurality of the elements that it harmonizes—the truth of Being always being for Weil the unity of a plurality, from the cosmos and the social world up to the Trinity.

Once we have put order and rootedness together, we can then consider the list of pairs of contraries that Weil holds together. The first needs are "liberty" and "obedience," which appear themselves to be unified in "responsibility"; then in quick succession comes "equality" and "hierarchy," "honor" and "punishment," "freedom of opinion" and "truth," "security" and "risk," "private property" and "collective property." (The last pair today might be put as "private property" and "the common good.")

As we have seen above, this list is undoubtedly in Weil's mind not exhaustive. When we consult the various drafts of *The Need for Roots*, we know that there are variants and possible additions. What might be added, while remaining close to the pairs indicated above, are "intimacy" and "public life" (OC V.2 375), or "participation in a collective action," and "personal initiative" (OC V.2 376). There also appears a need whose singularity is, like order and rootedness, supra-categorial and cutting across all the others. This need is joy: "Joy is an essential need of the soul. The lack of joy, whether it is due to affliction or simply boredom, is a sick state where the intelligence, courage, and generosity are extinguished. Human thought is nourished by joy" (OC V.2 168). We might note in this passage how in this type of fragment we are obliged to break with the idea that Weil was utterly fascinated with affliction and in a way which forbade all joy. But, what is of significance for us here is to see that joy does not number itself with the plurality of the needs, but, in a way analogous to rootedness, it appears as an immanent result of their satisfaction: "As the satisfaction of the needs of the body produce well-being, the satisfaction of the needs of the soul produce joy" (OC V.2 399). Joy is thus less a need itself than it is the vital satisfaction of the other needs, accompanying the sense of rootedness in the universe.[31]

According to the set of texts which we are treating, leaving aside the question of the list's completeness and definitiveness, we thus have

---

31. See the parallel remarks of Julie Daigle in Chapter 3.

nearly twenty needs of the soul.[32] One can see that, whatever possible additions there might be, all of them confirm the principle that demands that these needs of the soul, besides any synthetic or supra-categorial ones, are not contradictories but contraries, and are to be balanced. Thus liberty and obedience are needs of the soul, but neither of these terms can be absolutized. Rather, it is necessary to link them in order to see the truth of what these terms mean. It is the same with the other pairs, whose binary or bipolar qualities are unified transcendently. This anthropology and ontology of "polarity" is a thought that is original to Weil, but one will find a similar principle in other twentieth-century authors, such as Roman Guardini and Maurice Blondel, where the ensemble of the real is structured precisely by polarities, in opposition to the schemes of ontological monists and dualists that are so common in the history of philosophy.[33] It is now necessary to consider if this clarifies the properly political stakes of the theory of the needs of the soul.

An Original Model of Political Anthropology

At first glance, this list of the needs of the soul might seem to be quite neutral with regard to any political philosophy. It is hard to see how one could develop any political doctrine from it that is suitable to the modern context. There is also a second difficulty here in that this list does not bear any evident relation to the other dimensions of Weil's political reflections in London that are better known such as the relations between the person and the sacred, between true and false greatness (Chapter 7), and between politics and religion or spirituality.

Nevertheless, there is one characteristic that can help, if one pays attention to the fact that the principle of the union of contraries can be utilized in order to construct relations between the needs. That will lead us to let two major lines of thought intersect: (i) the one which looks back to *personal freedoms* (freedom/freedom of opinion/risk/private

---

32. In a fragment seeking to deepen "the notion of obligation-need," Weil clarifies this relative indetermination in a luminous way by writing: "This formula is as absolute as a principle and as flexible as life" (OC V.1 377). Whence, at the end of "the Profession of Faith" she says that "this study is always open to revision." See Appendix I.

33. See Emmanuel Gabellieri, *Le phénomène et l'entre-deux: Pour une metaxologie.* Herman: Paris, 2019; especially sec. 19, 174–183.

property/personal initiative/intimacy); (and (ii) the other which looks back to the inverse for *a social order* (obedience/hierarchy/punishment/truth/security/participation in the collective/public life).

The sought-for balance between these two axes seems obvious; it reveals *a principle of reciprocal subordination* between the person and the community. That can then give us a key that says something about the question of the apparent neutrality of the exposition. The neutrality is in effect only an apparent one. For everything makes sense if one views it from the point of view that it is trying to respond to a major conflict of modernity, which is nothing less, in the broadest sense, than the one between liberalism and socialism (or individualism/communitarianism if one is referring to this post-modern variant of the individual-society conflict). The setting out of the needs of the soul seems in a certain sense to ignore superbly this conflict while seeking to do it justice, if one can put it that way. There is thus, on the one side, the truth of liberalism (represented by the series of terms fleshing out the idea of freedom) and, on the other side, the truth of socialism (which is witnessed in the series "equality-collective").

This last observation, however, also has its limits. Distinguishing the two lines of thought then makes it appear that there is a *third series* of terms and values, either remaining outside the first two series, or one that gives prominence to certain terms classified in one or the other line. The decisive point being that these tertiary values, in relation to modernity, seem to be "pre-modern" ones, namely: order/obedience/honor/punishment/truth/rootedness/public life.

We thus come to meet up with, under a new angle, the old question of whether Weil's final political reflections are modern or anti-modern. For it seems evident that the table of categories that we have before our eyes is both at once, or, even at one and the same time, modern and pre-modern, if one wants to put it that way. But this way of speaking still isn't right. For Weil's thinking proceeds on two tracks: she wants to marry liberalism's truth with that of socialism (which, insofar as they are ideologies, are not contraries in the Pythagorean sense but terms that have become, in modernity, contradictories), and likewise wants to marry the truth of these two modern currents with values whose origins and models are ancient and medieval. In the process she ventures to posit a mixture that simply does not have any name in modern ideology, no more than it does in antiquity or the medieval. Such is the horizon given to "the new civilization" that the London writings are trying to sketch.[34]

This remark may well suffice to clarify what the stakes are in *The Need for Roots*. But, as we know, this theory of the needs of the soul is only one of the dimensions of the new political anthropology that Weil was trying to utilize in London, and that all the contributors of the present volume are trying to clarify. So, while remaining centered on the notion of the needs of the soul, we will now try to stress two of these dimensions, one that links these needs to a philosophy of public life, and the other clarifying again the relation of the theory of the needs of the soul to a desire for the Good that goes beyond public life.[35]

Vital *Milieux* and Public Life

When one considers the properly vegetal nature of the metaphor of rootedness, one is likely to take away from the idea of "roots" (especially if one is careless, as one finds in other political contexts) the sense of an ideological conservatism or even a "pagan" idolatry of the sun.[36] But

---

34. This situation ought to clarify the recurring debate of the last fifty years as to whether Weil's must therefore shed light, in our opinion, on the recurring debate in the debates for more than fifty years (and especially around *L'Enracinement* and the writings of London) to know if the thought of Weil is "modern" or "anti-modern." Everybody gives an opinion which no doubt sheds light on his or her own personal inclination, but not Weil's thought itself, at least, if we do not see that she seeks to shatter this opposition as such, by laying down the principles of a new historical vision: "post-modern" certainly, but one that still has not been named.

35. See: "every human being is made above all (however one could die without ever have done these things) for things infinitely higher than any ideal proposed to him by public life" (OC V.2 398).

36. This reading is notably illustrated in Phillippe Dujardin, *Idéologie et politique* (Grenoble: Presses Universitaires Grenoble, 1975.) But it has also been seen from another point of view in Emmanuel Levinas, whose ethical admiration for Weil remained closed with respect to the idea of rootedness; it was, in his eyes, pagan, and linked to what he saw as Weil's "anti-hebraism." I note two of my own studies on this subject: "Simone Weil Between paganism and the Bible: A Hermeneutic Dialogue with Ricoeur, Lévinas, Schelling and Pascal," in *Between the Human and the Divine, Philosophical and Theological Hermeneutics*, Andrzej Wiercinski éd., (Toronto: Hermeneutic Press, 2002), 456–470; and «Judaïsme et querelle des Alliances», *Cahier de L'Herne Simone Weil*, (Paris, Ed. de L'Herne), 2014, 358–69.

when one considers more closely Weil's attempt at a definition of "roots," two things appear that forcefully forbid this misreading.

The first is that rootedness appears as something temporal and historical before it is spatial. It expresses the relation between "a community which preserves in living shape certain particular treasures of the past and certain particular expectations for the future" (NR 43). From this point of view, this is not at all a reference to a territory that is at stake, but a sense of continuity between past, present, and future, crystallized in a culture. This is why, at least up to a certain point, a culture, a people can be something more than a state, that is, if they have the freedom to maintain their customs and their own culture. This is also why a nomad deprived of the desert, and kept from wandering, would be just as up-rooted as a citizen from a small Italian city thrown all at once into New York without any links to all that he might have been attached to before. Rootedness supposes, therefore, whatever might be the set of determinations to which that refers, a familiar way of life by which the soul and that which is outside it can be sensed to be in harmony.

But it is necessary that at the same time there be some sort of respiration[37] that goes on between interiority and exteriority. The loss of a sense of being at home is uprooting. But being enclosed in a sense of home and not having a sense of openness to the outside can also mean the death of the soul. This indicates another essential trait that we have already noted: rootedness supposes a notion of a vital milieu, which for Weil actually always refers to a plurality of milieux in life, as it does to a plurality of roots. "Every human being needs to have multiple roots. It is necessary for him to draw wellnigh the whole of his moral, intellectual and spiritual life by way of the environment of which he forms a natural part" (NR 43; OC V.2, 143). This plurality is fundamental. One rediscovers it here at a second level, but which was in fact already in the principle of the unity of contraries belonging to the theory of the needs of the soul, namely that they are plural.

This philosophy of a living milieu is interdependent with a notion of public life, which is often expanded by analogous formulas of "collective

---

37. A particular study should be developed here, analogous to what Pascal David has seen with respect to the notion of "atmosphere" so often presented in the London texts. See Pascal, David, *Simone Weil, Luttons-nous pour la justice ? Manuel d'action politique*, (Lyon: Ed. Peuple libre, 2017), 229–35).

life," or "the public good." These play in Weil the same role as "public space" does in Hannah Arendt.[38] Such expressions are used in the London writings, notably when it is a question for Weil of thinking out the conditions of collective action necessary to the French Resistance, or when reflecting on the future political structures of the Free French. But they go beyond this context, harkening back, for example, to the model of the *Notebooks* for making demands, and to the Assembly of 1789 where the fluidity of the milieu of ideas proper to philosophical revues is more appropriate than political parties.[39] And the usage of the expression "public life" since the texts of 1939–1940 recalls another model for Weil, namely, that of the civilization of Languedoc.[40] In all these cases, it is a question of what rises up from the depths of a people without the action of the State, of a "radiance" that invents its own kinds of action and expressions, according to the model of a "new saintliness" that Weil laid out in her sixth letter to Father Perrin on May 26, 1942.[41] This "radiance" only exists in the case of popular movements that have "grown up like a plant," that is, in a spontaneous way, independent of all ideologico-political structure.[42] It occurs where the idea behind an organization

---

38. Note my analyses first in Gabellieri *Etre et Don*, 468–75, and then deepened in «Vie publique et *vita activa* chez S. Weil et H. Arendt», *Cahiers Simone Weil* 1999, 135–52; «'Action' et'Inspiration' un double fondement du politique?» in «Amor mundi, Amor Dei. Simone Weil et Hannah.Arendt», *Théophilyon*, IX-2, 2004, 559–79; «Ethique et 'Vie publique' comme médiations entre Religion et Politique», *Annuario di filosofia 2009*; «Ritorno della religione? Tra ragione, fede e società", Ed. Guerini Studio, Milano, 2009, 119–38.

39. The abundant use of this expression is strikingly noted in "Légitimité du gouvernement provisoire," "Réflexions sur la révolte" and "On the Suppression of All Political Parties" (SAPP).

40. See "A Medieval Epic Poem" and "The Romanesque Renaissance," SE 35–43, 44–53.

41. "Today it is not nearly enough merely to be a saint, but we must have the saintliness demanded by the present moment." Maritain "did not feel all the miraculous newness the saintliness of today must contain…. A new type of sanctity is, indeed, a fresh spring, an invention … almost equivalent to a new revelation" (WG 99). These passages are of the same ilk as those cited above concerning her debate with Maritain, which has led me to propose seeing in this letter from May 26, 1942, and in the draft of the letter from May 14, the origin of the set of writings from New York and London seeking to define the "invention" of a new civilization.

42. "The Assembly of 1789, so to say, pushed up like a plant in the milieu of a fever of thought which shook France during those months. It multiplied from circles of free discussion…. No party discipline, no propaganda poisoned it. A lot of men really sought

does not deny spontaneity, and, reciprocally, "when such an organization has not been formed artificially, but has grown up like a plant in the midst of day-today necessities, having at the same time been molded with patient vigilance and with some particular good clearly kept in view. This constitutes, perhaps, the highest degree of reality" (NR 211–212; OC V.2 282). This unity is at once moving and a method for inspiration, reason, necessity, and is at the heart of an action entirely indwelt by its goal, capable of unifying the successive temporality of means in the superior temporality of the collective aspiration to the good: that is exactly the "vital milieu" that Weil calls "rootedness."

Let us return to our earlier question. Is this ethos of public life modern or pre-modern? It suffices to pose this question to see that, here again, Weil escapes what might be a dilemma. For if one looks back at the ancient concept of the *res publica* or of the common good, the center of gravity of her thinking would appear to be ancient and classical. But if one refers to the principle of the dignity of all people at the base of the need for participation in all public life, it is modern. Weil's thought appears therefore to confront the privileged way that modern thinkers such as Rousseau, Proudhon, Tocqueville, and Arendt try to straddle two sides by opposing the Ancients and the Moderns. For if one adopts such a point of view the question cannot help but touch on the relation between politics and religion, or between politics and the transcendent, whereas Weil's thinking paradoxically leads one both to distinguish these things and to connect them.

---

for justice and truth. This was the radiating of true thought. This radiance had the Assembly as its natural fruit. It held together for some months the inspiration from it proceeded for the invention of a Constitution. Who knows what the result would have been if the country were not thrown into the criminal folly of the war? "(OC V.1 387). The same example is given at OC V.1 402. I have noted in *Etre et Don* (473) that this vegetal sort of vocabulary was also used during the days of Solidarity in Poland: See for example, Joseph Tischner, *Ethique de Solidarité* (Paris: Criterion, 1983), which stresses that the Polish revolution, like "a word which is made clear" had grown up like the trees in the forest. The analyses of the Polish revolution by Claude Lefort also have noted this vital spontaneity. See his *L'Invention démocratique*, (Paris: Livre de poche, 1981).

The Needs of the Soul and the Absolute Good: Transcendence and Secularity

We saw at the beginning of these analyses that Weil's criticism of Maritain was for his shooting too low in trying to lay a foundation for the "rights of man," instead of the "obligations towards every human being," and doing so in a concept of natural law. The modern concepts of rights and the human person that were mobilized against the Nazis appeared to Weil to be insufficient as they were a sort of mixture of the Roman juridical tradition and the liberal individualism that came from the Enlightenment. As she wrote in "What Is Sacred in Every Human Being?," what is sacred in a human being is not that which is in him or her that is strictly individual, and therefore personal.[43] Rather, "there is at the bottom of every human heart something that goes on expecting from infancy to the grave, that good and not evil will be done to us, despite the experience of crimes committed, suffered and observed. This above all else is what is sacred in every human being" (LPW 165).

The same thought is found in the "Profession of Faith," that opens the "Study for a Declaration of Obligations towards the Human Being," which ought to serve as the introduction to the text that we know now as *The Need for Roots*. Its real title ought to be, as recent critical editions have finally called it (but only as a subtitle) "Prelude to a Declaration of Duties towards the Human Being." For these obligations, these duties, are only unconditional for Weil insofar as they refer to an unconditional Good which is not a reality in the human being insofar as he or she is an individual, but something that is revealed "at the center of the human heart" in "this longing for an absolute good which is always there and is never appeased by any object in this world" (OC V.2 96; SE 219). If the anthropological assertion here implies a "metapolitical" plane, it is important then to try to give some precision to the sense of this "Profession of Faith." Is it a metaphysical claim? Is it an interjection of the religious into the political? Is it a return to Rousseau's idea of a "civil religion"?[44]

---

43. A man is not sacred, Weil writes, "insofar as his arms are long, or insofar as his eyes happen to be blue, or insofar as his thoughts happen to be common. Nor, if he is a duke, insofar as he is a duke. Nor, if he were a garbage man" (LPW 105).

44. See my "La double 'profession de foi' de Londres de Simone Weil á J.J. Rousseau et retour," which shows the parallels between Weil's profession of faith with two texts of Rousseau, namely "The Profession of Faith of the Savoyard Vicar" and in the last chapter

Moreover, whatever the case may be, is it compatible with modern principles of secularity or laicity? Is there not, as some people argue, a clearly anti-modern scheme at the heart of Weil's inspiration?

In the texts under consideration it is important, above all, to underline the intrinsic link between the assertion of "this reality situated outside the world" (but in relation to the human heart), and the absolute respect due, because of this link, to every human being:

> Whoever recognizes that reality recognizes also that link. Because of it, he holds every human being without any exception as something sacred to which he is bound to show respect. This is the only possible motive for universal respect towards all human beings. (OC V.2 97; SE 220)

A first remark is that, contrary to many philosophical traditions, the dignity of the human being and the respect due to the human being are not here founded on any particular faculty. For Aristotle and Plato, intelligence was the basis of human dignity. For St. Bernard of Clairvaux, it was above all, freedom. Beginning with Descartes, modernity founded this dignity on self-awareness. All of that is true enough, but it has to face, if one sticks with a theory of faculties, all the risks of inequality that the degrees of intelligence, freedom, or consciousness might result in when any given human being is directly, concretely related or compared to others. The desire for good is, on the contrary, at the root of every human being; it is true for the body as well as for the soul, both encompassing and transcending all faculties, and it gives value to every human being whoever he or she might be. Weil puts it this way: "All human beings are absolutely identical in so far as they can be thought of as consisting of a center, which is an unquenchable desire for good, surrounded by an accretion of psychical and bodily matter"[45] (OC V.298; SE 220).

---

of *Social Contract* on "Civil Religion" (*Cahiers Simone Weil*, XLIV n°4, décembre 2021, p. 435–464). Weil radically goes beyond the dualism existing in Rousseau (between a "pure" Christianity that would be "anti-political" and social existence). On the «enlargement» of Christianity at stake here, see also my study "Simone Weil, from the enlargement of metaphysics to the Enlargement of Christianity,» in Robert Chenavier and Thomas Pavel (Eds.), *Simone Weil, réception et transposition*, (Paris: Classiques Garnier, 2019), pp. 243–257.

45. A study should be done on all these formulas, beginning with early texts, according to which dignity consists in "being more" than one's act and thought (see, for example, LP 190–193).

This is why the dignity of the person is not defined by rights, but by a desire that is the same in everybody, a fundamental *need* for good and not evil given to human beings, and which is not expressed in terms of rights and "in a tone of contention," but as a cry or sorrowful plaint. It is not therefore a cry of "Why does he have more than I do?" but a cry relative to justice of "Why has someone done evil to me?"[46] (LPW 124; OCV.1 232).

Such a principle, and this is our second remark, leads to a philosophy of the union of soul and body, as we are obliged to pose a concrete link between this desire for Good and human sensibility, but in such a way that the respect of the relation to the unconditioned cannot be direct.[47] For "[t]he respect inspired by the link between man and the reality outside the world can be expressed to that part of man which exists in the reality of this world" (SE221; OC V.2. 99).

The possibility of indirect expression of respect towards the human being is therefore founded on "the connection in human nature between the desire for good, which is the essence of man and his sensibility.... Because of it, when a man's life is destroyed or damaged by some wound or privation of soul or body, which is due to other men's actions or negligence, it is not only his sensibility that suffers but also his aspiration towards the good. Therefore there has been sacrilege towards that which is sacred in him" (SE 221; OC V.2 99).

The universal and unconditional need of the human soul is therefore paradoxically found linked to an infinite variety of mediations, of

---

46. This is why rights belongs to those words which belong to the "middle" range of values (LPW 128). "The concept of rights is linked to that of sharing out, of exchange, of quantity. It has something of the commercial to it. It evokes legal proceedings and pleadings. Rights are always asserted in a tone of contention; and when this tone is adopted, force is not far behind to back it up, otherwise, it would be ridiculous" (LPW 113). This also frees us from the abstract dimension that does not allow the precision contained in the of the relation of obligations and needs: "If someone said, 'human beings need liberty' and one asked 'what is this liberty that human beings have a right to?', the notion used would not furnish any method to seek out the right answer. On the contrary, if one says: 'we are obliged to give to human beings what they need, and he needs freedom; and ... in this case, on the contrary" (OC V. 2 377).

47. I make this point in a way analogous to that of Martin Steffens who has strongly emphasized it in his commentary on the needs of the soul: *Les Besoins de l'âme—extrait de l'Enracinement*, (Barcelona: folioplus—philosophie, 2007), 106–11. See also Pascal David, «Le témoignage indirect du respect», S. Weil, *Luttons-nous pour la justice ? Manuel d'action politique*, (Lyon: ed. Peuple libre, 2017), 201–07.

metaxu, by which each culture refracts the values of the spirit into the order of space and time. Such a perspective is inscribed in a sense in the Kantian principle that human beings ought to be recognized and treated as ends and never as means. However, Weil's principle entirely avoids the risk in that position wherein the person might be seen an absolute in himself, no matter what he desires. It also avoids the risk that Kant himself did not avoid, namely—because of the separation between duty and sensibility—separating a transcendental consideration of the nature of human beings from a practical and cultural consideration of that nature. Here the Platonic desire for the good is linked to a consideration of human nature as sensible needs by which "the eminent dignity of the body is, as in the attention given to the afflicted, to be judge between souls."[48]

But, thirdly, it is necessary to ask about what this thirst for the Good is that is never fully realized here below. This transcendent good is not defined, except negatively, insofar as it does not belong to the reality of this world. It appears therefore above all as an Otherness in relation to which it is impossible to absolutize any natural or social reality, whatever it may be. To assert that the absolute good transcends the world simply means that no individual and no collective are absolute, while yet, as we have seen, there is "a link which attaches every man without exception to that other reality" (SE220; OC V.2 97). Thus, the preamble that Weil wants to put at the top of the future constitution has to assert the relation, indeterminate but real, of each human being to a transcendent instance transcending any political order, but without giving to it any particular philosophical or religious form. This "Profession of Faith" is not confessional; it is formulated in universal terms that do not imply any particular form of belief. It is defined, as numerous diverse fragments show, by the notion of "aspirations" (rather than values) "in terms to which an atheist could adhere with integrity, yet without taking away anything specific from these terms" (OC V.2 380).

So, we have a first response to the question of whether or not this profession of faith is in line with the modern principle of secularity. This way of defining human dignity is neither secular (if one means by that the negation of all transcendence) nor is it confessional (if one means by that a denominational determination of this transcendence). It escapes

---

48. This would also spell out all the affirmations according to which salvation would not be accomplished "if there isn't some bodily action which might unite it to the regeneration of the soul" (OC V. 4 339).

the dilemma between "freedom of conscience" and "duties to God" often enunciated by both sides, making them either exclusive or indifferent to each other. In Weil's case, in the perspective just shown, if one wanted, for example, to refer to the expression "duties towards God" nothing is denied by the state's neutrality or political neutrality. But the two sides are mediated and indirectly respectful of each other by a more immediate consciousness of the obligations towards human beings, insofar as this awareness maintains the dignity of the desire for Good (and therefore of "the image of God) that constitutes it.

One, nevertheless, might argue that both contemporary democracy and secularity can only admit such a perspective with a great deal of difficulty. While what Weil is proposing is not confessional, it does require one to recognize the link between each human being and transcendence. A response might be that since the beginning of the twenty-first century a "heteronomic" dimension has already been imposed on democratic societies, obliging us to modify radically the structure of modern humanism. It is a question of the necessity that, in order to honor the obligations toward the human being, one also has to define our "duties towards nature." That necessity has for a number of decades now been imposed on all minds (that is, modern ones). This forces us to break with the anthropocentrism of the Enlightenment; it is the recognition of a relation, which, if not a transcendent one, is at least one that at bears on how we look at the universe. For, to recognize that nature itself is a condition for human beings, to recognize that the universe is "provident," isn't this still indirectly a way of linking us again to the anonymous Logos which is the heart of the both the universe and of life? Isn't there also here a duty to recognize a Good going beyond the human? This is a situation that is totally novel for modern anthropocentrism, and its novelty has led to a resurgence of pagan religiosities (e.g., New Age ones) that modernity thought had forever disappeared. But this situation is not all that novel for a thinker like Weil, who, while she may not have seen the contemporary ecological crisis, at least seemed to have sensed it, as she could not conceive a human existence that did not recognize the universe as a whole—that true country of the human being.[49]

---

49. Recall this sort of passage in "The Implicit Forms of the Love of God": "Christianity will not be incarnated so long as there is not joined to it the Stoic idea of filial piety for the city of the world, for the country of here below which is the universe. When, as

Nevertheless, if one does not want the post-modern revenge of nature on modern humanism that imperils human self-transcendence, it is then without doubt imperative to assert for human beings a link to a Good that transcends them and that alone can give a basis for human dignity, and which, at the same time, prevents a "redivinization" of nature that would absorb the human into the purely physical. The need to be rooted, a fundamental need of the soul, is at once a social need, a cosmic need, and a metaphysical need in the sense that the human being is the "celestial plant" defined by Plato,[50] a part of which sinks its roots into the earth, and another part of which sinks its roots into the sky. Thus the political can and ought to refer to what goes beyond the political, without ever imposing a religion, but while opening the ethico-metaphysical space of the soul, allowing it to link again the different spheres of existence with the different levels of being.[51]

Translated by Eric O. Springsted

---

the result of some misapprehension, very difficult to understand today, Christianity cut itself off from Stoicism, it condemned itself to an abstract and separate existence" (WG 175).

50. Plato, *Timaeus*, 90a.

51. An important conversation, still to come, would be one between the thought of Erich Voegelin, whose vision of a deep convergence between Platonism and Christianity led him also to refuse the modern opposition between philosophy, religion, and politics, without, however, resorting to pre-modern theologico-political schemas. As with Weil, the recovery of the Platonic understanding of the soul as a *metaxu* (leading us to leave behind "compact ontologies"), leads us to see "the entire domain of the spiritual (*daimonion*)" as being "midway between (*metaxu*) God and the human. Thus the in-between, the *metaxu*, is not a blank space between poles, but the reality of the dialogue between humans and the gods, the mutual participation (*methexis*) of humans in the divine reality, and of the divine reality in the human world." Eric Voegelin, Ellis Sandoz, ed., *The Collected Works of Eric Voegelin: Published Essays: 1966–1985*, Louisiana State University Press (1990), vol. 12, 279.

CHAPTER 3

Politics, Joy, and the Needs of the Soul

Julie Daigle

In the first part of *The Need for Roots*, Weil tells us of the existence of an "eternal," completely "unconditional" obligation that is recognized universally and expressed by humanity's perennial writings. This obligation, writes Weil, is "performed" by the respect of the needs of human beings. These needs are of two types: physical needs or needs of the body, which are quite easy to identify and refer to things like the "protection against violence, housing, clothing, heating, hygiene and medical attention in case of illness"; and the needs of the soul, or moral needs, which are much more difficult to distinguish, but equally important (NR 5–7). True needs, Weil believes, whether physical or moral, can be defined by two characteristics. First, they are limited: like the bread that brings satiety to the hungry person, all needs eventually generate a feeling of satisfaction in the individual. Second, inspired by the Pythagoreans (see Chapter 2) Weil defends the idea that these needs present themselves in what she calls "antithetical pairs" that balance each other when they are combined. Contrary to the Aristotelian view that virtue consists in a golden mean between two extremes,[1] Weil believes that the complete and consecutive satisfaction of both needs is necessary for true balance to be attained (NR 12).

---

1. See Book II of *Nichomachean Ethics*.

75

Weil then goes on to provide us with a carefully thought-out list of the needs of the soul. Those that she identifies are order, liberty, obedience, responsibility, equality, hierarchism, honor, punishment, freedom of opinion, security, risk, private property, collective property, truth, and the need for roots. One might notice that not all of these needs seem to present in perfect pairs. Some pairs are quite obvious, like liberty and obedience, while others are less so. Many readers have attempted to understand Weil's intentions here (including some of my colleagues in this book), but since this is impossible to verify, we will simply add one important observation: Simone Pétrement, Weil's close friend and biographer, notes that these pairs are much clearer in another text written at around the same time as *The Need for Roots*, Weil's "Draft for a Statement of Human Obligations."[2] Pétrement observes that what makes the list presented in *The Need for Roots* less clear is that equality seems to have two opposites: responsibility and hierarchy. For Pétrement, this is because these two needs are related. In addition, contrary to the other opposite needs, freedom of opinion and truth aren't mentioned together. Given that *The Need for Roots* was practically written in one fell swoop, Pétrement believes that the separation of freedom of opinion and truth is probably due to Weil initially forgetting to add the need for truth, an oversight that she immediately remedied.[3]

The only needs for which there are no corresponding ones are the need for order and the need for roots. These two needs present another difficulty: both seem to be of chief importance. The need for order is the first need presented to us. Weil also adds that it is the first in that it is the most important. It "stands above all needs" because "[t]o be able to conceive it, we must know what the other needs are" (NR 12). Weil seems to

---

2. For a comprehensive overview of this text and the three versions Weil had envisioned of it, see Eric O. Springsted's "Introduction." The final draft of Weil's essay is included in Appendix I.

3. Simone Pétrement, *La vie de Simone Weil* (Paris: Fayard, 1973), 654. In a footnote, Pétrement adds that in her "Carnet de Londres," Weil specifies: "Manuscrit: ajouter: besoin de *vérité*" [Manuscript: add: need for truth]. Surprisingly, the paragraph where Pétrement explains this wasn't translated in the English version of her biography of Weil. Consider alternately Emmanuel Gabellieri's insight (Chapter 2) that responsibility, rather, unifies liberty and obedience, or Eric O. Springsted's view (in his "Introduction") that: "It is to Weil's philosophical credit that she recognizes that balanced lists have certain virtues, such as not allowing excessive weight on any one need, but lists and perfect symmetry should not rule one's thinking."

accord equal importance to the need for roots, about which she writes that it is "perhaps the most important and least recognized need of the human soul" (NR 43).

In a nuanced article, Eric O. Springsted writes that an important key to unlock this apparent contradiction between the need for order and the need for roots is the absolute originality of Weil's understanding of the notion of order.[4] As discussed below, he is certainly right. In fact, the enterprise of *The Need for Roots* consists in a systematic rethinking of most of its essential concepts. This is true, for example, of the notion of "*patrie*,"[5] which Weil explicitly states that she is considering for the first time (NR 101–102). However, it is true as well for all of the needs of the soul, at the heart of which we find rootedness, a notion that, in Weil's time, had been highjacked by right-wing thinkers such as the French novelist and politician Maurice Barrès.[6]

Paradoxically, although for most of her life Weil circulated amongst trade-unionists, communists, and leftists of all stripes, several of the terms that figure in *The Need for Roots* have been deemed conservative or right-wing. To this day, Weil is frequently misread by new conservatives that offer facile, often faulty, interpretations of her work.[7] The ideas that she defends in this book, and especially the needs of the soul that figure in her list, are surely some of the most controversial in her *oeuvre*. Philippe Dujardin, for example, writes that Weil's analysis of uprootedness in France is reactionary, and he sees totalitarian inclinations in her ideas on public freedoms and the organization of political power.[8] Dujardin also stated that Weil defends a morality of passivity and resigna-

---

4. Eric O. Springsted, *Simone Weil for the Twenty-First Century* (Notre Dame, IN: University of Notre Dame Press, 2021), 159–174.

5. The term "*patrie*" is quite difficult to render in English. Arthur Wills translates it here as "patriotism," which connotes something different than "*patrie*," the former evoking a form of ideology instead of an institution. Wills does translate "*patrie*" elsewhere in the book as "country," which translates into French as "*pays*".

6. See Maurice Barrès, *Les Déracinés* (Paris: 1897).

7. On June 23, 2018, Robert Chenavier, Oliver Mongin, and Jean-Louis Schlegel signed an open letter in the French daily newspaper *Le Monde* decrying these "mediocre interpretations" as gross travesties of Weil's thought. https://www.lemonde.fr/idees/article/2018/06/23/lisons-donc-simone-weil-sans-la-recuperer-par-de-mediocres-instrumentalisations_5320161_3232.html.

8. Philippe Dujardin, *Simone Weil. Idéologie et politique* (Grenoble: Presses Universitaires de Grenoble, 1975), 170.

tion.[9] For his part, Conor Cruise O'Brien argued that Weil was essentially a religious thinker who despaired of politics, and he criticized the impossibility of the political program that she defended in *The Need for Roots*.[10] O'Brien recognized, however, the political and moral value of Weil's criticism of nationalism. He praised her sensitivity towards the destructive forces of collective life, even if he ultimately condemned her for vilifying all forms of collectivity. For this, he accused her of being "antipolitical" and a "pure intellectual."

In all fairness, there are certainly some claims and propositions that Weil makes in *The Need for Roots*—and especially in the introductory section on the needs of the soul—that are surprising if not disturbing.[11] Though Weil's style could be direct and illuminating, it is also sometimes riddled by hyperbolic language. So, too, there is undeniably a measure of hubris in some of her writing. But as surprising as Weil's choice of words and phrasing could be sometimes, speaking in terms that often were and still are the equivalent of taboos, she tends to get to unexplored truths.

To truly appreciate the originality and conceptual depth of the specific needs that Weil identifies in *The Need for Roots*, we must adopt a hermeneutic of generosity. That is, we must look at these needs through the lens of Weil's wider writings and life experiences. There, we can find keys to better interpret her often surprising use of language. This is particularly helpful to understand one of the pairs of needs that is arguably the most controversial in Weil's list: *liberty* and *obedience*. This pair is truly exemplary of the union of opposites that the human needs represent for Weil, and of the idea that opposite needs find balance in their unity. As we will see, inspired by a long philosophical tradition, Weil had been thinking about obedience in conjunction with liberty ever since her very first essays in the early 1930s. Preoccupied by a certain leeriness

---

9. *Ibid.*, 58.

10. Conor Cruise O'Brien, "Patriotism and *The Need for Roots*. The Anti-Politics of Simone Weil," *The New York Review of Books*, vol. 24, no. 8 (1997), 23–28.

11. Take for instance Weil's thoughts on punishment: "Just as the musician awakens the sense of beauty in us by sounds, so the penal system should know how to awaken the sense of justice in the criminal by the infliction of pain, or even, if need be, of death" (NR 22). For a critical discussion of Weil's understanding of punishment consider Ronald Collins & Finn Nielsen, "The Spirit of Simone Weil's Law" in Richard H. Bell, ed., *Simone Weil's Philosophy of Culture: Readings Toward a Divine Humanity* (New York: Cambridge University Press, 1993), 250–252.

of obedience that she observed in her contemporaries, and would no doubt still identify in our liberal democracies if she were alive today, Weil sought to renew our understanding of the *relationship* between liberty and obedience.

What's more, looking at Weil's broader understanding of obedience and liberty can allow us to gain a more profound grasp of what she is actually doing by proposing a list of the needs of the soul. Specifically, we argue that Weil's list should be understood in the context of her unique conception of politics as a form of both labor and art that consists in the impossible and tragic collective task of identifying or (to use a concept more attuned to her work) "read" true necessities. The identification of these necessities to which human beings are called to consent to aims, ultimately, at establishing a social order that is continuously called to be thought anew. For this reason, the process of elaborating a list of the needs of the soul should be viewed, much like the institution of laws, as a constant work in progress. Indeed, reifying Weil's list is not in the spirit of her understanding of politics, which calls instead for creativity and steady renewal. Lastly, we want to highlight another need not included in the list Weil provides in *The Need for Roots*, one that she considered equally important for the soul: the need for joy. Understood in a particular Weilian fashion, joy provides us with an important key by which we can judge the quality of the specific needs identified, their satisfaction, as well as the rootedness of individuals.

Liberty and Obedience

The first pair of needs presented to us by Weil is liberty and obedience. Weil's conceptions of liberty and obedience in *The Need for Roots* are very much informed, modelled, and inspired by her experience and observations of physical labor, stemming from her involvement in the labor movement as well as the time she spent working in three factories during the 1930s. Liberty, for one, was at the heart of Weil's first *magnum opus*, her *Reflections Concerning the Causes of Liberty and Social Oppression*,[12]

---

12. Hereafter referred to as *Reflections*.

penned in 1934 when she was only twenty-five.[13] Here, almost a decade before she wrote *The Need for Roots*, Weil espoused what she called a "heroic" conception of liberty, viewed not as the satisfaction of whims or desires, the absence of constraints or freedom from natural and social necessities, but rather as a relationship between thought and action: "the absolutely free man would be he whose every action proceeded from a preliminary judgment concerning the end which he set himself and the sequence of means suitable for attaining this end" (OL 85). In this sense, liberty, for Weil, consists in being able to represent to oneself the necessities of life, and adapting one's thoughts and actions to them. Seeing liberty as a form of conscious submission to necessity, Weil adhered to Bacon's precept that "'[w]e cannot command Nature except by obeying her'" (OL 107).[14]

While Weil recognized that such a high standard of liberty is, in reality, impossible to accomplish, she believed that we should nevertheless aspire to such an ideal: "Perfect liberty is what we must try to represent clearly to ourselves, not in the hope of attaining it, but in the hope of attaining a less imperfect liberty than is our present condition; for the better can be conceived only by reference to the perfect" (OL 84). Perfect liberty, for Weil, can never be realized; it is always a project, a utopia. However, nothing is more important for societies than this type of utopia of reason (OL 106). It is precisely what allows us to work towards eliminating injustices and social oppression.

When Weil wrote *The Need for Roots* almost a decade after her *Reflections*, she described the need for liberty as "the ability to choose," adding that this liberty should be limited by rules (NR 12). She specifies, however, that liberty in no way depends on the extent of these limits. It de-

---

13. Although we focus here solely on Weil's conceptions of liberty in her *Reflections* and in *The Need for Roots*, we must note that liberty—much like obedience—is one of the most polysemic and nuanced concepts in Weil's work. In addition to what she calls "supernatural liberty," which encompasses the most metaphysical implications, we can also find an implicit definition of liberty in her work that echoes the understanding of liberty as non-domination of Republican thinkers. See Julie Daigle, "Thoughts on a Weilian Republicanism" in Sophie Bourgault and Julie Daigle, eds., *Simone Weil, Beyond Ideology?* (Cham: Palgrave MacMillan, 2020), 227–252.

14. The Latin version of Bacon's maxim, *Homo naturae parendo imperat*, appears several times in Weil's work and is consistent with another expression she sometimes recalls in her first notebook by Tacitus: *Omnia serviliter pro dominatione*, meaning "servile in all his actions for the sake of power" (OC VI.1 74, 79 et 96).

pends, rather, on certain conditions: rules should be simple enough so that people understand both their purpose and reason for being; the authority from which these rules emanate should be loved; and finally, these rules should be "stable, general and limited in number for the mind to be able to grasp them once and for all." Weil concludes that "[u]nder these conditions, the liberty of men of goodwill, though limited in the sphere of action, is complete in that of conscience" (NR 13). This definition of liberty is consistent with the one we find in *Reflections* as a relationship between thought and action. Both involve consent to the social and natural necessities that limit actions, and view arbitrariness and blind submission as contrary to freedom.

To be free, then, individuals must recognize the necessities of a social and political order, so that they can consent to them in full consciousness. This consent is essential to obedience—the second need listed by Weil—which is of two kinds: "obedience to established rules and obedience to human beings looked upon as leaders." Consent "given once and for all, with the sole reservation [...] that the demands of conscience be satisfied" is crucial, for Weil, because it allows us to distinguish obedience, which involves a type of submission that can be seen as service, from servility, which she ties to oppression (NR 14).

The Resistance to Obey

That obedience is included in Weil's list was controversial, especially at a time when it was precisely the obedience of some of her contemporaries that led to the tragedies of the Second World War. However, the presence of obedience in this list remains just as contentious today. Indeed, it is disobedience that is a much more legitimate subject, widely discussed in both the general public and in academic circles. But if Weil thought that it was important to include obedience in her list of the needs of the soul, it is likely because she had become increasingly aware of a certain resistance to obey in her contemporaries. In fact, she first described this resistance during her involvement with the French labor movement.

At the beginning of the 1930s, the French Left was split between socialists, radicals, and communists. In 1934, however, and following Stalin's efforts to become closer to democratic countries, it formed a unified coalition: the Popular Front. In effect, Stalin encouraged the French Communist Party to form an alliance with the radicals and the socialists in the hopes of countering the rise of fascism in Europe.[15] The previous year, Hitler became chancellor of Germany, a country that, like France, had massive unemployment rates. Efforts had to be made to avoid the emergence of fascism in France. In the wake of the anti-fascist movement, the trade unions united and the unionization rates of workers were at an all-time high.[16] The Popular Front won the legislative elections in May of 1936,[17] bringing the socialist leader Léon Blum to power. During this same month of May, the impatient working class initiated one of the biggest strike and occupation movements in history. In June, with more than 1,800,000 strikers,[18] the movement led to the signing of the Matignon Agreements, ensuring, inter alia, the 40-hour work week and 15 days of paid vacations for all workers.

Weil believed that the victory of the Popular Front radically changed the working-class reality she had witnessed in the factories. It represented, namely, a "burst of dignity" [*un sursaut de dignité*],[19] that morally and psychologically transformed the workers and employers and eliminated all of the conditions on which the organization of factories were founded.[20] Weil also observed a transformation in the psyche of workers, who now felt that they had the power to disobey.[21] Whereas before 1936, the organization of factories was based on terror and slavery, the decisive issue, for Weil, was to determine on what order the reformed factory should be founded. Now that the authority of both the employers and the trade-unions was equally recognized, Weil noticed, not without

---

15. Stéphane Courtois, «Les intellectuels et l'antifascisme» in Jean-Pierre Rioux, ed., *Le Front populaire* (Paris: Éditions Tallandier, 2006), 44.

16. At the beginning of 1937, the C.G.T. (General Confederation of Labor) had more than four million members (OC II. 2 390).

17. Weil was thrilled with the electoral victory of the Frente popular, the Spanish equivalent of the Front populaire, in February 1936. When the Franquist rebellion broke out in July of the same year, she decided to join the Republican ranks in the Durruti Column. Her stay in Spain was nevertheless short-lived, since she soon returned to France, without going to combat, this after badly burning her left leg.

18. Jean-Pierre Rioux, «Repères chronologiques» in *Le Front populaire* (Paris: Éditions Tallandier, 2006), 144.

19. OC II.2, *La déclaration de la C.G.T.*, 384.

20. OC II.2, *Remarques sur les enseignements à tirer des conflits du Nord*, 423.

21. *Ibid.*, 424.

worry, a resistance of workers to obey their superiors. She saw that the employers had to make a considerable effort to be obeyed.[22] All of this led her to conclude that both the workers and the employers needed to learn *how* to obey, and that obedience and hierarchy were necessities of social life.

This same concern with obedience appears in *The Need for Roots*, where Weil observes a reluctance in her compatriots to obey. She worries that the French people will be reticent to obey even a legitimate source of authority because they will have been too accustomed to slavery and the obligation to disobey during the German occupation: "Victory is going to liberate a country in which everyone will have been almost exclusively occupied in disobeying, from either good or bad motives. [...] How are people going to be made to understand that all this is finished, that henceforward they have to obey?" (NR 154). Weil restates her worry about this problem on the next page, where she writes: "The government which arises in France after the liberation of the country will have to face a triple danger caused by this blood lust, this mendacity complex and this inability to obey" (NR 155).

To be clear, Weil always expressed her opposition to a type of obedience that had deleterious effects on the human soul, the "condition of beast of burden,"[23] that she observed in herself and in her coworkers during her time in the factories. What Weil deplored was the constant subordination and passive obedience that the conditions and nature of factory work imposed on the workers. However, she viewed neither obedience nor subordination per se as problematic. What she observed in the factories was a kind of obedience that didn't reflect the true needs of human beings,[24] that didn't respect their freedom of thought and action, and so denied their dignity. These working conditions led to the commodification of workers, who were treated like machines of flesh and blood [*machines de chair*],[25] without any real capacity for thought.

---

22. OC II.2, *Crise d'autorité*, 456.

23. These are the words Weil used to describe this negative type of obedience in her "Factory Journal" (FW 180), and in a letter to her friend Albertine Thévenon (*La Condition ouvrière*, présentation et notes par Robert Chenavier (Paris: Gallimard, 2002), 59.

24. Weil first used the expression "needs of the soul" in 1938, in a draft article titled "À propos du syndicalisme 'unique, apolitique, obligatoire'" (OC II.3, 273).

25. The expression appears in an open letter Weil wrote to unionized workers (OC II.2, *Lettre ouverte à un syndiqué*, 392).

Workers were considered passive beings whose actions were entirely dictated by another. They were reduced to a mindless obedience, without the opportunity to exercise their autonomy or creativity. Hence, they perceived the tasks with which they were charged as constraints and inescapable necessities. Such subservience was antithetical to Weil's ideal notion of obedience.

The Consent to True Necessities

Weil believed that when those who command recognize the capacities of workers to accomplish their tasks with intelligence and humanity, obedience and subordination could be legitimate. Obedience could be dignified and just if it respects the capacity for thought of individuals, which defines their humanity. Weil thus lays out the conditions for obedience to be synonymous with liberty. In fact, she views true liberty as a form of obedience, and obedience as authentic liberty. They are synonyms, so to speak, since they both require the consent of individuals. Weil explicitly makes this connection in an essay written at around the same time as *The Need for Roots* titled "Are We Struggling for Justice?": "Where obedience is consented to there is freedom: there, and nowhere else. [...] Where obedience does not have everywhere a daily and permanent flavor of freedom, there is no freedom. Freedom is the flavor of true obedience" (SWW 126). For Weil, who remained faithful to the lessons of the Stoics, the right attitude for workers faced with industrial necessities wasn't blind submission, but rather the *acceptance* of true necessities. The acceptance of true necessities takes into consideration the liberty of individuals, while blind submission reflects a situation of servitude. If acceptance and consent[26] include critical thought, the type of submission that Weil criticizes excludes it.

What difference does Weil make between "true" and "false" necessities? The distinction appears in a few of her essays.[27] First, in a draft ar-

---

26. In her later writings, Weil seems to prefer the term *consent* over *acceptance*. See, e.g., NR 14–15.

27. Robert Chenavier calls attention to this crucial distinction in *Simone Weil. Une philosophie du travail* (Paris: Cerf, 2001), 350–351.

ticle from September 1937, she refers to a distinction, that is difficult to establish, between a necessity that concerns the nature of things [*la nature des choses*] and another type of necessity that has to do with human relationships [*les rapports humains*]. Weil specifies that the first type is the only true necessity, whereas the second type is false.[28] In a later article titled "The First Condition for the Work of a Free Person," written at the end of her stay in Marseille in April of 1942, Weil carefully distinguishes "forms of suffering that are written in the nature of things" and "forms of suffering that are the result of our crime" (LPW 141). Whereas the first forms of suffering must be accepted as an inherent part of human existence, the other forms stem from an injustice and so must be combatted by social reforms. For Weil, a certain type of servitude should even be considered an inherent part of human existence. She writes: "There is in the work of human hands and, in general, in the skilled performance of a task, which is work properly understood, an irreducible element of servitude that even a perfectly just society cannot remove.[29] This is because it is governed by necessity, not by finality." (LPW 131). Finally, another draft article on Étienne de La Boétie's *Discourse on Voluntary Servitude* (1577) mentions the existence of a false type of necessity: "There is nothing spiritual about the pitiless necessity which has kept, and goes on keeping, the masses of slaves [...] on their knees; it corresponds to everything that is brutal in nature. And yet it is apparently exercised in virtue of laws which are contrary to those of nature" (OL 141). Once we admit the existence of a difference between true and false necessity, the question that surfaces is how this distinction is established. In the next section we will discuss how this is, in large part, the work of politics.

---

28. OC II.3, *La Condition ouvrière*, 259.

29. One can wonder why here servitude becomes acceptable when Weil had always stated that it should be avoided. An explanation can be found in the notion of "reading," which we clarify later, and the idea that attention has the potential to radically change the perception we have of necessity, from constraint to model of obedience to which we can grant our consent. See, for example, OC VI.3, 404.

The Art and Labor of Politics

We can assume that politics, for Weil, are directly inspired by physical labor. In fact, in the last pages of *The Need for Roots*, she writes: "A return to truth would make manifest, amongst other things, the truth of physical labour. [¶] Physical labour willingly consented to is, after death willingly consented to, the most perfect form of obedience" (NR 291–292). Hence, Weil applies to political life the lesson that she learned during her involvement in the labor movement that consented obedience can guarantee liberty. Much like perfect obedience in physical labor and death consist in consenting to the true necessities to which human life is inevitably submitted, politics, for Weil, can be defined as a form of labor that aims at distinguishing between the type of necessity that comes from the nature of things from the type of necessity that comes from the relationships between human beings. Indeed, Weilian politics do the work of identifying the true necessities to which individuals must obey and the false necessities resulting from social oppression and the use of force that must be combatted. They allow us to name sufferings that are useless because they are the consequence of necessities that are perceived to be real, but in fact aren't. In this sense, politics may be the only safeguard we have against the false necessity that crushes human beings and makes them slavish.

The "Reading" of Necessities

What particular method and skills do politics and the identification of true necessities ask of us? There is an important concept developed by Weil, one that she never discusses in *The Need for Roots*, but that is quite helpful in understanding the process of identifying true necessities. This is the notion of "reading." Weil developed this concept in a series of essays and notes written in the early 1940s.[30] She had even envisioned writing a book on this topic,[31] which attests to the importance she at-

---

30. In her *Diplôme d'études supérieures* on Descartes (1930), Weil had already begun to identify paths for reflection on the notion of "reading." See Béatrice-Clémentine Farron-Landry, «Lecture et non-lecture chez Simone Weil», *Cahiers Simone Weil*, vol. III, no. 4 (1980), 238; and Robert Chenavier, *Simone Weil. Une philosophie du travail*, 520.

31. See OC VI.1 170.

tributed to it. Her "Essay on the Concept of Reading" (LPW 21–27) appeared posthumously (1946) in *Les Études philosophiques*. With this
notion, Weil attempts to put words on the way that we interpret and
perceive the world.[32] The world, for her, is like a text that we *read*, and
readings are the different meanings that we find in the world.

Weil thus lays the foundations of a precise step-by-step method of
discernment, available to anyone who is willing to make the necessary
efforts. These steps refer to the different kinds of readings of the world
that allow us to approach the real—i.e. true necessity—or to know it.
Through a spiritual apprenticeship, involving supernatural attention and
what Weil calls "decreation," we can learn to read the world at three levels. We can learn to "read necessity behind sensation, order behind necessity, and God behind order" (NB 267). There would therefore be several levels of apprehension of the real: sensation, necessity, order, and
God. This is what Weil calls, following Plato's idea of domains,[33] "[l]evels
of readings, superimposed readings" (NB 51). None of these levels are
more or less important than the others: "What distinguishes the higher
states from the lower ones is, in the higher states, the co-existence of
several superposed planes" (NB 312). Hence, these readings are comprehensive and cumulative: all of the "superior" levels include the "inferior" ones. All of them give us access to the real, but in different ways.
At the "inferior" level of sensations (which, it should be stressed, simply means that it is limited in the sense that it is incomplete), we read
and believe what we read. We perceive or read the world through our
body that is like Descartes' blind man's stick (NB 40). The world appears to us through sensations and appearances, mediations through
which we interpret meanings. At this first level we are convinced that
our perception of reality *is* reality. We believe what we perceive through
our senses. We believe that the meanings that we read are reality; we
read "necessity behind sensations." We experience necessity by inter-
acting with it, either through the limitations it imposes on us or
through its malleability (IC 181).

This first, automatic, reading is subjective and self-centered. It consists in believing that our perspective is the reality of the world. But as

---

32. For Weil, the world, the real, and true necessity are synonyms.
33. NB 245. The idea is from Plato's *Timaeus*.

we access superior levels of reading through the decreative process,[34] we realize that our perception of reality is always, in one way or the other, biased. To reach the intermediate levels of reading[35] we must accept the subjective quality of our reading, but also the multiplicity of perspectives. In fact, we have already moved from the first level of reading when we realize that our spontaneous reading is fundamentally contradictory: while reality must exist because we experience it as an obstacle, we realize that we are always interpreting this reality through sensations and meanings that we read. And so, we begin to doubt the reality of these meanings.

Like all paradoxes, Weil claims that this one must be *contemplated.* This contradiction, this *mystery*, must not lead us to despair. In fact, Weil reminds us that Plato believed that contradictions "draw us upwards" (LPW 21–22). Weil often uses the metaphor of the lever to explain how we can access superior levels of reading: "Lever. Tears the being away from appearance. [...] Tears the will away from desire, or desire away from perspective" (NB 233). She writes as well: "It is always a question of rising above perspectives through the composition of perspectives" (*Ibid.,* 239).

Although everyone experiences the world in their own distinctive way, we are called to read reality accurately. Indeed, even if it is difficult to access, reality does exist. And this reality is shaped by necessity. Thus, by being attentive to the relationships between things, the second reading allows us to read "order behind necessity": "To think of necessity in a way that is pure, it must be detached from the matter which supports it and conceived as a fabric of conditions knotted one with the others" (IC 181). What this involves is a labor of composition and of coordinating the multiplicity of perspectives: "READINGS.—co-ordination in Time and with the readings of others. Co-ordination between simultaneous and successive readings" (NB 99). This level of reading consists in combining different readings in order to extract laws and relationships between phenomena. We can thus gain a certain knowledge of necessity and come to see it as obeying the laws of matter. "The obedience of Matter requires no law to illustrate it. But we have to have laws so as to be able to visualize it. Otherwise, since we run up against it in connexion

---

34. See Springsted, *Simone Weil for the Twenty-First Century,* 184–188.
35. Weil indicates that there are "many degrees" (NB 42).

with our desires, to which it shows itself either favourable or unfavour-
able, we would take it to be caprice" (NB 612–613). Through an apprenticeship that involves attention and discursive intelligence, what Weil
sometimes calls "natural reason,"[36] we move away from an understanding of reality as incomprehensible arbitrariness and capriciousness. In
fact, this second reading leads to science. Taking some distance from our
immediate experience means rising to the level of abstraction and of the
synthesis of all perspectives. This is precisely the object of mathematics—"*the* science of nature," the science of which all others are mere
applications (IC 181). Weil writes that the same principle applies to social and psychological phenomena, of which we can gain knowledge by
recognizing "a necessity analogous to mathematical necessity" (IC 182).

Why is this second reading important? Why must we combine readings? Weil's answer to these questions is significant and has important
political implications that she doesn't directly address. In a passage from
her *Notebooks* where she mentions the coordination of readings, she
writes:

> In the immediate present, and individually, everything is
> equally true. Why should such a co-ordination be necessary?
> Because here Good enters into the picture. I have got to be in
> accord with others and with past 'I', future 'I'. [¶] This accord
> represents reality. (NB 99)

The reason why the coordination of multiple readings is important has
to do with me being in agreement with myself and with others. Without
this coordination, no agreement can be reached. What's at play is the
recognition of the existence of the Good and of reality. When readings
are superimposed or coincide, the combination of readings is indicative
of reality and of the Good, of true necessity.[37] This is why Weil states that
the second reading is the "true reading" (NB 40).

Politics, for Weil—even though she never states it explicitly—involve
this intermediary level of reading, the level of "multiple perspectives," of
"composition on multiple planes" (NB 42). They imply the combination

---

36. On this see Chenavier, *Simone Weil. Une philosophie du travail*, 535–536.

37. We leave aside here, not because of its unimportance but for brevity purposes, the
third level of reading to which this points, and which consists in reading "God behind
order" (NB 267).

of different perspectives, with the aim of producing a collective *oeuvre* that consists in laws that can bring forth the Good and guide the *patrie*. Weil hints towards this in the third section of *The Need for Roots* where she considers both politics and political action an art. If politics are akin to the arts[38]—and more specifically, to poetry, architecture, and music, for Weil—it is because politics, like these other forms of art, require a great degree of attention.[39] The type of attention that is required is a "simultaneous composition on several planes." For Weil, this is both the law and proper difficulty of artistic creation (NR 214). It requires many different objects of attention to be considered at the same time. Weil gives us the example of poetry, in which these different levels of composition concern everything from grammar to musicality to the laws of versification.

Weil is aware that the type of attention that she is describing is impossible. In fact, she believes that human intelligence is incapable of following this method perfectly, and that the direct access to true necessity (understood as the "thought of God" [*la pensée de Dieu*][40] is impossible (LPW 22). However—much like the aspiration to true liberty she describes in her *Reflections*—she also thinks that this impossibility isn't a reason to despair from trying to apply it. Even though the actions and decisions that come from applying this faculty of composition on multiple planes will always be imperfect, our willingness to use this method and our desire for justice can increase the chances that they will be good (NR 215).

It is exactly this type of effort to identify true necessities that is deployed by Weil in her list of the needs of the soul at the beginning of *The Need for Roots*. Although Weil most likely understood these needs as historical and cultural invariables, it's important to insist on the fact that she recognized that her list was tentative. In one version of her "Draft for

---

38. Weil also mentions that they are, in this sense, similar to science (NR 213–216).

39. In the English translation of *The Need for Roots* Arthur Wills prefers "concentration" instead of *attention*, the French term used by Weil, which is surprising considering the importance of attention in Weil's body of work, and her opposition to a kind of concentration that evokes a tensing, muscular effort. Weil attempted to distinguish this kind of concentration from the true, supernatural faculty of attention that she saw, rather, as a kind of "negative effort," involving the suspension of our thoughts and making ourselves available to being penetrated by truth. See, for example, "Reflections on the Right Use of School Studies with a View to the Love of God" (SWW 95–96).

40. See OC VI.1 172.

a Statement of Human Obligations," she notes that the list of obligations should correspond to the list of needs established after a study that is always subject to revision (OC V.2 96).[41] From the outset of *The Need for Roots*, she writes that even though the needs of the soul are "much more difficult to recognize and to enumerate" than the needs of the body (NR 7), we must try to do so. Indeed, what she is offering are, simply and humbly, "a few indications" (NR 10) as to what a list of such needs could look like. She neither thought that the list she offered was complete, nor that it was perfect. We can't stress this enough.[42] And since Weil believed that the work of identifying necessities is never fully accomplished, it's likely that she offered her list as a proposal that can and should be thoroughly debated. Politics, like philosophy, for Weil, involve the deployment of creativity and a spirit of constant renewal. Weil is time and again prompting us to exercise our political imagination, as she is convinced that it is crucial for the expression of justice and truth.

The Establishment of a Social Order

Of course, the question of who should be tasked with revising this list is an important one. We can suppose that, for Weil, not all individuals would be entrusted with this responsibility. Only the most virtuous and wise would define these needs, like the laws to which all must obey. Here we can certainly see one of many resonances between Weil and Plato, whom, one could argue, Weil admired perhaps more than any other philosopher. The democratic character of this process can nevertheless be noted when we consider the importance for Weil of listening and being attentive to victims who, more often than not, struggle to be heard

---

41. Weil wrote several versions of this "Draft for a Statement of Human Obligations" (see OC V.2 95–105 and Annexe V.1, 369–377). The final version is included in "Appendix One" of this book.

42. Weil is a vanguard of recent philosophical efforts to identify universal needs. For example, Martha Nussbaum's version of the capability theory of justice defines a list of ten central capabilities. In spite of fundamental differences, several commonalities exist between Weil and Nussbaum's lists: they both aim at honoring human dignity, are destined to be included in national constitutions, and are open to revision. See Martha Nussbaum, *Women and Human Development: The Capabilities Approach* (New York: Cambridge University Press, 2000), 4–10.

and to express the injustices they suffer.[43] To overcome this difficulty, Weil offers a few suggestions in her beautiful essay titled "What Is Sacred in Every Human Being?" (LPW 103–129). First, public education must give individuals the capacity to effectively communicate their needs and the injustices they suffer. Weil also encourages a regime "where the public expression of opinions is defined less by freedom and more by an atmosphere of silence and attention" (LPW 106) to allow these inaudible voices to be heard. Lastly, public institutions should ensure that power is vested in the hands of individuals who have both the capacity and the desire to listen and understand, by "a tender and divining attention," those who struggle with the expression of their needs (LPW 106).

Though the work of identifying the needs of the soul is accomplished by individuals—since collectivities, according to Weil, are incapable of thought[44]—this labor is nevertheless a collective apprenticeship that aims at a shared reading. If Weil encourages differences and the "perpetual stirring of ideas" (NR 165) in *The Need for Roots*, it is precisely to come to this shared reading. She believes that a reading that combines all perspectives, instead of defending only one, is more likely to be closer to justice.

The main objective of this political labor is to establish a social order. Weil understands order as "a texture of social relationships such that no one is compelled to violate imperative obligations in order to carry out other ones" (NR 10). Social order ensures that all of the needs of the soul are fulfilled, and that they don't contradict each other. Consequently, an adequate social order would allow individuals to feel as though they are not obliged to disobey. They can freely consent and obey without thinking that, in doing so, they are acting in a way that is incompatible with their conscience. Weil was very preoccupied by the question of incompatible obligations. In fact, she tells us that her contemporaries lived in a time when the "incompatibility" and "confusion" between obligations was particularly present (NR 10). However, she adds that "we possess no method for diminishing this incompatibility," and that the possibility of

---

43. Weil was very sensitive to what we now call, following the term coined by Miranda Fricker (2007), epistemic injustices.

44. In Weil's *Reflections*, we find the following statement: "In the case of the mind, [...] here the individual surpasses the collectivity to the same extent as something surpasses nothing, for thought only takes shape in a mind that is alone face to face with itself; collectivities do not think" (OL 98).

a social order that would allow for no incompatible obligations to exist just might be a "fiction" (NR 10–11).

Weil recognizes that perfect social order is impossible. This is the tragic labor of politics that her thought brings to light. However, she also believes that both social order and the state are lesser evils, preferable to chaos and unleashed violence.[45] Although the means of politics can never completely eliminate the existence of force and oppression, they can try to limit it. With its perpetual call to tackle, renew, and clarify the questioning of necessities, the never-ending labor of politics is a constant aspiration to justice, and to "the unrealized good to which we aspire" (NR 11). When Weil writes about the unrealized good here, she is referring to a good that will ever remain in the realm of thought, in the most Platonic sense of the word. But we should not let ourselves be discouraged by the unrealizable quality of the good. On the contrary, believes Weil, when we turn our attention in its direction, what motivates us and directs our thoughts becomes hope. Hope that there is something more beautiful and more just to be accomplished. Hope that we can create a world where justice is more present in our relationships with others. Indeed, the disappearance of oppression and of force becomes the sole focus of our energy and collective efforts. "If we keep ever-present in our minds the idea of a veritable human order, […] we shall be in a similar position to that of a man travelling, without a guide, through the night, but continually thinking of the direction he wishes to follow. Such a traveller's way is lit by a great hope" (NR 12).

Weil believes that contemplating things like the beauty of the world, works of art, and our universal desire for the good can bring us hope because they reveal that it is harmony, and not what she calls "blind, mechanical force," that is sovereign in the universe (NR 11). In this way, Weil positions herself squarely against a view that we find in so-called Machiavellian "realist" politics,[46] one that views force as sovereign in both the natural and social world. Weil believes, instead, that the attentive contemplation of the universe reveals the truth of the Pythagorean

---

45. Weil reaffirms the necessity of social order, in spite of its inherent imperfections, as well as the perpetuation of the inevitable conflicts that result from this imperfection, in the conclusion of a commentary she wrote in 1937 on Étienne de La Boétie's *Discourse on Voluntary Servitude* (OL, *Meditation on Obedience and Liberty*, 138).

46. Then again, she appreciated his realist perspective provided one did not ignore the true realism of the workings of the world. See, e.g., NB 132 and SE 61–62.

idea of harmony. In the natural world, blind forces limit and balance each other into a beautiful whole. A social order that respects the human needs on all levels, Weil writes, would imitate this harmony.

However, politics, for Weil, don't consist in finding an ideal social order, absolute and universal, that can be imposed on any and all societies. In effect, Weil believes that the need for order can only be satisfied by the growing of the unique socio-historical roots of a people. If the needs of the soul are timeless and universal, they are nevertheless *expressed*—Weil uses the word "performed" (NR 4)—differently throughout history and different societies. Hence it follows from this, for example, that the best social order for Americans to be rooted would be very different from the one required by Canadians or Peruvians.

So how do we know when a social order is suitable for human flourishing? The answer to this question can be found in another need identified by Weil, one that she doesn't include in the list provided in *The Need for Roots*, but that is present in fragments and notes from the same time: the need for joy.[47] In the next section, we will show how joy is indicative of a social order that produces harmony and leads to the adequate rootedness of human beings.

The Need for Joy

A social order is a reflection of the harmony of the natural world when true feelings of joy are felt by individuals. Weil holds a challenging, original and, in a sense, unusual understanding of joy. In fact, a misunderstanding of Weil's conception of joy probably contributed to the harshness of several judgments of her person and her work, including Susan Sontag's 1963 reproval of Weil in *The New York Review of Books*.[48]

---

47. Weil identifies several kinds of joy in her *Notebooks*: "It is not joy and suffering which are in opposition to each other, but the types they respectively produce. There are infernal types of joy and suffering; healing types of joy and suffering, and celestial types of joy and suffering" (NB 230). What interests us here is the kind of joy that is celebrated by Weil. This is the kind of joy that she identifies as a need of the soul. See also FLN 8, 10, 69, 90, and 199.

48. Sontag doesn't mince her words towards Weil: "I am thinking of the fanatical asceticism of Simone Weil's life, her contempt for pleasure and happiness, her noble and ridiculous political gestures, her elaborate self-denials, her tireless courting of affliction; and I do not exclude her homeliness, her physical clumsiness, her migraines, her tuber-

But Weil's student, Anne Reynaud, has stated that joy might be the keystone of Weil's intellectual and spiritual life.[49] In fact, in writings that are contemporary to *The Need for Roots*, Weil tells us that joy is an essential need of the soul, and that the lack of joy is a state of disease where intelligence, courage, and generosity have disappeared. Joy, she specifies, isn't a fleeting impression of happiness that comes from the outside, either from the pleasures of the senses or the continuous distractions that we understand all too well today (OC V.2 398–399). There is, in this regard, a likeness between Weil's writings on joy and Étienne de La Boétie's criticism of the effects of distractions on reason, liberty, and on the capacity for attention of individuals in his *Discourse on Voluntary Servitude*.[50]

Joy, for Weil, comes instead from the inside. However, we cannot fabricate it ourselves, and it doesn't suddenly appear when we begin to look for it (OC V.2 399). To feel joy, it is not enough to say to ourselves that we are joyful, as would like to suggest today's defenders of positive thinking and their many avatars.[51] Robert Chenavier clarifies the specific meaning that Weil gives to joy when he writes that pure or perfect joy, for Weil, "has nothing to do with the expansion of our personal existence."[52] To give weight to this idea, Chenavier calls our attention to a passage from the *Notebooks* where Weil writes that "perfect joy excludes the very feeling of joy, for in the soul filled by the object no corner is available to say 'I.'"[53] In joy, the feeling of the self disappears, and makes room for another feeling that has nothing to do with the 'I' or the self:

culosis. No one who loves life would wish to imitate her dedication to martyrdom nor would wish it for his children nor for anyone else whom he loves." Susan Sontag, "Simone Weil," *The New York Review of Books* (Feb. 1, 1963).

49. "La joie chez Simone Weil," *Cahiers Simone Weil*, X. 2 (1987), 140. I am grateful to Emmanuel Gabellieri for calling my attention to this article. Gabellieri also signals the importance of considering the need for joy in Chapter 2 of this book.

50. La Boétie mentions how the tyrant Cyrus had succeeded in dumbing down and submitting the Lydians by multiplying amusements and hobbies. Etienne de La Boétie, *The Politics of Obedience: The Discourse of Voluntary Servitude*, intro. by Murray N. Rothbard, trans. by Harry Kurz (Auburn, Alabama: The Mises Institute, 1975), 64.

51. See on this question, A. Rebecca Rozelle-Stone, "Simone Weil, Sara Ahmed, and a Politics of Hap" in Sophie Bourgault and Julie Daigle, eds., *Simone Weil, Beyond Ideology?* (Cham: Palgrave Macmillan, 2020), 61–81.

52. Robert Chenavier, *Simone Weil. Attention to the Real*, trans. by Bernard E. Doering (Notre Dame: University of Notre Dame Press, 2012), 67.

53. *Ibid.* The passage can be found in NB 179.

the "sentiment of the real"[54] or the "feeling of reality."[55] In fact, Weil also notes that sadness signals the diminishment or the disappearance of the sentiment of the real (OC VI.1 79). As Chenavier puts it, joy, for Weil, doesn't come from the satisfaction of the demands of the self.[56] It's not joy that we would feel if the world were exactly as we wish. Understood as the sentiment of the real, joy is, instead, the love of the world as it is.

How can we understand this? Weil offers some clarity: "Joy is directed towards an object. I am full of joy at the sight of the sun shining, or the moon over the sea, or a beautiful city, or a fine human being; no 'I' obtrudes itself in the fulness of joy. On the other hand, 'I' suffer" (NB 291). Joy, then, is the result of something that is outside of the self: although it wells up from within, it nevertheless comes from the feeling of being filled by something outside of the self.

We can find another example of this relationship between the sentiment of the real, joy, and the disappearance of the "I" in a letter that Weil wrote to her friend Joë Bousquet, a writer and former officer that was paralyzed by a gunshot wound to the spine during the First World War.[57] Weil visited Bousquet only once at his home in Carcassonne, but this was enough to establish a solid friendship.[58] Weil wrote to her friend: "I am convinced that affliction on the one hand, and on the other hand joy, when it is a complete and pure commitment to perfect beauty, are the only two keys which give entry to the realm of purity, where one can breathe: the home of the real" (SL 141). Knowledge of the real, which amounts to the knowledge of true necessities, involves joy and affliction. Joy and affliction are the two faces of the relationship between the individual and the real. Both affliction and joy offer us an experience of the real, a real that reveals itself to be "perfect beauty" if we can look at it with attention and love.

What can prevent us from accessing the real is a type of madness that can appear insidiously. For Weil, it is impossible for a person who has gone mad and has lost contact with reality to be joyful. Conversely, pro-

---

54. "Joy is the fulness of the sentiment of the real" (NB 222).
55. NB 266.
56. Robert Chenavier, *Simone Weil. Attention to the Real*, 68.
57. The letter is dated 12 May 1942.
58. Simone Pétrement, *Simone Weil: A Life*, trans. by Raymond Rosenthal (New York: Pantheon Books, 1976), 456.

longed sadness can also make an individual vulnerable to madness.[59] Facing affliction and overcoming a long-lasting sadness without losing touch with reality through the imagination or lies[60] requires a rare supernatural courage that can be found only in the purest beings, those who have another type of madness, the true madness, the madness of love. Most people are incapable of such a feat. One of the most important examples for Weil of this courage to look reality in the face through affliction is Job,[61] a "blameless and upright"[62] man who remains just in spite of all of the hardship and suffering he endures. Weil writes about Job: "It was because he was so honest in his suffering, because he would not entertain any thought that might impair its truth, that God came down to reveal the beauty of the world to him" (WG 114). Beauty, then, is not an "attribute of matter"; like joy, "[i]t is a relationship of the world to our sensibility, the sensibility that depends upon the structure of our body and our soul" (WG 103–104).

For Weil, the satisfaction of the needs of the soul is one of the conditions of possibility of joy. The satisfaction of these needs favors the appearance of joy, without being a necessary or sufficient condition of it. Indeed, Weil writes that there is something mysterious in joy, something of the order of grace that escapes all explanation and understanding (OC V.2, 399). Hence, joy is not a need like the others; it is the consequence or the product of an adequate social order. Joy is precisely what makes it possible to verify that the needs of the soul are correctly identified and fully satisfied. "Any place where the needs of the human beings are satisfied can be recognized by the fact that there is a flowering of fraternity, joy, beauty, and happiness. Wherever people are lonely and turned in on themselves, wherever there is sadness or ugliness, there are privations that need remedying" (SWW 141). The better the needs are satisfied, the greater the feeling of joy. In fact, we could even go so far as to say that, for Weil, joy is proportional to the rootedness of the individual. Joy, as the true sentiment of the real or the feeling of reality, rises like a sap from the depths of the roots.

---

59. On the relationship between sadness and madness see OC VI.1 79.

60. "For him who is capable of preventing the automatic reaction of defense, which tends to increase the soul's capacity for lying, affliction is not an evil, although it is always a wounding and in a sense a degradation" (WG 134).

61. Jb, 1–42, The New American Bible.

62. Jb, 1, The New American Bible.

This is precisely the joy expressed by the character of Violetta in *Venice Saved*,[63] the unfinished play in three acts that Weil was writing around the same time as *The Need for Roots*.[64] Violetta's rootedness and her attachment to Venice come to light on the eve of the Pentecost when her father asks her if her apparent excitement is due to a love interest. She answers that it isn't due to any single person. While she is unsure where her excitement comes from, she says that she feels as though she will love, that she loves the whole universe, and she wonders at the amount of goodness and beauty in the world. Violetta's feelings of universal love and well-being are reflections of her particular rootedness and communion with Venice. They are demonstrations that the true love of country—the type of patriotism that Weil was attempting to think for the first time[65]—is, at the same time, a love of the world, of the other, and of the universe.

---

63. Simone Weil, *Venice Saved*, Silvia Panizza & Philip Wilson trans. (New York: Bloomsbury, 2019).

64. Another example illustrating why J.P. Little was right to note that *Venice Saved* is an artistic expression of what we find expressed theoretically in *The Need for Roots*. See J.P. Little, "Society as Mediator in Simone Weil's 'Venise Sauvée,'" *The Modern Language Review*, vol. 65, no. 2 (1970), 301.

65. This new patriotism is further discussed in the next chapter by Lissa McCullough.

CHAPTER 4

The Need for Roots

Lissa McCullough

Simone Weil's final essay, *The Need for Roots*, is uncharacteristically sprawling. It was composed rapidly—with no time to revise or re-think—over the last few months of her life in early 1943 while she was working in service of the Free France movement based in London under severely demoralizing conditions; German forces had by now occupied the whole of France and were aggressively waging war on both western and eastern fronts. The reader of the essay must struggle to discern its complex central thesis given that Weil does not declare her intentions in so many words, or at least such indications are hard to find and pin down. To assert that the essay is about "rootedness" is not much help because, as Weil affirms, the subject is inherently elusive. Certain main ideas recur repeatedly, but these seem to compete with one another as the core intent or purpose. We must observe how these recurrent key topics cohere with each other, how they braid together into a whole, and this entails a challenging effort of assimilation.

The animating quest of Weil's essay is to think through a new notion of *patriotism*, love of country, that is crucially and decisively distinguished from all forms of nationalism, chauvinism, and racist colonialism. True patriotism in her eyes is a spiritual-religious loyalty. In the wake of France's fall and occupation, Weil was striving to articulate a love of country that would rally the French in their country's defense. But even beyond that, she proposes, the French are "obliged to invent a new sort of patriotism" that thinks out what the world requires, for "the world requires at the present time a new patriotism" (NR 145). An authentic patriotism for Weil is one that is, and must be, universally defensible and perfectly just, not a product of nationalist chauvinism, or white European supremacism, or colonial expansionism. Authentic love of country, like any pure love, is ultimately in substance *religious*—an essentially spiritual matter—and this explains why the later pages of the essay are concerned with love of God, justice, and religious obedience. Her argument offers a whirlwind tour, passing from the vital needs of the soul, through the rise of monarchic despotism, the advent of the modern nation-state, the French Revolution, imperial colonial conquest, to questions of the true basis of morality and the ultimate indispensability of a notion of transcendent good for the life of *any* nation, not only for France.

Her leading question is: What about contemporary France is worthy of fighting and dying for, quite in despite of the grave sins and crimes it has committed over the previous centuries as an imperial-colonial state? What devotion to France rates as truly *spiritual*, as a living manifestation of the divine incarnation that embodies inherent worth as such, just as any beloved country does? Weil was primed for this question all her life, growing up as a child during the disruptions of the Great War—a horrible, grueling war during which France suffered untold trauma and loss. Now, as the Nazi occupation of France called out her patriotic best, she dedicated the last effort of her life to this line of inquiry, seeking viable answers. There is only one remedy, she forcefully asserts: "[T]o give French people something to love; and in the first place, to give them France to love; to conceive the reality corresponding to the name of France in such a way that as she actually is, in her very truth, she can be loved with the whole heart" (NR 155).

It might come as a surprise that Weil would seek to validate patriotism at all. But that is exactly the point. In the essay she is descrying a justified and justifiable patriotism: an ardent homeland-defending love of country—"a bright, pure flame of patriotism" (NR 109)—that holds to universal criteria that *any* culturally rooted society at *any* time in history would be justified to hold. Here her aim is to argue consistently on the basis of an ethical-religious universalism. The prerequisite for France to recover authentic value and valor in the current context of war and German occupation is "nothing less than a question of refashioning the soul of the country" (NR 148). A renewed basis for patriotism is needed, a pure and transparent understanding of what an authentic love of country looks like, and what its essential duties are (NR 101–103). France's war effort must be nourished by what Weil refers to as its veritable genius: "The unique source of salvation and greatness for France lies in regaining contact with her genius in the depths of her distress" (NR 212).

Cultures that are uprooted, spread uprooting. Weil is profoundly disquieted that under the effects of war the "disease of uprootedness has taken on such a sharp increase throughout Europe as to leave one legitimately appalled" (NR 50). In the throes of resisting Nazism, an existential danger threatens France in victory as well as defeat. Nazism as an aggressive militarized nationalism is, per Weil's analysis, a product and consequence of modern uprootedness, and any national power aggressive enough to win victory is prone to be as uprooted and uprooting as the regime it is fighting. For indeed, France has shown its own tendencies in this direction historically, Weil argues (NR 146–47); its dreams of imperial conquest, ill-treatment of foreigners, and colonial greediness have led to a misfortune that is not undeserved (NR 86, 112). Whoever is uprooted, uproots others, she asserts, and whoever is rooted, does not uproot others (NR 48). Therefore the only hope to oppose the Nazi disease—an uprootedness that uproots—without becoming an equivalent uprooting force lies not in greater concentration of brute force but in strengthened organic loyalties, the sustaining native relationships that are concrete embodied incarnations rather than abstract ideological manipulations. The hope for France lies in roots and rootedness, in renewed love for—and willingness to sacrifice for—the concrete, the local, that particular portion of the incarnation that is intimately loved as one's native country, as opposed to the abstract and uprooted center of power: the nation-state. "A nation cannot be an object of charity. But a country can be, as an environmental source of eternal traditions" (NB 504).[1]

Weil interweaves several lines of argument to make this case: (1) an exploration of rootedness (*enracinement*), an elusive notion that nonetheless captures something essential about any organically formed society; (2) a critique of the modern nation-state, including its monetary

---

1. My thanks to Lawrence Schmidt for bringing to my attention this passage on patriotism in Weil's notebooks.

apparatus, as the primary agent of uprooting (*déracinement*) in the modern world through conquest, oppression, colonial rule, and exploitation; (3) a clarification of the obligations of the citizen to his or her country, rooted in appropriate loyalty to the physical land, to regional lifeways and cultural creations, and to the collective spirit of one's home place (*genius loci*); and finally (4) the vital role of religious inspiration in social and national life.

Vital Needs of the Soul

The essay focuses on non-physical vital needs that are "analogous to hunger." Of the vital needs necessary to human life, physical needs are relatively easy to identify and make explicit, whereas the "needs of the soul" are far more elusive, difficult to recognize and enumerate, and yet "everyone recognizes that they exist," she asserts (in an exuberant overstatement). They form a necessary condition of our life on earth, for "if they are not satisfied, we fall little by little into a state more or less resembling death, more or less akin to a purely vegetative existence" (NR 7; OC 5.2.114–15). Psychic-spiritual needs are never as palpable and visible as the need for food, yet they are fully food-like needs, she insists. One can touch a piece of bread, one can see the wasting effects of hunger, but it is possible to be oblivious to the lifelong scarring effects of violent abuse, dislocation, destruction of homeland, deprivation of dignity through humiliation, and like forms of trauma that stunt or shatter life just as surely as does physical trauma and starvation, but more invisibly. One's body can survive a trauma that one's soul cannot, producing a living death or literal death, a social death, an active or passive suicide.

After treating the first fourteen needs of the soul briefly (order, liberty, obedience, responsibility, equality, hierarchy, honor, punishment, freedom of opinion, security, risk, private property, collective property, truth), Weil turns to the fifteenth, stating that the need to be rooted (*l'enracinement*) is "perhaps the most important and most underrecognized" need of the soul, and she asserts that this is one of the most difficult of the vital needs to define (NR 43). In view of its importance and elusiveness, the rest of the essay is an attempt to articulate this need.

The fact that *enracinement* belongs to this listing as the fifteenth and final element was long obscured by an editorial mutation introduced in the first edition of *L'Enracinement*, published in 1949. The editors suppressed the number "15" (an Arabic numeral in Weil's text) that identified the need for roots as the final need in the listing, then arbitrarily separated off Weil's treatment of this need into a "Part 2" and "Part 3" of their own creation. The volume of Weil's *Oeuvres complètes* containing this essay, published under the direction of Robert Chenavier in 2013, finally clarifies and restores the original structure of the essay (see OC 5.2.142, the asterisked footnote). For more than sixty years, readers were left to wonder how the fourteen needs in the arbitrarily created "Part One" connect with this "perhaps most important" need of the soul that opens the arbitrarily created "Part Two," inexplicably severed from the preceding list, without comment, with the essential enumeration erased. In Weil's original manuscript there is no space or page break or heading separating off the fifteenth need from the listing of the first fourteen, nor is there any break in the manuscript to justify a "Part 3" (OC 5.2.142, 260). The original text is run together without division into parts.

The critical vitality of roots in human life is actually correlated with their elusive indefinability. A way to think about this is as follows: just as human gestation before birth is one of the longest in nature with good reason (as anthropologist Lewis Mumford notes, "we are a retarded animal"), so the factors promoting early development—mimetic inculcation, layered acculturation, and gradual emergence of the individual persona within its human community and natural environment—are processes occurring continuously over many decades of life.[2] These are truly lifelong developmental processes, not only processes of juvenile development, and the individual's development only terminates with death. Once launched at birth, the individual requires an intricate and complex natural-cultural nexus to nourish it with all it requires to develop a range of distinctively human facilities: motor skills, symbolization and language skills, social interpretation and interaction skills, critical reflection skills, creative aspirational goals, and so on, that mutate to new ones through the successive stages of life. Each of these realms of human development and learning is fathomless. This complex of infusions and influences interweaves a tremendous array of cultural variables to serve as "food" (*nouriture*), as Weil calls it, for developing indi-

---

2. Lewis Mumford, *The Transformations of Man* (New York: Harper and Row, 1956), 10.

viduality in community. Selected elements can perhaps be weaker or missing, yet the child still flourishes more or less. But if too many essential variables that sustain individual and communal development are denied, violently disturbed, or suddenly cut off, this often results in a shattered and shocked being, marked and scarred for life, not able to become whole or hale again.

L'Enracinement seizes on the metaphor of roots, the human need for roots, and the manner of their formation, yet perhaps the greater share of her analysis depicts the destruction and deficit of roots as a modern global affliction. She argues that imperial wars and colonial conquest, forces of violent uprooting, have plunged the Western imperial states themselves into a generalized state of uprootedness that constitutes an "almost desperate situation" (NR 51). The true mission of the Free France movement is therefore "a spiritual mission before being a military and political one"—even for the sake of military and political success. It is the deep-seated morale of the French people that will decide whether there is sufficient energy, devotion, and grit to fight to regain their freedom rather than succumb. This spiritual mission must serve as the "director of conscience on a national plane" (NR 213). In writing this essay as a resistance thinker and writer, Weil is seeking to spark such a new national conscience in the hopes it can be fanned into a flame by a regenerated collective spirit of authentic patriotic loyalty grounded in spiritual values.

On "Roots" Literal and Metaphorical

The metaphorical sense of "root" is fraught with interpretive challenges. We do well to keep close to Weil's own words and implications, attending to how she writes about roots and rootedness, why the theme matters as profoundly as it does to her, and what she wanted her readers to understand about the global uprootedness that she diagnoses. We ought not to take the root inspiration of the metaphor for granted. The French word *racine*, derived from the Latin *radix*, denotes a botanic organ in its most literal definition; only secondarily is it a metaphor. Root as metaphor, referring to *cause* or *origin*, is a usage dating to the high Middle Ages, and the mathematical sense of *root* (as in square root) begins in the mid-sixteenth century. Literal roots, while outwardly sessile, act as superefficient arterial superhighways for nutrient transfer and exchange that procure essential nourishment for the living biomass of land-based flora and fauna. Material roots in the earth's surface routinely fulfill this function for complex forms of life on land, channeling a communicative interchange of vital materials between relatively sessile elements (leaves, branches, trunk or stem, solid root structures, and soil). Though static-seeming, a root's core reason for being is as a conduit of life-aggrandizing flux.

Only rarely does Weil remark on literal roots in her writing, yet the essential "labor" of roots inspires what is for her an elemental metaphor. Solar energy is a condition of our existence that our bellies receive via rooted plants. She notes that all we can do as agriculturalists is to arrange seeds, soil, water, and fertilizer so that the sun may descend into plants more efficiently: "Solar energy descends into plants and animals as a living thing, but becomes a dead one before satisfying our needs.... It is a grace that we receive.... We don't actually do anything" (NB 543). Roots are life-proliferating organs of generation, growth, outreach, communication, interconnection, selection, distribution, absorption, resourceful redirection, and waste and toxin removal that sustain life that would otherwise perish of substantial lack and/or excess accumulation. So, let us duly remark that a *root* is not just any metaphor; it undergirds the miracle of life. It is fitting to keep in mind that even if rooted plants are sessile, roots are anything but static: they extend, search out, change route, and respond; they facilitate logistical transfer and biophilic interrelations in dynamic service of life. Weil reflects: "It is the light falling continually from heaven which alone gives a tree the energy to send powerful roots deep into the earth. The tree is really rooted in the sky" (SE 23).

One reason *root* used as a metaphor is elusive is that it has no literal aspect: no physical root serves as a gathering place for the symbolic sense of "rootedness." The metaphorical sense does not bear any isomorphism with the physical rootedness of plants for the obvious reason that human life is not sessile. Family, native tongue, and home place offer perhaps the closest isomorphism to physical rooting. Our DNA is the recombinant "offshoot" of our parents', our inculturation is mediated by the "root words" of our native tongue, our childhood is "rooted" in familiar places—all vaguely in the manner in which a plant is imbedded in soil. But these analogies only demonstrate how literalism fails: in human existence, rather than literal rooting there is *relationship*: intimate familial-familiar relationships that produce connection and identification, including a profound feeling of kinship, home, and homeland. The individual is encompassed in a sustaining whole by interrelations with other human and nonhuman lives, land and landscape, patterns and rhythms of life, languages and belief systems, aesthetic and practical inculturation.

Yet let us recall that a deracinated human life can also persist indefinitely in an abject state with roots violently severed, denuded of the sustaining concrete connections that identify us most intimately to ourselves. As Weil observes:

> I may lose at any moment, through the play of circumstances over which I have no control, anything whatsoever that I possess, including those things which are so intimately mine that I consider them as being myself. There is nothing that I might not lose. It could happen at any moment that what I am might be abolished and replaced by anything whatsoever of the filthiest and most contemptible sort. (SE 27)

In its extreme form Weil observes of affliction, "[t]he greatest suffering which allows some roots to remain intact is still infinitely removed from this quasi-hell" (NB 252).

Rootedness as metaphor is elusive because cultural roots function through inspiration not fixation; they function most effectively to the extent they are malleable, transformable influences, not a fixed and rigid conditioning of expectations. Even highly traditional cultures, despite their conservatism, survive by being dynamic and variegated. Modes of rootedness are differentially dynamic, responding in novel ways to sudden or long-term circumstantial changes. Their sustainability—and their power to sustain—is a consequence of multivalence, fluidity, creative mutation, not fixation. For Weil, the point of equilibrium is always found in motion, not in stasis. Conditional changes through time are the "motion" that cultural roots must adapt to and accommodate. Traditions and peoples have different tolerances for change, for shocks and shifts, which is to say they manifest differential adaptabilities. A cultural system is sustained by its success in achieving sustainability.

The metaphor of roots, I would suggest, intrinsically invokes the notion of *cultural sustainability*: the test of time that selects for those organic cultural systems that generate a realistic, grounded, time-tested practical wisdom. They are not shooting in the dark, not reinventing the wheel, not wasting slowly accumulated value, but are garnering limited resources and accepting constraints in order to live meaningfully under variable conditions of time and place.[3] They succeed, at least, until they are uprooted and destroyed by an *unsustainable* system of value such as the ones analyzed here by Weil: war, conquest, centralized mechanisms of power, and money-value. Coercive power, which wholly lacks the creative power to grow roots, is able to uproot overnight. The modern militarized nation-state is an abstraction bred by uprootedness, difficult to define exactly, yet it exercises an all-too-real power to uproot that is observable today in all corners of the earth (NR 114).

Body as World-Root

Reflection on the *real* was central to Weil's thinking all her life; it should inform our effort to unpack this "perhaps most important" of all needs of the soul: the need for roots. Contact with reality is an essential need of the human soul, yet because we are in some degree playthings of our own imagination and will, "[t]o become conscious of even the simplest realities one needs to pay attention" (SE 150). This speaks for the advisability of keeping mindful of the material grounding of intellectual and spiritual functions; or, to express this in Weil's words: "Matter becomes thought every day, in the sense that we breathe and eat; the energy liberated by chemical transformations becomes at any rate an instrument of thought" (NB165). For Weil, indeed, matter is no less mysterious than thought, no less miraculous (NB 405, 612; FLN 362).

Upon conception, the material grounding of a human life begins to complexify in the womb. The body that is knitted with great rapidity by recombinant DNA is our original and primary "root" in the world. The material world-root that is our body, that is *us*, remains our foundation

---

3. Two sources that may be of interest on this theme are Pascal David, "Qu'est-ce qu'un milieu? Enjeux politiques et spirituels," in *Un art de vivre par temps de catastrophe* (Valence: Peuple Libre, 2020), 140–68, and Eric O. Springsted, "A Theory of Culture," chapter 12 in *Simone Weil for the Twenty-First Century* (Notre Dame: University of Notre Dame Press, 2021), 175–93.

until the last of our days. We *are* this organizing construal of sensation, of perception of things and places; we are the body getting a lease on its powers to perceive and interact with the order of the world.[4] Being rooted is achieved by a nexus of influences that put the body-mind in touch with a composite natural-cultural reality, enlarging the individual's world and world-readiness. Yet, Weil maintained, we fail to grasp the real relations between things because our imagination filters contact with the world through our biases in the process of perception. Despite our naïve confidence that "seeing is believing," our perceptions are in part mixed with imaginative projection. For example, in a *propos* for Alain of 1925, the sixteen-year-old Weil asserted:

> We do not have consciousness of things, but of our attitudes in the face of things, which give us information about themselves inasmuch as we are in part constrained by them. But the imagination supplements that which is strongly insufficient for us about the exterior world, because it is exterior, and produces a compromise which we call perception.

Our direct perception comes to us compromised. She concludes the piece: "Without grounding in reality [*sans fondement dans la realité*] this imagination plays freely in the void" (OC 1:298; my translation).

Rootedness is what supplies the individual a supporting orientation to the world, grounding us in the "real" relationships between things. As cultures evolve, symbolizations become overlaid and patterned onto the embodied activities and relations that maintain everyday life. Mundane repetitions, cadences, rhythms, resonances, are commensurate with our bodies, our psyches.[5] The heart beats, cicadas buzz in the trees, organic repetitions are mimicked in symbol and ritual. Thus material presence and symbolic construals become coordinated in an organic nexus. The symbolic realm fuses with the material ground of life much as the eucharistic wafer is imbued with sacrality when blessed. The symbolic potency invested in an object, place, life pattern, or ritual enables these to func-

---

4. See Lissa McCullough, "Simone Weil's Phenomenology of the Body," *Comparative and Continental Philosophy* 4, no. 2 (November 2012): 195–218.

5. See, for example, NB 107. The theme of rhythms and cadences in labor is touched on by Simone Kotva (Chapter 9) in this volume and by Scott B. Ritner in "The Training of the Soul," in *Simone Weil and Continental Philosophy*, ed. A. Rebecca Rozelle-Stone (New York: Rowman & Littlefield, 2017), 198–99.

tion as analogous to food, nourishing the soul. Dual lines of grounding—natural and cultural—interweave in life patterns and rituals forming a shared world of "tried and true" relationships that sustain what is essentially a vulnerable conditional existence, both individual and communal. Weil understood that symbolic orders of this kind, grounded in concrete lifeways, feed the soul all life long, and the soul atrophies without them.

Weil asserts that "we owe our respect to a collectivity" such as country, family, or another because it provides nourishment analogous to food for a certain number of human souls; each such collectivity is unique, and if destroyed cannot be replaced (NR 8; OC 5.2.115); for "[t]here is nothing in the world so precious, but at the same time so frail and perishable, so difficult, or even impossible, to revive, as the living warmth of a human environment, that medium which bathes and fosters the thoughts and the virtues" (SE 79). Rootedness in community is a real, active, natural participation that is almost automatically produced by "place, conditions of birth, profession, and social surroundings," and from it one must draw almost the whole of one's moral, intellectual, and spiritual life (NR 43). It is the "particular function" of collectivity to achieve transgenerational continuity in time through family roots, connecting the present community with its ancestors in the past and its descendants to come in the future (NR 99–100).

Weil emphasizes that her notion of roots is not isolating but interactive. "Rooting in and the multiplying of contacts are complementary to one another" (NR 52). Every human being needs to have multiple roots, making possible reciprocal exchanges, but any one environment should receive outside influences as a stimulant intensifying its own particular way of life (NR 43–44). Each country, each province, has its own genius that proves to be a boon in exchanges with others, leading to mutual enrichment; differences should be encouraged. Even as one is rooted in one's own locale as "a certain particular vital medium," it would be natural to form "nuclei" for the free circulation of ideas and exchange of influences across provinces, regions, and nations (NR 160, 156, 161). Weil translates this into a need for France as a small country, potentially stifling, to interconnect with Europe and the wider world (NR 164–65). But she cautions that "[e]xchange is only possible where each one preserves his own genius, and that is not possible without liberty" (NR 161).

The Genius Loci of *Pays*

Local traditions arise in organic connection with place, family, community, and ecosystem: the language, the religious practices and festivals, the songs and poems, the local heroes and stories, the familiar places enjoyed and remembered in common, the feeling of communal pride in "how we do things here," ancestral loyalties, and so on. In carrying this sense of locality, specific "placedness," individual provinces speak louder than the collective name of a country. It is not the collectivity called France so much as Normandy, Provence, Lorraine, or Brittany that carry the scent and vitality of the "roots" Weil means to invoke (NR 105–108, 164). The modern French nation was the product of conquest of these regions, killing or at least undercutting and stifling their genius (NR 119, 143). Each locale, each region or province, constitutes a distinctive way of life, esthetic, and constellation of mores.[6] The genius loci comes to incarnate an almost mythic identity, one that is strictly inimitable. It is this unique identity of place that commercial tourism sells, and precisely by selling, more often than not uproots and destroys. Weil noted the conundrum during her spring 1937 sojourn in Italy that "everything in and around Assisi is Franciscan—everything, except what has been put up in honour of Saint Francis" (SL 85).

Uniqueness of place, uniqueness of organic cultural development in any singular locale, means that local virtues and beauties are not moveable or fungible; non-transferability is an essential aspect of the thing itself. One may take pains to prepare an exquisite caprese salad in California, for example, but one cannot—no matter the money spent or the chef hired—produce one equal to this supremely simple plate as it is served around Naples, Italy. A California-style emulation is the outcome, convincing no one who knows the difference. The unique gifts of locality are non-transferable because they are a complex fusion of non-substitutable materiality, geography and climate, cultural habits and mores, intergenerational tradition, intuitive savoir-faire, and local individual flair. Weil urges that we need to honor and cherish these "historical atolls of the living past left upon the surface

---

6. The contemporary philosopher Edward S. Casey has articulated a phenomenology of place along these lines in many works, beginning with *The Fate of Place: A Philosophical History* (Berkeley: University of California Press, 1997).

of the earth"; all these distillations of the living past should be jealously preserved everywhere, whether in Paris or Tahiti, for there are not so many remaining on the entire globe (NR 51; OC 5.2.149). Because "[t] he past once destroyed never returns, destruction of the past is perhaps the greatest of all crimes," Weil asserts, and preservation "of what little of it remains ought to become almost an obsession" (NR 52). "Loss of the past, whether it be collectively or individually, is the supreme human tragedy, and we have thrown ours away just like a child picking off the petals of a rose" (NR 119).

Weil's description of uprootedness as a "loss of the past" (NR 119) may come across as a bit abstract, yet what she means to invoke by le passé is wedded to—inextricable from—concrete place or locale: a complex nexus of natural-cultural embodied relations. She makes clear she is depicting a *living* past, a "past" in the present—alive in the souls of those who carry it, for example, in this quotation:

> The future brings us nothing, gives us nothing; it is we who in order to build it have to give it everything, our very life. . . . [W]e possess no other life, no other living sap, than the treasures stored up from the past and digested, assimilated and created afresh by us. (NR 51)

Of all the human soul's needs, none is more vital than this one of the past, referring to the relations an individual is born into, then grows to adulthood within, a local-cultural community that imbues a natural sense of transgenerational identity, belonging, and communal aspiration. Much of this past is preserved in living memory, in lifeways of family and local lore, in native approaches to education, and in sentimental loyalty. The loss of this past is the supreme human tragedy for the sake of which "peoples will put up a desperate resistance to being conquered" (NR 119).

In terms of healthy rootedness, the young of the nation are an especially critical factor, the budding promise that past will be carried forward into new life. Yet Weil detected a deeply worrisome fatigue among the young in France (NR 149). Those on the right were tending to uncritical nationalist devotion to the State, embracing the rooting metaphor as employed propagandistically by *Blut-und-Boden*-style ideologies; meanwhile, those on the left were embracing a working-class internationalism-cum-imperialism that only served to aggrandize the power and prestige of the State in the USSR (NR 150–52). Both competing doctrines, the nationalist right and the internationalist left, strengthened State power at the expense of the values embedded in longstanding traditions.

Weil points to three principal forces that destroy roots and spread the disease of uprooting: military conquest, money-power, and an abstract, ideological approach to education not grounded in concrete life experience (NR 44–45, 121, 124). Her essay proceeds to examine how workers, peasant farmers, and citizens in general are differentially subjected to uprooting by these forces. A cutting of the roots has occurred even for those who live a more traditional life in the countryside; since the First World War, peasants have become alienated and uprooted, breaking from their past and running away to join the ranks of proletarian workers (NR 78–83). Money and the State have destroyed all other bonds of attachment: the provinces have a self-regard as conquered territory reigned over by the centralized power of the State (NR 117, 119, 121); "[t]he family doesn't exist" except as a denuded nucleus (NR 99); monetized wage-labor and the threat of unemployment has cut away the roots of workers who, with the rise of class resentments and hatreds, feel at war with society (NR 123); and meanwhile the bourgeoisie pursues its private interests rather than the public good and has at best a feeble attachment to country (NR 49). In society at large, real education is almost extinct, and there is a deficit of loyalty, gratitude, and affection (NR 121).

The Bane of Centralization:
Nation-State versus Country

Centralization of power, prestige, and cultural influence kills roots; it is the primary force in history responsible for the killing of spiritual values, including love of country: "[A]ll progress in the direction of centralized power implies irreparable losses in everything that is really precious" (SE 80). Centralized power dominates through a combination of brute force (conquest, policing), coercive authority, and the erosive abstractions of money, ideology, and abstract ideological education. The diametric contrast between uprooting and rootedness is one between *killing* versus *sustaining* collective life: the natural-cultural synergies that constitute rootedness are real inasmuch as they *really* sustain the bodies and souls of individuals within transgenerational communities. Centralization will have killed "all sorts of precious things whose preservation would have been essential if the next dispensation was to be a living intercourse between diverse and mutually independent centres instead of a dreary chaos" (SE 79).

A clear imperative of Weil's text is that the concrete relations and lifeways that sustain a people in particular local traditions deserve to be prized and cherished over abstract, alienated, severed, and impoverished relations. Much of the essay is therefore an attempt to tease out the essential distinction between country (*pays*) and the nation-state (*état*) so that a legitimate form of patriotism (devotion to *patrie*) can be based on the former rather than the latter. Failure to distinguish between France as a nation-state and France as a country leads not only to their confusion but their fusion with disastrous consequences (NR 127). Authentic patriotism is a devotion to one's country (*pays*) as the natural-cultural locale in which one is rooted, nourished from birth; patriotism in its rootless form is attachment to the nation as an imperial power structure. The deep problem is that both are called "France."

Weil asserts that the State's proper duty is to "make the country, in the highest possible degree, a reality," ensuring the country becomes a "life-giving agent" offering really "good, root-fixing ground" (NR 163). Since its inception in the seventeenth century, however, the French state (*état*) has conquered, subjected, and parasitized France as a country (*pays*) consisting of highly individuated provinces, and this is a consequence of the centralized power structure that is the essence of the modern nation-state. The French State idolized by Cardinal Richelieu was neither the crown nor the public good but a "blind and anonymous machine for manufacturing order and power" (SE 94). Thus Richelieu's devotion to the State uprooted France. Obsequiousness before the sheer power and prestige of the State, Weil observes, whether on the early model of Richelieu or the later one of Charles Maurras, has in the course of time displaced the affection that heartfelt love of country once inhabited (NR 115, 122, 166). In the course of this evolution, even the word *nation* has changed its meaning:

> In our day, [the word *nation*] no longer denotes the sovereign
> people, but the sum total of peoples recognizing the authority
> of the same State; it is the political structure created by a State

[*état*] and the country [*pays*] under its control.... [N]ot only is the State in question not the sovereign people, but it is the very self-same inhuman, brutal, bureaucratic, police-ridden State bequeathed by Richelieu to Louis XIV, by Louis XIV to the Convention, by the Convention to the Empire, and by the Empire to the Third Republic. And what is more, it is instinctively recognized and hated as such. (NR 127)

The cold mechanism of the State, its steely brutality and bureaucratic indifference, cannot be loved and yet is able to command self-sacrifice of citizens in the name of "France"—the natural-cultural homeland to which one owes one's native identity and loyalty. What results is a "loveless idolatry—what could be more monstrous....?" (NR 127). Each successive regime—from absolute monarchy to the Revolution to the Third Republic—destroyed local and regional life at an ever-increasing rate until the citizen was left nothing else, no intermediate collective structures—such as extended families, towns, groups of villages, provinces, or regions—to which to direct loyalty (NR 121, 114, 117–18, 129): "[T]he State has morally killed everything, territorially speaking, smaller than itself" (NR 122). Thus, uprooting breeds idolatry, especially idolatry of the State and, in consequence, the cult of the great leader "who is the personal magnet for all loyalties" whose appeal is in part that he is made of flesh and blood as the cold concern of the State is not (NR 68, 114–15).

Though proponents of the Revolution imagined they were breaking once and for all with monarchic despotism, during the successive waves of counterrevolution and terror the forces of centralized power concentrated in the administrative apparatus soon reasserted authoritarian control. Even as monarchy was overthrown, the centralized legal and administrative structures that were erected under absolutist monarchy proved resilient and resistant to overthrow. The Revolution, to save itself, reached for this core of power. As a consequence, more or less overnight, one despotic regime was replaced by another—though to speak more accurately, the same elements of authoritarian structure were simply taken over by a new head, a new doctrine or ideology, a new label. Anonymous structures of power all too often outlast the political ideologies and historical actors that imagine themselves to possess them. Thus a government portraying itself as a democratic republic proved to be as despotic and parasitic upon the citizenry as was absolute monarchy, and "the illusion of national sovereignty showed itself to be manifestly an illusion," the people were indubitably not sovereign (NR 111). Weil depicts the strange paradox of the Third Republic that few were able to recognize at the time: a democracy in which all public institutions were openly hated and despised by the entire population. "[T]he whole series of political institutions were the object of disgust, derision, and disdain. The very word politics had taken on a profoundly pejorative meaning incredible in a democracy" (NR 121).

A classic study that supplies illuminating historical context and support for Weil's argument at this point is Alexis de Tocqueville's *The Old Regime and the French Revolution* (1856)—here referenced as *L'Ancien Régime.*[7] Tocqueville's inquiry, like Weil's, was animated by a vivid patriotic concern for revealing authentic liberty as against servility in the spirit of the French people, and he also harbors the abiding worry that absolutism and despotism have triumphed in the order of the day. Both Tocqueville and Weil trace out the continuities between the despotism of the *ancien régime* and the uprootedness of post-Revolutionary France as increasingly subjected to "repressive apparatus" of the French State (NR 120). In *L'Ancien Régime* Tocqueville anatomizes the historical preconditions of the Revolution in order to trace the events, mistakes, and misjudgments that led the French to "abandon their original ideal," turning their backs on freedom and proceeding to "acquiesce in an equality of servitude under the master of all Europe"—that is, under "a government, both stronger and far more autocratic than the one which the Revolution had overthrown, centralized once more the entire administration, made itself all-powerful, suppressed our dearly bought liberties, and replaced them by a mere pretense of freedom" (AR xi).

Both Weil and Tocqueville emphasize the fierce resolve of the 1789 revolutionaries to effect a clean *break* with the past, using violence as needed to achieve it (AR x, NR 109). In Tocqueville's words, they sought to make "a scission in their life line and to create an unbridgeable gulf between all they had hitherto been and all they now aspired to be," and they "spared no pains in their endeavor to obliterate their former selves"

---

7. Alexis de Tocqueville, *The Old Regime and the French Revolution* (1856), trans. Stuart Gilbert (New York: Doubleday, 1955).

to make sure of imparting nothing whatever from the past into the new regime. Tocqueville's study traces out how this first idealist phase of the revolution was quickly supplanted by a second realist phase that "took over from the old regime not only most of its customs, conventions, and modes of thought, but even those very ideas which prompted our revolutionaries to destroy it ...; they used the debris of the old order for building up the new" (AR vii). The old regime of the seventeenth century was, Tocqueville notes, already "highly centralized and all-powerful," and this immanent reality of the bureaucratic State reemerged full force in the second phase of the revolution, as many of the laws and administrative methods that had been suppressed in 1789 reappeared a few years later (AR x–xi).

Weil's political orientation as a former syndicalist-activist and lover of Rousseau inclines her to defend republicanism in principle, but she espies a historic betrayal of the French people in the way the Revolution consolidated power in a central State apparatus unresponsive to the needs and aspirations of the provinces as distinctive regions, cultures, and ways of life in need of support rather than repressive exploitation. The aspiration to absolute rupture with the past was a grave error on the part of the revolutionaries because it rendered the Revolution a *rootless* beginning point, making a bid to quash all longstanding deep-rooted loyalties—to land and family and lord and king (NR 105)—with brute force, rather than building up republican feeling nourished by living historical roots and regional loyalties. Revolutionary spirit was conceived not as embodying a love of the French past but as a violent break with and erasure of that past. But Weil insists that opposition of future to past or past to future is absurd; one cannot turn one's back on the past and expect to begin with nothing. Love of the past in the form of loyalty to one's country has nothing to do with a reactionary political orientation; on the contrary, she argues, all loyalties are treasures of infinite value and rarity because they honor roots, the "living sap" out of which the future is created (NR 51, 164).

Post-revolutionary France, therefore, has suffered this paradox of patriotism founded not on the past but on the most violent break with the past (NR 109, 110). This Weil considers deeply problematic because even the spirit of revolution must maintain itself out of the past: "Like all human activities, the revolution draws all its vigour from a tradition" (NR 51, 54, 110). Bereft of a sustaining loyalty to the past, embracing in its place the abstract tabula rasa of "Year One," the ideal of power to the people—self-government—rapidly degenerated into expedient centralized power *over* the people. The pure flame of patriotism that fueled the Revolution was siphoned off toward national sovereignty, the power of State, not toward national liberty. Whereas the Revolution should have stood firm against all idolization of state power and empire (NR 164, 166), the demands of empire and conquest trumped the republic (NR 147, 109, 112, 119). The upshot is that France has never been a self-governing republican nation, shored up by the strength of its variegated regional identities, but one marked by a culture of servility, distrust, and contempt for government. She diagnoses a "far more acute form of uprootedness" in France than in other countries due to "a far older and more intense form of State centralization" (NR 129).

Oppression of the *pays* by the State is not an end in itself but a means to extract and deploy national resources in service of the centralized power structure, as Tocqueville also attests: "Unhappily our kings' one desire was to keep power in their own hands at all costs and they turned a blind eye to the needs of modern civilization."[8] Weil repeatedly addresses how the sundry regions and diverse peoples of France were colonized as a means of aggrandizing imperial power to engage in wars and colonize abroad (NR 109, 133, 80–81): "[T]he national unity had been brought about almost exclusively by the most brutal conquests" (NR 143). The organ of State, far from serving the public good by enhancing the health of regions and provinces, betrayed this charge by erecting administrative structures of systematic oppression, subjection, and extraction: "[T]he development of the State exhausts a country. The State eats away its moral substance, lives on it, fattens on it, until the day comes when no more nourishment can be drawn from it, and famine reduces it to a condition of lethargy" (NR 119).

This is the root source of the "inertia," "apathetic stupor," "drowsiness," and "general malady" displayed by France in face of German aggression: the long-term sapping of the *pays* by the centralized State. The sudden collapse of France in June 1940, which surprised observers all over the world, Weil observes, simply showed the extent to which the country was uprooted: "A tree whose roots are almost entirely eaten away falls at the first blow. If France offered a spectacle more painful

---

8. Tocqueville, *L'Ancien Régime*, 221.

than that of any other European country, it is because modern civilization with all its toxins [*ses poisons*] was in a more advanced stage there than elsewhere, with the exception of Germany" (NR 49, 50, 86, 100–102). While uprootedness was taking an aggressive malignant form in Germany fueled by an ideology of fake roots, *Blut und Boden*, the specific form of uprootedness in France became manifest in its abject exhaustion and paralysis. The country that behaved the best by far was the one in which tradition is strongest, Weil notes, where the strengths of cultural rootedness were still alive: that is, England (NR 49).

In terms of the political order, the crucial contest for Weil is not between monarchy and republicanism, but between legitimate versus illegitimate forms of sovereignty, whether that sovereign be a king or the people; indeed, she defends legitimate monarchical sovereignty, the king who was a representative of God (NR 269–70, 275). A legitimate political order stands in equilibrium with the root-system of the larger society, whereas a parasitic centralized State exploits peoples and lands, domestic and foreign alike, for the ulterior purpose of aggrandizing power for power's sake. Weil had already argued in "Analysis of Oppression" (1934) that the essential nature of power implies that it can never be secured. This inherent insecurity and instability of any power structure entails that it is only able to maintain itself as a *means* to power, a power to obtain power, never as an end; hence all ends of whatever kind are converted into means to aggrandize power in a relentless quest and competition that takes the place of all ends (OL 67–69; NR 216). This inversion of means and ends is the very essence of all evil in society (NB 495). The centralized power of State uproots in all directions, outwardly and inwardly, converting every resource it can assimilate into an additional means to power.

In this light, Weil explores the deracinating impact of conquests in history by powerful imperial states: those of Rome, Louis XIV, Mussolini, and Hitler. "Conquests are not of life, they are of death at the very moment they take place" (NR 51). Relentless pressures on the imperial State to expand its power through wars and conquests necessitate imposition of authoritarian mechanisms of internal control, colonization, repression, and extraction within a nation. The resources needed to project power outward are conscripted from within and without simultaneously, using parallel forms of oppression and control: "[T]he totalitarian phenomenon of the State arises through a conquest carried out by the public authorities of the people under their care ... in order to possess a better instrument for carrying out foreign conquest" (NR 119). Wars and conquests require the State to concentrate power with relentless brutal efficiency; it has no choice. "France devoured and digested so many lands" (NR 142): it became a mechanism for exploiting the provinces—conquered earlier in history—to conquer and exploit lands abroad in the Americas, Africa, the Middle East, Indochina, and Oceania.[9] She decries the reflex celebration of France's past conquests without questioning whether in its growth it has not annihilated "things that were worth as much as she," and the way the nation is granted a superior prestige, an absolute value, exempt from moral considerations and bound up with the exaltation of war (NR 129–30, 137–38, 142). To renew itself, she urges, France must put an end to "the terrible uprootedness that European colonial methods always produce" and foster a recovery of roots wherever that is possible (NR 52, 160).

The destruction of the past effected by centralized State power—first under the crown's despotic rule in the seventeenth century, then under the "diffused terrorism" of the police-ridden modern State—has produced a gaping vacuum of true patriotic loyalty in the French people (NR 155). Nor does Weil trust the feeble resurgence of patriotism that occurred in response to fall of Paris in June and July of 1940 following the "collective act of cowardice and treason" that was the Franco-German armistice (NR 49–50, 100–101, 113; SL 158). In her analysis, the French have grown permanently accustomed to disobeying a repressive and rapacious State that they regard with animosity and contempt. Only a deep-rooted love of *country* as opposed to State can begin to change this. Hence Weil's aim in the essay is to stir the hidden roots of France—vessels of wisdom, nobility, and worth—in order that France might recognize its old face and redeem itself as an intrinsically multicultural country inhabited by free and grounded citizens, a constellation of resilient peoples situated within a larger European community (NR 164), not as a political territory united by conquest into a cold, monocultural nation (NR 99). Unfortunately, a clear depiction of the problem by Tocqueville and Weil, in unison, almost one hundred years apart, does not constitute a solution. The power to uproot is violent and rapid, whereas the power to cultivate roots entails a slow, creative sedimentation conditioned by a myriad of "frail and perishable" variables.

---

9. See J. P. Little, ed., *Simone Weil on Colonialism: An Ethic of the Other* (Lanham: Rowman & Littlefield, 2003).

Money-Value: Fungibility as Uprooting

Rootedness as placed, located, organic relations that are everywhere specific and particular means that everything that exists is *essentially* unique; inherently nothing is fungible, nothing can be taken for—*mistaken for*—an equivalent of something else. Each point in the divine incarnation that is the world has its just and rightful place. Money, however, sets up an abstract system of universal fungible exchange of these intrinsically nonfungible qualities. It is crucial to grasp this core reason why money is uprooting: it is a system of abstraction that per se constitutes a revolutionary revaluation (obfuscation) of unique values. As a universal accounting of false (unreal) equivalences, it liquidates all ends in favor of means. A quantitative rule of measure trumps the immeasurability of qualitative difference.

In 1943, as Weil was writing this essay in London, American anthropologist-historian Lewis Mumford was analyzing how early modern capitalist enterprise inaugurated a new abstractive value-system that turned the focus of productive activity "from tangibles to intangibles," substituting money-values for life-values, instilling new habits of abstraction and calculation. The means of exchange, money, usurped the function and meaning of the things that were exchanged, Mumford writes; money itself became a commodity and money-getting became a specialized form of activity: "[W]hat are called gains in capitalist economics often turn out, from the standpoint of social energetics, to be losses; while the real gains, the gains upon which all the activities of life, civilization, and culture ultimately depend were either counted as losses or were ignored because they remained outside the commercial scheme of accountancy."[10]

Exercising an ever increasing hegemony, money-value has been granted free rein as a *means* liberated from any concern with honoring or protecting nonmonetary *ends*. As an abstract value-system—a system of abstract valuation—it systematically subjects all things to a common standard of equivalency. In the form of debt, moreover, it reigns as a major force of destabilization; Weil points to "the subversive role consistently played, ever since money existed, by the phenomenon of debt" (SE

---

10. Lewis Mumford, *Technics and Civilization* (New York: Harcourt, Brace, and World, 1934; reprint, 1963), 23, 373; quotations that follow are on 24, 379.

149). Money as a means of abstract equalization has been empowered to run roughshod over all unique qualitative differences, all unique ends in themselves, ultimately over life itself, as we are seeing in the widespread societal and environmental havoc wrought by economic financialization around the globe, a world in which the rentier-class is demonstrably in quest of absolute dominance and control.

Mumford defines money as "the quest for power by means of abstractions." Because money is the sole form of wealth that is "without assignable limits," money as a system of valuation gives license to unlimited abstraction. Nothing is allowed to resist being expressed in financial terms, and this rampant abstraction fuels a historically unprecedented power dynamic. Mumford, as profound a humanist as Weil, calls for a countervailing cultural force that would "frame a comprehensive scheme of ends"; there is need to banish the life-menacing pillaging abstractions of money-value. Weil calls for something quite similar, expressed in terms of rootedness: natural limits, harmony, proportion, physical embodiment within the order of the world—all of which are ultimately a religious concern connected with honoring the incarnation, the order of the world, and "the order of the world is the same as the beauty of the world" (NR 291). Weil identifies order as a vital need of the human soul, and this means proportionality, balance, just limits, appropriateness of relations—finally, beauty in all its forms.

The Greek Example?

The ancient Romans and Hebrews serve as paradigms of uprootedness for Weil (NR 47, 131). These she frequently contrasts with the ancient Greeks who represent the epitome of rootedness, as expressed, for example, in a 1940 letter to her brother André: "In the eyes of the Greeks, the very principle of the soul's salvation was measure, balance, proportion, harmony; because desire is always unmeasured and boundless. Therefore, to conceive the universe as an equilibrium and a harmony is to make it like a mirror of salvation" (SL 125). To conceive the universe in all its apparent chaos and injustice as an equilibrium and a harmony is to make it into a "mirror of salvation" in that it abolishes the uncontrolled and unlimited, replacing it with a cosmic image of justice. The Pythagoreans' key idea, Weil posits, is that the "good is always defined by the union of opposites" (NB 447, SL 137). Harmony or proportion is achieved through the unity of contraries qua contraries. Such harmony is impossible if the contraries are either brought together forcibly, inappropriately, or unduly mixed; rather, the genuine "point of unity has to be found." This is achieved by an intellectual-spiritual effort of contemplation: one must contemplate the object in question until one arrives at the secret point where the contraries converge into one and the same thing (SE 51).

But Weil based her judgments of "Greece" on its literature (e.g., SE 133) and was nescient of Greek history, failing to recognize the profound continuities between Greece and Rome as fully monetized chattel slave societies. As Kostas Vlassopoulos's comprehensive cross-cultural study confirms, chattel slavery was the dominant form of labor in the social world of the Homeric epics: "The earliest evidence we have for Greek history, the Homeric epics and Hesiod, make it abundantly clear that slaves constituted the main labour source from which Greek elites derived their wealth."[11] The groundbreaking work of classicist Richard Seaford has shown ancient Greece to have been the first fully monetized society in world history.[12] Historian David McNally, building on Seaford's research, argues that the Greek economic complex of war, slavery, market, and monetization constituted the very soul of uprooting in antiquity.[13]

Ironically, then, ancient Greece perfectly exemplifies Weil's argument about the uprooting impact of war, conquest, monetization, and cultural chauvinism (most Greek slaves were "barbarians" from Thrace, the Black Sea region, Asia Minor, Syria). By the time of Homer, war, slavery, and monetary market exchange were systemically connected in Greece. The Homeric adjective indicating that an individual is free, *eleutheros*, actually refers to a state of belonging to others and to the community; to be free is to belong, whereas the unfree lack belonging. Only war-pillaged goods from new territories, including slaves, could be treated as booty from outside these Maussian networks of gift-obligation. Slavery

---

11. Kostas Vlassopoulos, *Historicizing Ancient Slavery* (Edinburgh: Edinburgh University Press, 2021), 181–82.

12. Richard Seaford, *Money and the Early Greek Mind: Homer, Philosophy, Tragedy* (Cambridge: Cambridge University Press, 2004).

13. David McNally, *Blood and Money: War, Slavery, Finance, and Empire* (Chicago: Haymarket, 2020).

was heavily gendered because men were killed, women were captured, sold, deracinated; moreover, the slave status of the mother legally predetermined the slave status of her children.[14] A captured foreigner was ripped out of her community of mutual obligation and protection; she inhabited a realm of disconnection and ruthless subjugation under the recurrent existential threat of social death.[15]

The economy of Athens in the fifth and fourth centuries was predominantly based on chattel slavery and, as historian Peter Garnsey notes, Athenian democracy and democratic ideology fed off slavery. No one was burdened with defending it because no one was confronted with the view that slavery is wrong, it was held to be the natural order of things.[16] Slave auctions were held monthly in the Athenian agora, offering an abundant and relatively cheap commodity (as compared with prices in the Near East), allowing slave ownership to extend far beyond the elite. Slavery achieved deep acceptance among the propertied classes who formed the social and political elite, including the likes of Plato.[17] Plato's *Republic* argues that it is in accordance with reason that the higher-born rule over the lower-born, masters over slaves, the strong over the weak, the wise over the less wise, and men over women.[18]

Rome was not the worst place to be a slave in the ancient world, as Weil asserts (SE 78); arguably, rather, Greece was.[19] When identifying "Greece" in her mind's eye, Weil invokes the literary classics of Greece, much as when identifying "Israel" she invokes the Hebrew Bible.[20] This

---

14. McNally, *Blood and Money*, 19–44; Vlassopoulos, *Historicizing Ancient Slavery*, 171–72.

15. Both McNally and Vlassopoulos employ Orlando Patterson's concept of slavery as social death, but Vlassopoulos modifies it along lines suggested by Vincent Brown (*Historicizing Ancient Slavery*, 107, 111–112).

16. Peter Garnsey, *Ideas of Slavery from Aristotle to Augustine* (Cambridge: Cambridge University Press, 1996), 3, 9–13. Aristotle wrote in *Politics* 1.4, a slave is a living possession that wholly belongs to his or her master, and he who is by nature not his own but another's man, is by nature a slave—a remarkably convenient tautology.

17. McNally, *Blood and Money*, 36; Vlassopoulos, *Historicizing Ancient Slavery*, 180, 125–26.

18. Vilho Harle, *Ideas of Social Order in the Ancient World* (Westport, CT: Greenwood Press, 1998), 112.

19. Garnsey, *Ideas of Slavery*, 6–7, 88; Vlassopoulos, *Historicizing Ancient Slavery*, 129, 171.

20. See Emmanuel Levinas, "Simone Weil against the Bible," in *Difficult Freedom: Essays on Judaism*, Séan Hand, trans. (Baltimore: John Hopkins University Press), 133–141.

literary identification is problematic on both counts, and we ought not to give it a pass, however much we value Weil's work. To accept this uncritical approach is like identifying the soul of antebellum slave-driving America by invoking Thoreau's *Essay on Civil Disobedience*. Great literature is not history, even if it is produced in history. "Greece" is not the *Iliad* and the tragedies of Sophocles; Greece was a war-mongering, enslaving and slave-trading, thoroughly monetized, uprooting civilization, yet it was romanticized by Weil as precisely the opposite: a civilization bathed in the golden light of wisdom.

Religion: Taproot of Civilization

We can outline Weil's reasoning as it is presented in the text in order to reconstruct her argument about roots. This is an attempt to gather Weil's thinking about rootedness into a comprehensive account in a series of theses (even if certain of Weil's historical claims are dangerously unsound, as just suggested):

Phenomenological Phase of Argument:

1. Beauty and truth are our avenues to the Good in this actual world ("here below").
2. The relations that constitute beauty and truth are not data given in the world; rather, our incarnate body-mind constructs them using inculcated principles of proportion and appropriate measure provided by culture, not nature.
3. In this work of ordering our experience, the thinking-perceiving body is like a compass that constructs a circle—but in this analogy we should imagine an intelligent compass that is able to *think* the circle it draws. The body conjoins real and ideal; real data are organized according to a coherent pattern or general concept provided by thought. The thinking body "describes" the circle by connecting the points of data given in perception.
4. The descriptions created by our body-mind allow us to "discover" order in the world; this order is not intrinsic, but is nonetheless "real" because the data are empirical.

5. Real relations are thus constituted as they are perceived. There are more and less adequate ways to describe relations; there are completely inadequate ways that perpetuate falsehood and illusion.

Historical Phase of Argument:

6. This manner of perceiving truth and beauty in the world was widely understood and practiced in the ancient world, both Eastern and Western. It was a universal Axial Age wisdom widely shared and held in common. In the West, the Greeks were masters of it, beginning with the Pythagoreans and Stoics, reaching a zenith in Plato.

7. Christianity absorbed this ancient wisdom and carried it forward in a new mythic expression with a new set of symbols and rituals, but the Romanization of Christianity under the late empire and its aftermath hijacked the young religion in its early development, recasting it in a direction toward power and force, away from love, justice, and consent.

8. In the wake of late-medieval power struggles of the corrupt and illegitimate (power-seeking) Christian church, the rise of virulent capitalism, colonial imperialism, and contesting nationalisms in the vacuum left by the decline of Christianity, the Western world is now in implosive crisis. It can only save itself by revivifying the ancient roots that first teach us how to read harmony and unity in the midst of chaos and disorder, how to direct ourselves methodically toward good and away from evil.

9. Our need for roots is like the pilot's need for knowledge of navigation. Without the practical insight and methodic discipline of longstanding wisdom traditions—which are the key to cultural sustainability—civilization is bereft of the ability to act in accordance with practical reason and in obedience to grace. It loses the capacity to be self-ordering and is abandoned to a chaotic aimlessness that leads to destruction.

The sixth thesis points to a "mother root" or taproot of civilizations (a taproot is a major root from which other roots sprout laterally). In a

1942 letter to her colleague Jean Wahl, Weil depicts ancient Mediterranean wisdom as a taproot that grounded a whole family of religions and spawned the origins of Greek science and geometry (SL 159–61). She believed such a universal wisdom pervaded ancient civilizations, and this fueled her wide-ranging readings and researches in her last years into the *Bhagavad Gita*, Buddhism, Daoism, and various wisdom traditions and folktales. In the course of her own deepening conversion to Christian faith, Weil continued to credit diverse non-Christian and secular traditions (of Greece, Egypt, ancient India, and ancient China) and the pure reflections of beauty in art and science with having done as much as, or more than, overtly Christian ones to deliver her "into Christ's hands as his captive" (WG 48).

In Weil's essentialist outlook, most of the major world religions and wisdom traditions celebrate the order of the world as universal obedience to the divine will (NR 281–90). Any religion that loves the order of the world purely implicitly loves God purely; therefore, "[i]f there exists another thinking species, there will always be the same God for it, only another Word" (NB 233). Just as only one capable of friendship can take heartfelt interest in the fate of a stranger, Weil insists, so must we have given all our attention, faith, and love to a particular religion in order to regard any religion not our own with the high degree of attention, faith, and love that is proper to it (WG 119). Weil does not recognize any essential difference between Christian love and pure *amor fati*, asserting that such genuine stoical love of the order of the world is as commonly found outside Christianity as inside. The universal criterion of divine renunciation and self-sacrifice—the cross—is implicit for Weil in all "true religion," and she saw evidence of this (correctly or not) in most religions: "The religions which have a conception of this renunciation, this voluntary distance, this voluntary effacement of God, his apparent absence and secret presence here below, these religions are true religion, the translation into different languages of the great Revelation" (WG 89, cf. 117–18).

But modernity has lost this wisdom, this universal revelation. In a final blow, when the fiercely anticlerical revolutionaries of 1789 mounted a violent attack on religion, they imposed by force a rootless and uprooting secularity, and although Weil admits that secularization (*laïcisation*) is better than ersatz Christianity, it is infinitely worse than what she esteems to be real Christianity (NR 90–91). In the twentieth century, "religious life has been subordinated to that of the nation as never before," treated as a private affair and relegated to a more or less capricious choice, "something like the choice of a political party, or even that of a tie" (NR 123, 125); whereas Weil maintains that the proper place of Christian religion is suffusing all of life (NR 118).

Detachment:
We Must Uproot Ourselves

Weil's religious thought is concerned in an Augustinian fashion with the proper ordering of our actions by a proper weighting of our loves, for "man always devotes himself to an order" (NB 279). Religious conceptions prove their value for Weil by their effectiveness in bringing about an attitude of *amor fati*: this implies humility, obedience, longing for justice, and action that is consistent with the ineluctable truth of finitude and death. There is an imperative to embrace *limit* in the physical realm, in our desire for earthly things, because only then do we become capable of being just. The unlimited is the evil principle; in relations between human beings, the good consists in abolishing the uncontrolled and unlimited—that is what justice is (SL 125). Yet there is need to embrace the *unlimited* in the spiritual realm since love is and must be essentially unlimited. It is our spiritual task and obligation to sort out this essential difference in the way we love: the dialectic between limited and unlimited.

The dialectic is as follows: The insatiable desire for good that constitutes the core of the human being can be commensurate only when directed toward a good that is unlimited, absolute, unconditioned (FLN 143); that is, directed toward a good that is absent. But love is not real unless it is directed toward a particular object; it becomes universal only as a result of analogy and transference (WG 119). The principal virtue of the name of God is that it points beyond all finite conceptions and namings to a universal love that is essentially anonymous *because* it is universal. Creation is a kenotic act in which God *self-empties* into the concrete particularity of the entire world (NB, vol. I, 283–84, 262, vol. II, 424; IC 183). God *descends* into the particular; the link between the universal and the particular is a descending movement, never an ascending one (NB, vol. I, 307). The very notion of divine *incarnation* images a love of concrete particular existence as against an empty, unreal universality. We, in the image of God's love, are called to direct our love to the all: "[A]fter having torn the soul from the body and having passed through death to approach God," Weil writes, "the saint must incarnate himself, as it were, in his own body so as to shed upon this world, upon this earthly life, a reflection of the supernatural light" (SNL 112).

Once the soul has espoused God it redescends into the body and the world (NB 383): "Our love should stretch as widely across all space, and should be as equally distributed in every portion of it as is the very light of the sun.... Every existing thing is equally upheld in its existence by God's creative love. The friends of God should love him to the point of merging their love into his with regard to all things here below" (WG 50). Because the mind is not forced to believe in the existence of anything, Weil asserts, the only organ of contact with existence is acceptance, love. To believe in the reality of the outside world and to *love* it are one and the same thing; the organ of belief is supernatural love even in regard to earthly things (NB 308–309, 298). Though I am merely an atom in this world, when I desire that this world should exist—exactly as it does exist—I become a co-creator with God (NB 297).

This is why ultimately, spiritually, we must outgrow our need for roots, and in the process of doing so we must uproot ourselves, banishing all attachments while still loving the incarnation as such in the order of the world. Our love must become as universal as God's love:

> One must uproot oneself; cut down the tree and make of it a cross, and then carry it always; uproot oneself from the social and vegetative angles; have no native land on this earth that one may call one's own.
> To do all that to other people, from the outside, is an ersatz form of de-creation; it is producing unreality....
> But in uprooting oneself one seeks a greater reality.
> One must acquire the feeling of being at home in exile.
> The city is a μεταξύ [*metaxu*] for the purposes of uprooting.
> If, under the stroke of affliction, one is deprived of one's roots before one has even begun to transfigure them (or if one has never had any), what possible hope can there be? (NB 298, cf. 312)

When supernatural love is our mode of seeing, the universe as a whole is our country. Yet even so one bears a special obligation to one's specific native country for providing the "vegetative roots" that made this cosmopolitanism possible. Even after one's own need for roots is transcended, others do need roots—the young, those on the way—creating an indelible obligation. An infinite duty can be rooted in a finite domain. True patriotism stems from a sacred vocation, and it is this vocation that Weil spells out, meanderingly, in the last few dozen pages of the essay (NR 212–98).

Weil acknowledges a contradiction inherent in patriotism, even when it stems from a sacred regard for one's country that is untainted by adulation of the power of State. One's country is something limited, yet under certain circumstances its demands become unlimited. It may happen that one's obligation toward an endangered collectivity such as one's country reaches the point of entailing a total sacrifice (NR 8, 158). Here the distinction that pertains between two goods—the finite good of one's country and the infinite good that is God—seems to become confused (NR 155, 130). She judges it to be one of the basic contradictions belonging to our human condition, arguing that an infinite sacrifice for a finite good is not idolatrous when it constitutes obedience to the sacred dimension rather than the social (NR 156–57), for "the state of being rooted is altogether different from the social element" (NB 296). When love of endangered neighbor or country becomes a reason for ultimate sacrifice, at issue is a spiritual embrace of incarnation, a love of the world qua formed and loved by God, including the blessings embodied in one's homeland and one's people. As Julie Daigle writes in this volume (Chapter 3), "true love of country is, at the same time, a love of the world, of the other, and of the universe."

Contact with the order of the world, when that order is "read" as the divine will to incarnation, inspires religiosity and works against the evil of social forces. The only appropriate response to the ubiquity of force is obedience to a universal sacrality: "Christ ransomed the vegetative domain, but not the social one. He did not pray for the world. The social domain is unreservedly that of the Prince of this World. We have but one duty in regard to the social element, which is to try to limit the evil contained therein" (NB 296). One is rightly called to defend one's country because of special obligation to that locale in all its intimately known corporeal specificity, not due to arbitrary preferentialism or chauvinism. The roots that nourish the body-soul generate a transgenerational obligation: they are *metaxu* connecting individuals into community, and communities into the order of the world.

The rootedness invoked by Weil is another way of articulating contact with reality, integration within a greater whole, inspiration by the order of the world, *amor fati*, acceptance of necessity, and this discipline with regard to one's real embodied relationships is ultimately aimed toward salvation, wholeness, a revelation of divine incarnation as crucifixion. We must love the order of the world, Weil insists, but what does that mean? The order of the world is *incarnate*: absolutely particular and located. Real relations are essentially particular and located. The integral need for roots is a need for *incarnate* existence and *embodied* communal relations predominating over abstract, alienated, severed, or inexistent relations. Religion and humane culture nourish the real, concrete, vital threads that constitute us, body and soul, in our natural-cultural environ. Yet when metaphorical roots achieve their ultimate purpose—maturation, readiness, fruition—they give way to wings. Just as an umbilical cord or a larval cocoon materially nurtures the organism's freedom to outgrow them, so the natural-cultural roots of the *genii locorum* nurture an ability to abide in the joy of God unrestricted by these food-like relations and attachments. A nurturing apprenticeship by one's roots finally makes possible obedience to the poet's command: "Go love without the help of any Thing on Earth" (William Blake).

In her letter to a pupil quoted earlier, Weil comments that in factory work she feels she has "escaped from a world of abstractions" to find herself among *real* human beings, good and bad (SL 11). The factory is a primary site of uprooting, yet she found herself constrained to encounter a "more real" world in this industrial hell. There is no daydreaming in the factory; illusions are hard to maintain. This points to a basic structural conundrum that conditions every human life: Where illusions are ripped away and brute necessity bares itself, the natural joys perish in deprivation, stunting the soul's capacity to aspire to salvation. On the other hand, where the comforts of life are superabundant to a degree that they insulate one from brute necessity, ersatz perceptions and illusions flourish, overtaking and blotting out contact with reality, the order of the world, and one's vocation to decreate. Weil struggles to articulate the elusive equilibrium that makes possible a humane life lived in its natural-cultural nexus in a sanely ordered society, pursuing the good in a spirit of truth, achieving contact with reality, the order of the world, and via these real relations is situated to experience contact with the good.

But as Weil forewarns in the essay, emerging worldwide was an ever aggrandizing dominion of money-value, power quest, militarization, and uprooting rootlessness. Some eighty years later we must grimly observe an unprecedented global arms race; escalating nuclear threat; epic inequality between haves and have-nots that is increasing by magnitudes; involuntary mass migration due to war, ethnic conflict, and climate change; environmental catastrophe; nationalist brutalities and genocidal apartheid; unhinged ideological warfare; crumbling civic institutions of "democracies" never truly democratic; intensifying assault on indigenous peoples, lands, activists, and journalists; dirty drug wars; rampant global substance abuse; rising homelessness; mental breakdown; deprivation; and despair. The young, just coming of age, are left to pick up random fragments in an attempt to build a life in this chaos. They have no root system to feed them.

Though Weil was off-base in her romanticization of ancient Greece, she was spot on in her predictions of where the world was speeding. Shortly after her death the Nazi regime fell to a more powerful, more centralized uprooting power: the rising American empire, which in the wake of the Second World War has driven a military-industrial-financial competition for global dominance among continental powers that threatens life on earth in the third millennium.[21] Only a sea-change rising out of the life-sustaining root systems of the earth can arrest and disarm this great beast, *le gros animal*, that Weil saw coming with extraordinary prescience: "As for the American continent, since its population has for several centuries been founded above all on immigration"—strangely, Weil doesn't mention genocide and slavery—"the

---

21. See Weil's important remarks on American promises of "guns and butter" (NR 96). Even as the U.S. Congress approves hundreds of billions of dollars annually for the so-called defense budget, the real sum exceeds one trillion per year according to policy analysts William D. Hartung and Mandy Smithberger, "America's Defense Budget Is Bigger than You Think"; https://www.thenation.com/article/archive/tom-dispatch-america-defense-budget-bigger-than-you-think/. See also Michael Hudson, *Super Imperialism: The Economic Strategy of American Empire,* 3rd ed. (Islet, 2021), and Giovanni Arrighi, *The Long Twentieth Century: Money, Power, and the Origins of Our Times* (London: Verso, 1994).

dominating influence which it will probably exercise greatly increases the danger" (NR 50, cf. 155), meaning the danger that uprootedness may achieve an ultimate victory over life on earth.

CHAPTER 5

The Degradation of Human Justice

Lawrence Edward Schmidt

As Lissa McCullough has elaborated in Chapter 4, the problem of uprootedness is intimately related to the distortion of human justice in human society. That distortion has been caused in turn by the inauthenticity of France's love for itself, its idolatrous nationalism which has falsely replaced its patriotism. In *The Need for Roots*, Simone Weil argued many times that the rise of Adolf Hitler in the thirties provided a perfect illustration of the problem of uprootedness (Chapter 4) and the degradation of human justice. And it illustrated the need to question his greatness. "The unhappy peoples of the European continent are in need of greatness even more than of bread, and there are only two sorts of greatness: true greatness which is of a spiritual order and the old, old lie of world conquest. Conquest is an ersatz greatness" (NR 97). Thus, she maintained that we must transform our notion of greatness in our very selves if we hope to change our understanding of Hitler (Chapter 7).

Some seventy-five years after Adolf Hitler's death our fascination with the Nazi dictator continues to grow.[1] Clearly, we are still trying to come to terms with Hitler, who is the most extraordinary figure of the twentieth century.[2] This coming to terms with Hitler among the reading public as well as among professional historians requires us to leave be-

---

1. John Lukacs, *The Hitler of History* (New York; Alfred A. Knopf, 1998), 2.
2. Ian Kershaw, *Hitler, 1889–1936: Hubris* (London: Allen Lane, Penguin Press, 1998).

133

hind simplistic views according to which Hitler was a "'demonic'—at least by inference, an inhuman and ahistorical—phenomenon [as opposed to] "a historical figure, incarnating various human characteristics and endowed with recognizable talents."[3]

A Deeper Understanding of Hitler

A re-examination of Simone Weil's writings may contribute to our understanding of this historicizing process and a deepening of our understanding of Hitler. Weil was not interested in detailing his life. Rather, she wished to understand his "greatness" in the light of a political theory that would enable us to pass judgment on the pathology of the spirit that infected the civilization which in turn gave rise to his dictatorship. That civilization suffered from four major deficiencies: "our false conception of greatness; the degradation of the sentiment of justice; our idolization of money; and our lack of religious inspiration" (NR 216). Weil was crucially aware of Hitler and the rise of National Socialism from the time when she visited Germany (to examine the labor movement) in 1932. But it was only in the period before and during World War II that she began to write extensively about him (SE 89–144). In all her writings she resisted the common temptation to see the Nazi dictatorship as anomalous or discontinuous with the rest of European history. She also refused to downplay Hitler's abilities or to see him as insane. And she rejected the temptation to mythologize him as a "primitive" leader.

Weil saw that Hitler's rise to power was not an accident or an anomaly. As surprising as it might appear from a purely biographical perspective, Weil argued that Hitler's emergence as a national leader should be considered continuous (and consistent) with the values of Western civilization. The origins of Hitlerism are in Imperial Rome in the policies perfected by such "heroic" figures as Caesar, the elder Scipio, Marius, and Sulla. Those policies were based on prestige, perfidy, and terror. "The Romans conquered the world," according to Weil, "because they were serious, disciplined, and organized; because their outlook and methods were consistently and continuously maintained; because they were convinced of being a superior race, born to command. And also

---

3. Lukacs, *The Hitler of History*, 5.

because they successfully employed the most ruthless, premeditated, calculated, systematic cruelty, combining or alternating it with cold-hearted perfidy and hypocritical propaganda" ("The Great Beast," SE 102). In the modern period, the absolutism of Louis XIV, the idolatry of the state by Richelieu, the expansionism of Napoleon who incongruously and incomprehensibly wanted to liberate the world by conquering it, and the militarism of Frederick II of Prussia—all can be considered as laying the groundwork for the emergence of Hitlerism. Spanish, Dutch, French, and English imperialism set the pattern until Hitler determined to use the German state to build his own thousand-year Reich.

Weil secondly argued that Hitler was neither mediocre nor a maniac who suffered from delusions of grandeur. He was a man of real knowledge and genuine talent. "Before the age of twenty-five he had such a clear vision of German foreign policy, especially as regards the inopportuneness of a war fleet and as regards the danger of an Austrian alliance."[4] Weil's sober evaluation of Hitler has been confirmed by most of his biographers, including Percy Schramm, who became the editor of the War Diary of the High Command of the *Wehrmacht* in 1943. In *Hitler: The Man and the Military Leader* Schramm asserted that "his remarkable memory, together with iron diligence and a strong power of concentration, had enabled Hitler in the course of the years to acquire knowledge of a scope and detail that again and again amazed persons talking with him, and earned him sincere admiration."[5] With regard to the Nazi dictator's mental stability, Weil argued in 1939 that "there is no reason to regard Hitler as a maniac with an obsession of grandeur.... The appetite for power, even for universal power, is only insane when there is no possibility of indulging it; a man who sees the possibility opening before him and does not try to grasp it, even at the risk of destroying himself, is either a saint or a mediocrity. Even if in the pursuit of it he repudiates morality, and his plighted word and everything hon-

---

4. Simone Weil, "Observations Concerning the Essay on Hitler," an unpublished essay quoted in Simone Pétrement, *Simone Weil: A Life* (New York: Pantheon Books, 1976), 511.

5. Percy Ernst Schramm, *Hitler: The Man and Military Leader* (Chicago: Quadrangle Books, 1971). 70.

orable, we have no right to conclude that he is a barbarian, a madman or a monster."[6]

In *The Need for Roots*, Weil argued that Hitler was merely being more consistent than the rest of us in pursuing the type of greatness he saw praised in his society. "That is exactly the sort of greatness he has achieved, the very sort before which we all bow down in servile admiration as soon as our eyes are turned toward the past. We don't go beyond a base submission of the mind in regard to it; we haven't tried like Hitler to seize it with both hands. But in this respect he is a better man than any of us. Once one recognizes something as being a good, one should want to seize it. Not to want to do so is cowardly" (NR 223).

Hitler set out to play a role in history as a world leader. In Weil's view he succeeded so brilliantly not because he was "primitive" but because he was thoroughly modern. It should be noted, however, that, for her, "primitive" was not a pejorative adjective. "Primitive leaders ruled legitimately, that is to say within the bounds set by traditions."[7] Hitler did not. Regardless, Hitler had a certain talent or genius which enabled him to exploit the social disintegration of his times. Weil wrote at the height of his power in 1942:

> It seems to me difficult to deny that Hitler conceives, and conceives clearly, the laws of a kind of physics of human matter, laws that he has not invented but that before him were presented so forcibly and distinctly by men of genius. He possesses an exact notion of the range of the power of force, something that the average man *never* has....
>
> Nothing could be less primitive than Hitler, who would be inconceivable without modern technique and the existence of *millions of uprooted men....* Hitler's power is unlimited; this is where he becomes part of a nightmare.[8]

The laws of a kind of physics of human matter. This is an odd and ambiguous phrase; on the surface it appears contradictory. Human beings are

6. Simone Weil, "Observations Concerning The Essay on Hitler," an unpublished essay quoted in Pétrement, *Simone Weil*, 511.

7. Zygmunt Bauman, *Modernity and the Holocaust* (Ithaca, New York: Cornell University Press, 1991), 13.

8. Simone Weil, "Observations Concerning The Essay on Hitler," an unpublished essay quoted in Pétrement, *Simone Weil*, 511 (itals. in original).

not matter, or at least they are not merely matter. Surely Weil is not say-ing that they can be comprehensively understood in terms of the laws of physics. But the phrase effectively evokes the horrors of the slave labor camps that Weil clearly knew about and the sense that somehow the bottom had fallen out of the moral universe in Europe. The human body was given a precise dollar value as a piece of matter. Dental fillings were carefully salvaged from emaciated bodies of concentration camp vic-tims. Human skin was used to make Himmler's furniture.[9] All this was consistent with the laws of a kind of physics of human matter. Equally striking is the contention that "Hitler possessed an exact notion of the power of force." It is clear that Weil is not referring to physical force (as understood through the laws of physics) but to psychic and social force (understood as the ability to use all psychological and sociological mechanisms present in the souls of human beings and in human society devoid of any aspiration towards what is good). "There is not on earth any force except force," she wrote. "That could serve as an axiom. As for the force which is not of this earth, contact with it cannot be bought at any lesser price than the passing through a kind of death" (NR 218).

The Rule and Role of Force

It is the earthly force that rules in the Great Beast. The implication is that, subjected to enough social pressure, human beings are capable of anything. Weil put it this way: "Everything points to the fact that, unless supernatural grace intervenes, there is no form of cruelty or depravity of which ordinary, decent people are not capable, once the corresponding psychological mechanisms have been set in motion" (NR 223). At a so-cial level, Weil understood force as having no essential relationship to what is good or just:

> Force is not a machine for automatically creating justice. It is
> a blind mechanism which produces indiscriminately and im-
> partially just or unjust results, but by all the laws of probability,
> nearly always unjust ones. Lapse of time makes no difference;

---

9. See Gitta Sereny, *Albert Speer: His Battle with the Truth* (New York: Alfred A. Knopf 1995), 309–10.

it doesn't increase in the functioning of this mechanism the infinitesimal proportion of results which happen by chance to be in conformity with justice. Where force is absolutely sovereign, justice is absolutely unreal. (NR 240)

Weil argued that the conclusion of modern science is that laws of force determine all phenomena. Hitler accepted these conclusions. Weil quotes him from *Mein Kampf*:

"Man must never fall into the error of believing himself to be the lord and master of creation.... He will then feel that in a world in which planets and suns follow circular trajectories, moons revolve round planets, and force reigns everywhere supreme over weakness, which it either compels to serve it docilely or else crushes out of existence, Man cannot be subject to special laws of his own." (NR 237)

Weil concluded that "Hitler's entire life is nothing but the putting into practice of that conclusion" (NR 237).

And the Nazi conception of justice was developed on that basis. It "rests upon the conviction that, for all who are slaves by nature, servitude is the condition that is at the same time the happiest and the most just" (NR 241). This, as Percy Schramm points out, led Hitler to develop his own categorical imperative, the opposite of Kant's:

The guiding principle for National Socialist legislation was not to be the standard of moral relationships between men, but rather what was to be the laws of nature. Whoever objected that they were ruthless missed the point; whoever regarded the new standards of morality for human's behavior, derived from "eternal" laws as brutal, failed to realize that all living beings are subject to the harsh laws of nature. The first commandment of Hitlerian morality was therefore the preservation of the collective vital force of the German people; the misgivings of an older culture were simply brushed aside.[10]

---

10. Schramm, *Hitler*, 96.

The Bureaucratic State

Though Weil claims that the origins of Hitlerism (and its basic methods) are to be found among the Romans for whom she never ceases to express her contempt—I leave aside here the question of the accuracy of her treatment of them—she is not unaware that Hitler perfected those methods thanks to the "achievements" of the modern world. The most important of these is the creation of the bureaucratic state that began with Cardinal Richelieu (1585–1642) and culminated in twentieth-century Germany. During Weil's life the bureaucratic state gave rise in turn to the cult of the leader. She accounts for this cult as follows:

> The State is a cold concern which cannot inspire love, but itself kills, suppresses everything that might be loved; so one is forced to love it, because there is nothing else. That is the moral torment to which all of us today are exposed.
>
> Here lies perhaps the cause of that phenomenon of the leader, which has sprung up everywhere nowadays and surprises so many people. Just now, there is in all countries, in all movements, a man who is the personal magnet for all loyalties. Being compelled to embrace the cold, metallic surface of the State has made people, by contrast, hunger for something to love which is made of flesh and blood. This phenomenon shows no sign of disappearing, and however disastrous the consequences have been so far, it may still have some very unpleasant surprises in store for us. (NR 114)

The bureaucratic state called for the charismatic leader, and Hitler used the state to achieve his revolution. As Führer, he was able to use the power of suggestion, the separation of (and conflict between) governmental powers, the specifically modern techniques of propaganda, etc., to harness the authority of the state in the service of his ideological goals. Weil argued that Hitler was a genius at suggestion. For her, suggestion "is a form of coercion. A great part of its efficacity is due, on the one hand to repetition, and on the other hand to the strength at the command of the group whence the situation originates, or which it aims to acquire" (NR 189). That strength, the strength of Hitler's vision, was imposed through the same managerial techniques used in all modern bureaucracies. These bureaucracies, it is commonly acknowledged, made the Holocaust possible—in roughly the same way as modern engineering made the construction of the ovens of Auschwitz possible.

Following Simone Weil's line of thought and taking up the insights of Zygmunt Bauman, I want to propose that the normal operations of bureaucracies in Nazi Germany (which in no way differ from our own bureaucracies, except perhaps that they had a lower level of complexity) made the Holocaust more likely and more horrible. This might be explained by attending to Weil's understanding of the evil effects of autonomous technique:

> Speaking quite generally, in any sort of sphere, it is inevitable that evil should dominate wherever the technical side of things is either completely or almost completely sovereign.
>
> Technicians always tend to make themselves sovereign, because they feel that they alone know what they are about; and this is perfectly natural on their part. The responsibility for any evil overtaking them, as a necessary consequence, has to be exclusively borne by those who have allowed them full rein. (NR 203)

In bureaucracy, the technical is almost completely sovereign, and when the goal of the organization itself is evil, there is no braking—indeed there may be an accelerating—force on that evil.

Zygmunt Bauman comes at this topic as a sociologist forced by his wife's experience to try to understand Hitler's "Final Solution." In *Modernity and the Holocaust*, he begins by calling into question modern sociological theory according to which all immoral behavior is understood as the result of the failure of the civilizing process whose task it is to tame our animal nature. According to this view, humanity is emerging from pre-social barbarity. This "etiological myth" (which Weil would call the myth of progress) is backed by such ideologies as the "Whig view" of history, Max Weber's vision of rationalization, the psychoanalytical promise to tame the animal in man, Karl Marx's grand prophecy of life and history coming through technology under full control of the human species, and Émile Durkheim's understanding of society as the moralizing force par excellence. According to the etiological myth, in whatever form it takes, the Holocaust represented a failure of modern civilization's most cherished products: "its technology, its rational criteria of choice, its tendency to subordinate thought and action to the pragmatics of economy and effectiveness."[11]

"Progress" and the Modes of Modern Civilization

Bauman disagrees: Modern civilization is the problem. More of modernity will make the problem worse. Bauman concurs with Christopher Browning: "The Nazi mass murder of European Jewry was not only the technological achievement of an industrial society, but also the organizational achievement of a bureaucratic society."[12] And bureaucratic society is one that produces moral indifference. Bauman is forced to this conclusion by an examination of the literature on the Holocaust. Late nineteenth and early twentieth century Germany was perhaps the least antisemitic nation in Europe; the Jews were more assimilated and integrated into German society than elsewhere. The Holocaust was not a product of antisemitism or heterophobia which were constant elements throughout European history; it was rather a product of racism which is a distinctively modern ideology. According to Bauman:

> Racism differs from both heterophobia and constant enmity. The difference lies neither in the intensity of sentiment nor in the type of argument used to rationalize it. Racism stands apart by a practice of which it is a part and which it rationalizes; a practice that combines strategies of architecture and gardening with that of medicine—in the service of the construction of an artificial social order, through cutting out the elements of the present reality that neither fit the visualized perfect reality, nor can be changed so that they do. In a world that boasts the unprecedented ability to improve human conditions by reorganizing human affairs on a rational basis, racism manifests the conviction that a certain category of human

---

11. Bauman, *Modernity and the Holocaust*, 13.

12. See Christopher R. Browning, "The German Bureaucracy and the Holocaust" as quoted in *ibid.*, 13.

beings cannot be incorporated into the rational order, whatever the effort."[13]

Bauman explains convincingly that the racism of the Third Reich
makes sense only as part of an exercise of social engineering on a grandiose scale. This social engineering included the forceful elimination of
unwertes Leben, valueless life, useless eaters. "For the Nazi Designers of
the perfect society, the project they pursued and were determined to
implement through social engineering split human life into worthy and
unworthy: the first to be lovingly cultivated and given *Lebensraum*; the
other to be distanced, or—if the distancing proved unfeasible—exter-
minated. Those simply alien were not the objects of strictly racial policy."[14] This social engineering approach to reality that has its origins in the
Enlightenment formed the background to Hitler's revolution. Bauman
points out that

> well before they built the gas chambers, the Nazis, on Hitler's
> orders, attempted to exterminate their own mentally insane or
> bodily impaired compatriots through "mercy killing" (falsely
> nicknamed "euthanasia"), and to breed a superior race through
> the organized fertilization of racially superior women by ra-
> cially superior men (eugenics). Like these attempts, the mur-
> der of the Jews was an exercise in the rational management of
> society. And a systematic attempt to deploy in its service, the
> philosophy and precepts of applied science.[15]

Moreover, Bauman contends that neither a social engineering approach to reality, nor the propagation of a racist ideology using all the
techniques at their disposal, was able to carry out the Holocaust. "In
spite of the enormous resources devoted by the Nazi regime to racist
propaganda, the concentrated effort of Nazi education, and the real
threat of terror against resistance to Nazi practices, the popular acceptance of the racist programme (and particularly of its ultimate logical
consequences) stopped well short of the level an emotion-led extermi-
nation would require."[16] But what the passion of a pogrom (or a *Kristall-*

---

13. Bauman, *Modernity and the Holocaust*, 65 (itals. omitted).
14. *Ibid.*, 68.
15. *Ibid.*, 72.
16. *Ibid.*, 65.

nacht) could not achieve, the bureaucracy of the German state effected. "To be effective, modern exterminatory antisemitism had to be married to modern bureaucracy.... The *Führer* expressed his Romantic vision of the world cleansed of the terminally diseased race. The rest was a matter of a not at all romantic, coolly rational bureaucratic process."[17]

Bureaucracy is, in the twenty-first century, an essential element of work. And the modern work process, Simone Weil argued in *Oppression and Liberty*, destroys human freedom. It requires the dissociation of thought and action as work is divided up into manual and mental labor. Freedom cannot exist for most of the manual and mental laborers in modern industrial society. Due to the division and coordination of labor which in turn is a function of the techniques of production, there is a virtually complete divorce between thought and action. The manual laborer is not free, is dehumanized and reduced to a slave, not because he or she performs physically laborious tasks but because such tasks exclude the possibility of thought. Mental laborers, those who form the essential bureaucratic structure by which the activity of the individuals subject to a given collectivity are brought into coordinated relation, may be as enslaved as the manual laborers themselves. For their thought is ordinarily divorced from any direct action, and often does not involve a dialogue with those whose lives they order.

The Nazi bureaucracy, Bauman claims, was made up of normal people; they were not criminal, sadistic, or fanatical. Their loyalty to their gory task was a derivative of their loyalty to the organization. The civilizing process had taken only too well. But to Bauman this meant that the process had "succeeded in substituting artificial and flexible patterns of human conduct for natural drives, and hence made possible a scale of inhumanity and destruction which remained inconceivable as long as natural predispositions guided human action."[18]

The civilizing process here includes an integration into a modern bureaucracy and with it the dissociation of action from moral evaluation. Pre-modern chain of command (like that practiced in Imperial Rome or in a medieval guild) brings with it the hierarchical effects of a linear graduation of power and subordination. It creates some distance between the individual's action and the collective results. But insofar as

---

17. *Ibid.*, 77.
18. *Ibid.*, 95.

they share in the same occupational skills, the superior worker or soldier understands what is demanded of the inferior. This is no longer the case in a modern bureaucracy where there is a meticulous functional division of labor. "In a functional division of labor, everything one does is in principle multi-final; that is, it can be combined and integrated into more than one meaning-determining totality. By itself the function is devoid of meaning, and the meaning which will be eventually bestowed on it is in no way preempted by the actions of its perpetrators. It will be 'the others' (in most cases anonymous and out of reach) who will some time, somewhere, decide the meaning."[19]

The modern division of labor also means that executives will inevitably give commands without full knowledge of their effects. This obviously contributes to the creation of moral distance from the effects of an executive's actions. One is reminded here of the story told by Gitta Sereny about Albert Speer, who was Hitler's second in command and by the end of the war had over 14 million workers under his authority. In 1943 he went to the Hartz mountains, not far from Buchenwald, to inspect the underground installations (called 'Dora") where Wernher von Braun's V-2 rockets were being produced. Speer had himself previously authorized the use of slave labor from Buchenwald for this task. The prisoners lived in appalling condition in the caves with the rockets. "After [Speer's] inspection was over he found out that thousands had already died. 'I saw dead men … they couldn't hide the truth,' he said. 'And those who were still alive were skeletons.' He had never been so horrified in his life, he said. 'I ordered the immediate building of a barracks camp outside and there and then signed the papers for the necessary materials.'"[20]

Because of the functional division of labor Speer, as Reichminister of Armaments and War Production, could claim ignorance about the effects of his actions—and at the Nuremberg trials he was spared the death penalty because he claimed (falsely in Sereny's view) not to have known about the death camps. But those in the middle of a meticulous functional division of labor can also claim not to be responsible for the final outcome of collective activity. In a modern bureaucracy, they have only a technical rather than a moral responsibility. "Technical responsi-

---

19. *Ibid.*, 100.
20. See Sereny, *Albert Speer*, 309–10.

bility differs from moral responsibility in that it forgets that the action is a means to something other than itself," Bauman explains. "As outer connections of action are effectively moved from the field of vision, the bureaucrat's own act becomes an end in itself. It can be judged only by its intrinsic criteria or propriety and success."[21]

Bauman notes one last effect of bureaucratization: the dehumanization of the objects of operation. "Thanks to distantiation the objects at which the bureaucratic operation is aimed can and are reduced to a set of quantitative measures."[22] The functionaries then have common cause for they are forced to deal with human objects as a nuisance factor resisting the smooth flow of their bureaucratic process. Their success in dealing with the dehumanized objects gives them a positive moral self-evaluation. They "see themselves as companions in a difficult struggle, calling for courage, self-sacrifice and selfless dedication to the cause.... The functionaries may successfully serve any goal while their moral conscience remains unimpaired."[23]

Hitler was not a management expert. Schramm points out that he was totally unfamiliar with the daily workings of government. "He had never spent a single day of his life employed in an administrative office of government and had had contact only with the very lowest echelon of the military bureaucracy during the First World War."[24] It was not he who designed or implemented the solution to the Jewish problem as a rational-bureaucratic technical task not dependent on feelings and personal commitment. But he does seem to have understood that his vision of a Germany cleansed of Jews could be realized through modern bureaucratic techniques in a social organization as passionless, as "ice cold" as the workings of his own mind. As Simone Weil suggests, Hitler does seem to have possessed "an exact notion of the range of the power of force."

---

21. Bauman, *Modernity and the Holocaust*, 101.
22. *Ibid.*, 102.
23. *Ibid.*, 104.
24. Schramm, *Hitler*, 96.

On Money and Machines

Weil argues in the modern period the power of force has become monstrous because of the expansion of the importance of money, mechanization, and algebra as I have said. She is not making a timeless critique of cash, tools, or mathematics that were important elements in all pre-modern civilizations. She is criticizing money's function in the modern context. It was initially subordinate to machines even in the life of industrial society. But with the increased importance of speculation as a means to wealth, money created "a gulf between the thought of one term and the thought of the other.... [W]hile industry at least puts money into relation with things, speculation is a relation between money and itself" (FLN, 30). This has meant the succession of the industrial era by the financial era. With the invention and the implementation of the computer, the percentage of economic transactions that have to do with the purchase of things as opposed to those that manipulate money itself, that is those that are purely speculative in nature, has declined to less than 10%.[25] For Weil, the financial era inevitably led to decadence because it made it impossible to envisage the relationship between effort and the result of effort.

As for the second monster of modernity, Weil argued that machines, with the exception of those hand tools used by skilled artisans, have eliminated the need to employ methodical thought in the course of work. In order to encourage methodical thought "the analogy between the techniques employed in various tasks would have to be sufficiently close, and technical education sufficiently widespread to enable each worker to form a clear idea of all the specialized procedures; coordination would have to be arranged in sufficiently simple a manner to enable each one continually to have a precise knowledge of it, as concerns both cooperation between workers and exchange of products" (OL 99). But this in turn would mean that machines and methods would have been designed to subordinate the complex to the simple. We would not be able to use the more complex method unless we understood the simpler basis of it. "[A] thing is simpler than another thing when it is impossible to think the second thing without having already thought the first" (FLN

---

25. See William H. Vanderburg, *Living in the Labyrinth of Technology* (Toronto: University of Toronto Press, 2005), 274.

25). (It should be noted that a "user friendly" technology must subordinate the simple to the complex so that there is no need and, in most cases no opportunity, to understand the methods that we employ.)

Money and machines have become monsters in the modern context because of algebra. Simone Weil asked early in her Notebooks whether algebra was an "error of the human spirit" (NB, I, 9). For those of us who identify algebra or calculus with mathematics, this seems like an odd question to be posed by a Platonist for whom mathematics is the quintessential language with the aid of which images of necessity may be revealed to the mind. The question is based on the distinction between ancient geometry and modern calculus or algebra. James Calder explains the distinction in this way: "With geometry we are capable of representing relations that are lucidly perceptible to the human intelligence. The virtue of geometry, as a form of human language, is that its limits are the limits of representation and hence, scientifically, of thought. In geometry, language is as closely tied to thought as possible.... As a form of language an algebraic mathematics constitutes an entirely different case. In algebra the signs are combined into formulae according to the laws governing the things (or processes) to which they correspond."[26]

Nihilism and the Modern Science Project

Simone Weil, according to Diogenes Allen, "preferred geometry to algebra because it is conducive to readings that give us contact with the notion that nature consists of a tissue of limits and ratios, ideas which we have already seen are rich in aesthetic and religious significance."[27] But we should not minimize the point and ignore the monstrous social consequences: Weil was arguing that the development of algebra as the language of mathematics applied to physics took modern science off the track. Algebra made physics a "game for scientists and a collection of recipes for technicians" ("Reflections on Quantum Theory," SNL 37).

26. Calder, *Labour and Thought op. cit.*, 157.

27. Diogenes Allen, "The Concept of Reading and the 'Book of Nature'" in Richard Bell, ed., *Simone Weil's Philosophy of Culture: Readings toward A Divine Humanity* (Cambridge, Cambridge University Press, 1993), 108.

In "At the Price of an Infinite Error: The Scientific Image, Ancient and Modern"(LPW 155–198), Weil argued that in its first phase, from the seventeenth to the end of the nineteenth century, modern science understood the physical world on the analogy of physical labor. Algebra allowed the physicist to deal with infinitely complex transformations of matter (that is, process) through signs. These algebraic signs offered partial and incomplete representations of matter as if they were pictures rather than thoughts or images of actual phenomena. The pictures developed in terms of the rigor and fixity (relations of necessity) of algebraic equations were mistaken for the structure of nature itself. In twentieth-century science, that is quantum mechanics, the impoverished pictures themselves were abolished as was the notion of necessity itself.

Classical and modern science (with the aid of money, machines, and algebra) have produced technological wonders but have in the process destroyed the human scale of social life. These technological wonders have gone a long way towards destroying human freedom. Weil argued that a revolution is required if human freedom is to be recovered.

But the revolution proposed by Weil does not advocate the violent destruction of technology or the letter-bombing of some of technology's major adherents. The revolution required is the perennial revolution advocated by philosophy. It is a revolution which seeks to bring thought and action into relation within the life of the individual. Such a revolution can only take place through the educational appropriation of language, thought, and culture by the workers. It will perforce issue in a critique of the work situation and the division of labor insofar as they exclude the possibility of thought. Simone Weil did not think that decentralization could be brought about short of civilizational collapse. Her revolutionary task was not to help bring about such a collapse but to bring her thought to bear on the scientific achievements of her time and to bequeath it to those who might survive the collapse.

Weil contends that nihilism is at the heart of the modern technological project. She would agree with the recent post-modern appraisal of globalism made by Zygmunt Bauman: "Contrary to the widely shared view of modernity as the first universal civilization, this is a civilization singularly unfit for universalization. It is by nature an insular form of life, one that reproduces itself solely by deepening the difference between itself and the rest of the world by a self-assertion that "disenchants", disempowers and demeans that rest now transformed into the grazing ground. Such a self-assertion is not a reparable blunder of political thick-headedness or unalloyed greed; not a temporary myopia that can be forced or negotiated out of existence through the imposition of a stronger will or through political consensus reached by reasonable actors. Modernity cannot survive the advent of equality. Endemically and organically, modernity is a parasitic form of social arrangement which may stop its parasitic action only when the host organism is sucked dry of its life juices."[28]

The nihilism deplored here destroys the freedom of human beings and eschews the task of drawing up any rational criteria by which scientific projects or technical innovations could be evaluated. Pragmatism and utilitarianism are the respectable masks worn by this nihilism. Weil, on the other hand, has a Platonic commitment to thought and persuasion and education. In her *Notebooks* she wrote: "Plato. Intelligence dominates necessity through persuasion. Image of the inward order. Non-active action upon the self. Non-violence with regard to the self. Beauty is the image of this persuasion" (NB,I, 248). Simone Weil offers us, I suggest, an alternative to nihilism in our response the dead-end of technological progressivism.

In "Reflections Concerning the Cause of Liberty and Social Oppression," she explained that, thanks to the rise of Baconian science and the development of technology, modern civilization has given human beings more and more collective power over nature. But this collective power has not meant human liberation but servitude: "If in fact the human collectivity has to a large extent freed itself from the crushing burden which the gigantic forces of nature place on frail humanity, it has on the other hand, taken in some sort nature's place to the point of crushing the individual in a similar manner" (OL 79).

Platonic Anthropology

According to Weil, the human collectivity crushes the individual not by denying a person the opportunity of going through the so-called "power process" but by imposing on him/her a type of manual or mental

---

28. Zygmunt Bauman, *Postmodern Ethics* (Oxford: Blackwell, 1993), 215.

labor which precludes or excludes thought. Gabriella Fiori explains it in this way:

> Society, which has mastered the method that has eluded the individual, has apparently freed him from enslavement to nature and offered him the satisfaction of his primary necessities. The individual, clothed and fed, finds himself, on the contrary, in the condition of an "everlasting minor," enslaved to collectivity. How can we set him free? Asserting the rights of the individual against society is as ridiculous as "sustaining ʼthe rights of the gram in relation to the ton."[29]

In Weil's view, modern science, which is itself a collective enterprise (a prescriptive technology based on specialization), has itself crushed the individual scientist whose function is to add to the pool of knowledge rather than to become wise. In her pre-war notebook, Weil wrote: "Specialization. We take over not only *results* but *methods* which we do not understand. Indeed, the two go together; because algebraic results provide methods for the other sciences (e.g. infinitesimal calculus). [¶] So even in this sphere, too, the individual is crushed" (FLN 28, itals. in original). By that Simone Weil meant that individual thought is crushed in modern science as in so-called "scientifically managed" labor. As she saw it, the proper conditions of work are the direct opposite of those found in the technological society:

> In order that there may be a maximum of freedom, [two] *distinct* questions are involved:
> 1. that the individual should have *as little need as possible* of the collectivity
> 2. that the collectivity should have *as much need as possible* of the individual, i.e. of thought (which is the one thing that cannot be abstracted from the individual). (FLN 27, itals. in original)

Simone Weil's critique is rooted in her Platonic anthropology. For Weil, "thought" is a technical term. Thought is not language, and contrary to the view of many anthropologists, linguists, and information

---

29. Gabriella Fiori, *Simone Weil: An Intellectual Biography*, Joseph Berrigan, trans. (Athens: University of Georgia Press, 1989), 112.

theorists, thought cannot evolve.[30] Language clearly can and does evolve, but its evolution may render human action and human society more and more thoughtless. To the extent that it does evolve in this way, language makes it more and more difficult for human beings to remain in touch with necessity.

Language, as an aid to memory, gives us things in time. Language—whether oral, written, mathematical, scientific, or digital (that is, computational)—places the sun, the earth, the moon, and stars at our (imaginative) disposal.[31] But in so doing, language has no way of assuring us—even at the level of perception[32]—of the reality of what we imagine until we act. Action gives us things in space. Language allows us to act methodically and thus shows itself to be both indispensable and inadequate for thought, for it is only in methodical activity that we encounter contradiction. And contradiction (or dialectic) is the occasion of thought.[33]

---

30. Contrast Robert K. Logan, *The Fifth Language: Learning a Living in the Computer Age* (Toronto: Stoddart, 1995), 68–73.

31. See Calder, *Labour and Thought in the Philosophy of Simone Weil*, 56.

32. See Simone Weil, "The Pythagorean Doctrine" (IC 178):

It is surprising to read that number gives a body to things. We would sooner expect a form. But Philolaus' formula is literally true. All concise and rigorous analysis of perception, of illusion, of fantasy, of dream, of those states more or less near to hallucination, show that the perception of the real world differs from the errors resembling it, only because the real includes a contact with necessity. (Maine de Biran, Lagneau and Alain have shown the greatest discernment upon this point.) Necessity always appears to us as an ensemble of laws of variation, determined by fixed relationships and invariants. Reality for the human mind is contact with necessity. There is a contradiction here, for necessity is intelligible, not tangible. Thus the feeling of reality constitutes a harmony and a mystery. We convince ourselves of the reality of an object by going around it, an operation successively producing varied appearances which are determined by the immobility of a form which is different from all the appearances, exterior to them and transcending them. By this operation we know that the object is a thing and not an apparition, that it has a body.

33. As James Calder explains, the relationship between language, action, and thought is an epistemological mystery. The word mystery is not used in order to mystify:

If we remain on the simple level of anthropological description what appears to happen is this: images of necessity come into the mind "as in a flash" and out of nowhere discernible; all that we can say is that they are "revealed" to the mind in the silence of our mute contemplation of reality. And, miraculously, we find that they are partially applicable within the scope of human activity within the world.

A thought is an image of relation that is revealed in the mind from nowhere discernable, when our attention is directed away from process toward the realm of language. The revelation of thought through attention is purely a function private and unique to the individual. Through expression, however, thought is expropriated from the individual and embodied in things: in texts, techniques, skills, habits, customs of all kinds, and in the very organization of society itself. Language is such that these expressions of thought can serve as the basis of activity without being rethought by the individual.

The Death of Methodical Thought and the Degradation of Justice

Money, machines, and algebra have brought about the degradation of justice because, on Weil's account of justice, justice pertains not to the way in which people orient their will or predispose themselves to act toward each other, but, first and foremost, to how they see the other, and how they see themselves in relation to the other. If people see a world with themselves at the center, they will not see what is at stake in their relations with others; they will not see limits. This is why, for Weil, the language of modern political and moral theory was ultimately inadequate: it was grounded in the language of the will. The basic assumption of modern liberal thought is that each individual seeks, by calculation

---

Calder, *Labour and Thought*, 76. These images of necessity that are revealed in thought have the character of a fixed relation between two variables. They do not correspond to anything within the external tangible world and yet they illuminate it in this mysterious way. This simple description of thought acknowledges the basic discontinuity between the particulars of sense experience and the universals of the conceptual level, without pretending to understand the origin of thought in putative unconscious processes. The mysterious nature of the revelation of thought is elaborated by Weil (in a way that is beyond the scope of this chapter) by reference to the notion of reading. It leads her to reject the ancient skepticism of Cratylus, for whom the world cannot be read as meaningful, as well as the modern (Kantian) freedom to imagine a foundation of sense in human experience, or the existentialist liberty to allow the mind actively to manufacture meaning in our lives by projecting reason into the void, into the perfect discontinuity between one event and another. See *ibid.*, 89. For Weil, then, epistemology as securely founded upon the nature of thought as revelation is justified because it provides a description of the phenomenon that is consonant with our consciousness of it and is experimentally verifiable.

and contrivance, to extend his own claim, to realize his own narrow interests, to self-actualize. This language gives rise to the illusion of being without limits.

In the society in which we are living, "the rattle of everything that leads to the future"—what Flannery O'Connor calls the world's tumult—is more deafening and frenetic than ever. It constitutes for us the very matrix of myth and illusion which, for the heroes of the *Iliad*, took the form of the self-perpetuating violence of war. Accordingly it is a principle of limitlessness which blinds us to the true nature of reality. There is a sense of vertigo in the pace of technological development, expanding markets, the proliferation of new forms of media and advertisement. As Ernest Becker in his *Escape From Evil* observes, "modern man, in his one dimensional economics, is driven by the lie of his life, by his denial of limitation, of the true state of natural affairs."[34]

But running counter to the force of these illusions we also have what George Grant called "intimations of deprival."[35] These may take the form of traditions and narratives which contain within themselves accounts of justice which are *not* subject to the world's tumult. Or they may occur amidst those experiences of otherness in which an unconditional claim is made on us. These "moments of grace" seem to find no expression in the language of our public life, and yet, for most of us, at some point in our lives, their reality and importance cannot be denied. To Weil, the force of illusion in social life, particularly in advanced industrial societies, manifests itself precisely in the inadequacy of our language to convey such truths. In "What is Sacred in Every Human Being?" she wrote, "[m]any indispensable truths that could save human beings are not spoken for this sort of reason; those who could speak them cannot formulate them, those who could formulate them cannot say them." She concluded that "[t]he remedy for this evil should be one of the pressing problems of a true politics" (LPW 116).

---

34. Ernest Becker, *Escape From Evil* (New York: The Free Press, 1975), 89.
35. See George Grant, *Technology and Empire* (Toronto: House of Anansi, 1969), 139.

The Language of "Rights" and Modern Liberal Discourse

Weil thought that the language of "rights" was a prime example of the inadequacy of modern liberal discourse. Liberal theory, particularly in its Lockean form, starts from the conception of a person essentially as an autonomous property holder. Weil felt the language of "rights" corresponded to this conception. "The concept of rights is linked to that of sharing out, of exchange, of quantity. It has something of the commercial to it. It evokes legal proceedings and pleadings" (LPW 113). The notion of rights, the emergence of which she associates with the French Revolution, is "intrinsically inadequate." The real problem, for her, with the notion of rights is that it does not capture the sense in which a human being is both limited and limit. As a precondition of any kind of political justice, limits must be observed within the social world. Weil explains that any "imaginary extension of these limits is self-indulgent, and thus there is sensuousness in all that makes us forget the reality of these obstacles" (LPW 105–106). The language of rights ultimately obliges this human desire to obscure the truth of limit.

In contrast to the idea of rights that is so central to all modern political thought is Weil's idea of *obligation*. Obligation as a principle in human relationship and in the larger social world is grounded in "a reality outside the world, that is to say, outside space and time, outside man's mental universe, outside any sphere whatsoever that is accessible to human faculties" (SE 219). The human longing for good which is "never appeased by any object in this world" corresponds to this transcendent reality. Central to Weil's critique of rights was the observation that "[r]ights are always found to be related to certain conditions," whereas, "[o]bligations alone remain independent of all conditions" (NR 4).

Weil's language of obligation unearths two different aspects of the human experience for which modern political and moral philosophy has no words. The first is the experience of injustice as something more than just the thwarting of one's will, or the disregarding of one's legitimate claims, but as something akin to a "sacrilege." The second aspect is the sense of being bound unconditionally to another in a way which is not simply to be understood in terms of utility. They direct our attention to the truth of limit.

The language of rights emerged from the liberal assumption that the essence of a human being is her/his freedom. Weil's language of obligation, on the other hand, is founded upon an ontology of limit from which it may be deduced that it is in fact a higher "good" for human beings to know that they are limited. This knowledge directs their attention toward their ultimate end. The recognition of the other as a limit to the claims of the self is accordingly a condition of the realization of life's highest purposes. The poverty of liberalism is evidenced in its failure to address these concerns.

Politics: A Double-Edged Sword

The beauty, amidst the hardship, of being unconditionally claimed by something outside of ourselves—caring for someone who is dying, parenting a disabled child—is, in public terms, inarticulate. In the same way, we have a profoundly diminished language of responsibility. Because we do not have words with which to speak publicly of these "goods," neither can we speak of our failings with regard to them. With the concepts of *limit* and *obligation*, Weil invokes a new language of public life which expresses, in the clearest terms, an account of justice which goes far beyond that of modern humanism because it contains within it an answer to the question: to what end? It is the task of language, art, religion, a certain kind of science, and an inspired politics to draw attention, in public terms, to this deeper level of concern. Because good, beauty, and truth are given only in "lightning flashes ... moments of pure intuition" (NB, I, 156), a public language of good becomes crucial for us though we may often fail to notice its absence.

Politics is, for Weil, thus a double-edged sword. On the one hand, it represents the ever-present danger of blinding ideology and illusion, the obscuring of limit. On the other hand, politics is the art of preserving, through meaningful language, a connection to conceptions of good and justice. Weil uses, as an analogy, the art of the poet. Politics, like poetry, is an art requiring concentration and receptivity. "In order to write verse that contains some beauty, one must have had the ambition to equal by the arrangement of words that pure and divine beauty which, according to Plato, lies on the other side of the skies" (NR 215). Weil asserts the principle that a person, striving to be virtuous, cannot succeed by struggling to be less imperfect, but only by being attentive to the idea of perfection. Accordingly, a society does not move closer to justice when its attention is directed toward anything less than perfect justice.

CHAPTER 6

On Method:
Education and Inspiration

Robert Chenavier

Simone Weil was always preoccupied with questions of method, no matter what the field it was on which she was reflecting: society, the sciences, work, or technique. *The Need for Roots* mulls over three of them.[1] First of all, there is the search for a method of public action, which is also in her terms, a "method for breathing an inspiration into a people" (NR 185). Then there is the search for a "method to be followed in spiritual matters and in everything connected with the soul's welfare" (NR 186), which is to say, a method for defining the "needs of the soul." Finally, she employs a method of reading the past which is also of importance for our subject.

Weil ideally would like to figure out a unique and universal method that could resolve problems in different domains, on several levels, while keeping an eye on multiple actions and facts. Descartes' inspiration

---

1. In her other writings from London, Weil seeks out the principles of a materialist method that will avoid the mistakes that Marx made. Weil insisted very soon on the divergence, in the case of Marx, between the scientific point of view and the moral point of view: Reluctant to "allow two separate men to go on living in him—the revolutionary and the scientist [...] he insisted on making of his method into an instrument for predicting a future in conformity with his wishes. To achieve this, he was obliged to give a twist to the method and to the ideal, to deform the one and the other." "On the Contradictions of Marxism" (OL 148).

hangs on here, even despite her critiques of him in 1935–36.[2] Before her "second *grand* œuvre" Simone Weil had already posited some elements for reflection. She noted with respect to the subject of work, in her first cahier: "multiple action for [a] single method. [D]ivisible action (which may be spaced out through several hours) for [a] single method" (FLN 7). In the domain of knowledge, she posed an analogous principle with a caveat: "[M]ethod: if a method has been understood once for all and employed many times, and if it then, even in the domain of abstract signs, produces *unforeseen* results, and these results are accepted without being understood, then, from that moment, the method has become a mere formula or recipe" (FLN 26). Descartes sought a method, but there is a hole in his work, she thinks; he "never found a way to prevent order from becoming, as soon as it was conceived, a thing instead of an idea," Weil wrote to Alain in 1935 (SL 3). In effect, while the author of the *Rules for the Direction of the Mind* had established that signs should be kept in their place as simple instruments (SL 3), he did not succeed in avoiding their being substituted for what they signified and becoming an end in themselves. Method is then reduced to an art of manipulating signs, to "a game for scientists, and a collection of recipes for technicians" (FLN 9). The mind consents in this way to its own abdication (FLN 217) since it renounces its own function of coordination, insofar as the manipulation of signs according to a rule makes the result appear "like a miracle,"[3] as Weil observed in a letter to Robert Guihéneuf.[4] When method has signs as its domain instead of thought, the facility of working with the rules of signs replaces just and true reasoning. It is in this way that "Descartes' venture turned out badly" she says in her letter to Alain (SL 3). Yet, with this reservation about the idea of a unique and universal method, Weil still habitually spoke of *the* method, in the singular. Thus, she writes in *The Need for Roots*, "The method merely differs according to the different sphere. The higher one goes, the more rigorous and pre-

2. See André-A. Devaux, "Présence de Descartes dans la vie et dans l'œuvre de Simone Weil," *Cahiers Simone Weil*, vol. XVIII, no. 1, 1–23.

3. "One thus finds oneself in the position of having solved a problem by a species of magic, without the mind having connected the data with the solution" (OL 94). In a letter to R. Guihéneuf (*Cahiers Simone Weil*, vol. XXI, nos. 1–2, 9–10). Weil gives as an example the calculus of Fermat, see OC. V.I 94 and OC 1, 358–359.

4. *Cahiers Simone Weil*, vol. XXI, no. 1, 1–2, 13, 19.

cise it becomes" (NR 186). One just has to be rigorous in moving from one level to the other.

Those comments on method then allow one to see what the search for a method of public action in the "second *grand œuvre*" of 1943 is about. At the heart of this search is the question of inspiration: "We cannot be made better except by the influence upon us of what is better than we are" (SE 44). As we will see, the study of even this influence is not beyond method, not even when the inspiration in question implies a reference to the manifestation of the supernatural across human societies. So, how does this manifestation work? This is the question of public action, with which we will begin.

A Method to Breathe Inspiration into a People

Simone Weil always held fast to a principle from her early philosophy: "Action *after* discovering the method" (OC VI.1 77). In a text from 1926, Weil as a student tried to show that "after geometrical thought the first model of thought is the thought that immediately precedes action" (OC I 316). If it were possible to know all the conditions of our action, method would be infallible. All the elements for success would be given, "known and manipulable as signs are for a mathematician;" thus, "in order to get the desired result, it will suffice to put these elements in relation to each other using the methodical direction that would impress itself on thought ... to effective movements ... which would leave their mark on the world" (OCII.2 74). Such is the methodical mind which permits us to prepare carefully our actions.

The Need for Roots crosses a threshold and goes quite a bit farther when it seeks to sketch a "method of political action ... [that] goes beyond the possibilities of the human intelligence, at least as far as those possibilities are known" (NR 215). "From this analysis a method may be derived for making men—peoples and individuals, and oneself to begin with—better, by modifying the conceptions in such a way as to bring the purest motives into play" (NR 249). Such a raising of reflection to a new spiritual level requires a touchstone here below, so that the conditions of the descent of the supernatural, of the Good, may be created, for, she says, the Good descends "only to the extent to which certain conditions are in fact fulfilled on earth" (NR 261).

Weil believes that the "problem of a method for breathing an inspiration into a people is quite a new one" (NR 185), despite some "allusions" found in Plato's *Statesman*, and then notably in Rousseau. What is needed is to propose pathways for reflection while avoiding nonsensical or dangerous solutions. There is a real difficulty, in effect, in finding a good method. For example, "[i]n our own day, people have investigated and penetrated deeply into the problem of propaganda" (NR 185–186). Of course, though, propaganda does not aim at "creating an inspiration"; on the contrary, propaganda "closes, [and] seals up all the openings through which an inspiration might pass." Thus, the use of propaganda is fundamentally excluded as a method. Nor "is it a question of adopting reverse measures" (NR186) in the name of a simplistic causality. Another error would be to think that "the inspiring of a people is a mystery reserved to God alone, and for which, consequently, no method exists"[5] (NR 186). While "[t]he supreme and perfect state of mystical contemplation is something that is infinitely more mysterious still," nonetheless, St. John of the Cross wrote "treatises on the method of attaining to such a state, which, by their scientific precision, are far and away superior to anything produced by the psychologists or professors of our own time" (NR186). However, one cannot underestimate the difficulties. Weil adds that the sort of transformation itself undergone by the mystic "keeps one from hoping to see it accomplished by a whole people" (OC V.1 254). What one can hope for, though, is that the life of a people might "be imbued by a religion which is thoroughly oriented towards mysticism" (*Ibid.*). Her insistence on this last point is important, for it rules out all attempts at the spiritual inspiration of a people by trying to proselytize them, or by propaganda, or by bad education.[6]

Such methods would be inappropriate and would lead to a religious dictatorship that would inevitably blur social and spiritual levels, resulting in a religious society run entirely by fundamentalists. Weil dreaded above all an institutional religion that would bring about a "society of

---

5. The possibility of a method, with respect to matter, supposes that God himself does not govern pastorally, he governs as a sovereign over the world through principles. See NR 281.

6. As was the case with the measures imposed by the Vichy government. (NR 91).

divine pretensions"[7] capped by a sort of appeal to "ecclesiastical interests"[8] analogous to the authority claimed by official "interests of the
State." Indeed, it needs to be recognized publicly that "religion does not
consist in anything other than in a way of looking," or else it will be "shut
up inside churches," or entirely stifled wherever it might be found. "Religion should not claim to occupy a place in society other than that
which rightly belongs to supernatural love in the soul" (WG 141). Paradoxically—but it is only a paradox for the mind who does not understand the mode of action of the supernatural[9]—in order for religion to
be present everywhere, it "must not only not be totalitarian," but must
"limit itself strictly to the plane of supernatural love which alone is suitable for it" (WG 105). Then, it will penetrate everywhere by virtue of its
purity,[10] and not because of its institutional weight as a "social entity."[11]
The reference to the supernatural which should pervade the world does
not mean, in consequence, a supernatural which ignores specific social
situations, nor an erasure of the social by the supernatural. That would
mean forgetting the most important aspect of Weil's philosophical
method, namely, distinguishing levels.[12]

It is precisely the absence of any distinction of levels which led "the
men of 1789" to err as they did. They made rights the principle of the
French Revolution, and that was the origin of the failure of democracies.
They thought they could begin with the notion of rights and *at the same
time* pose absolute principles, which was a conceptually incoherent
move. This "confusion of language and ideas [...] is largely responsible
for the present political and social confusion" (NR 4). This is why *The
Need for Roots* opens with a critique of the lack of openness to the tran-

---

7. "A society with divine pretensions, like the Church, is perhaps more dangerous
still by virtue of the ersatz Good that it contains than by the evil that defiles it" (OC VI.2
419).

8. The expression is that of Patrice Rolland in *Simone Weil et Hannah Arendt: Christianisme et politique* (Paris: Klincksieck, 1996), 59.

9. See a sketch of "Is There a Marxist Doctrine?" (OC V.1 608).

10. Following this last citation, Weil writes: "The Bible says 'Wisdom penetrates everywhere because of its perfect purity" (See *Wisdom* 7:24). See also OC VI.3 131.

11. Weil writes to Father Perrin that the Church creates fear as "a social structure"
(WG 10).

12. "The ability to distinguish between levels is a matter of supreme importance" (OC
VI.2 487). The Platonic inspiration is clear: "The distinction of realms. Essential idea of
Plato" (OC VI.2 348).

scendent that characterizes rights. Weil takes up the work of reflection that dominated revolutionary thinking in 1789. Every difficulty comes back to *inventing* institutions that would point to the absolute in this world. Of course, institutions protect rights, persons, and liberties that already exist; what is needed, therefore, is to invent new ones "above them," ones destined to "abolish everything that in contemporary life crushes souls under injustice, lies, and ugliness" (OC V.1 236; LPW 128). Note that Weil says "above" and not "in its place." She wants to give a foundation to the "middle realm of values" (OC V.1 226 LPW 118). Thus, we again note, the institutions that protect rights, persons, and liberties "have a proper use in their own region" (LPW 128). This proposal surprises us, inasmuch as we see in the upholding of these values, especially the notion of rights, our recourse against totalitarianism. But we also should at the same avoid a hasty reading which would understand her "spiritual inspiration" as a matter of replacing every institution and positing *the* solution to every political and social problem.

What is important in this move towards a social power that would have a spiritual dimension, is not, on the political side, solely a matter of doing something to the institutional and juridical dimension; it is not on the spiritual side, adding a clerical and theological dimension. A spiritual politics is enjoined where we encounter a subjective dimension—e.g., the "needs of the soul" or a "revolt springing out of the depths of a few faithful hearts" (NR 191). It ought to be a specific form of public action where the "unheard thoughts" or the "unheard needs" of an entire people (the collective dimension) and of each person (the personal dimension) come together. Weil observes in "What Is Sacred in Every Human Being?": "Many indispensable truths that could save human beings are not spoken . . . ; those who could speak them cannot formulate them, those who could formulate them cannot say them. The remedy for this evil should be one of the pressing problems of a true politics" (LPW 116). One sees in such a proposal that it is a question of establishing the conditions for a politics of truth. It is a question of defining a new "'regime'[13] of truth which would be inseparable from a 'regime of attention.'" It falls to those who govern to advance this kind of regime. Michel Foucault calls a "'regime of truth' one where 'truth' is linked circularly to the systems of power which produce and maintain it, and to the effects of

---

13. This expression is used in a passage from "The Factory Journal" (OC II.2 267).

power that it induces and that flow back to it."[14] For Simone Weil, it is a question precisely of internally detaching "the power of truth" from the social, political, and cultural forms in which it normally functions. It is the condition of becoming attentive to the "indispensable truths" secretly present in souls, but which ask to be seen so that they can be expressed in appropriate language.

Weil faces here the principal difficulty of politics as Rousseau found it, namely, of knowing how to reinforce in human hearts a sense of obligation that is indispensable for their social being. The end of *The Social Contract* gives this care over to "the civil religion." Weil does not use this expression, although it is indeed within a religious perspective that she seeks to inspire individuals with a sense that an appeal to reason could never reveal. The reinforcement of the sense of obligation in the human heart is inevitably done in imperfect conditions since these conditions are social ones. It is nevertheless necessary "to accept the situation provided for us, and which subjects us to absolute obligations in regard to things that are relative, limited and imperfect" (NR 157). It is always necessary to refuse to mix the perfect and the imperfect. To do that, one needs to recognize this fundamental truth of Christianity: "[P]rogress towards a lesser imperfection is not produced by the desire for a lesser imperfection. Only the desire of perfection has the virtue of being able to destroy in the soul some part of the evil which defiles it"(NR 215).

This desire for perfection lies, as we shall see, on the level of motives; its application is always played out in imperfect situations; but this application has no chance of success if the inspiration is not perfectly pure. As is often the case with Weil, it is necessary to hold onto the two extremes of any idea while at the same time harmonizing them and respecting the proper level of each. Otherwise, one falls into a simplification that flattens the real into a single dimension. Such is the difficulty of finding a method which can breathe an inspiration into the political and the social.

---

14. Michel Foucault *Dits et Écrits II*, (Paris: Gallimard, 2001), 114. See also, more generally, 112 *sq.*

A Way of Educating an Entire People

Let us consider from this point of view the notion of public action, conceived as a way of educating "an entire people." Weil insists that it "must be given a permanent place in the mind." "It demands an all the greater effort seeing that it is, for us, a completely new idea," for, since the Renaissance, "public activities have never been visualized in this light, but solely as a means of establishing a particular form of power regarded as desirable for one reason or another" (NR 188), such as "being in the State's interest." "Politics are practically never looked upon as an art of so high a category." Indeed, it is a vulgar conception of politics that sees it as a "technique for acquiring and holding on to power" (NR 216) that Weil wants to go beyond in order to go towards a superior form of action. Against the Roman forms of power found in the State and the Church, she argues, with respect to the political projects that a liberated France should undertake, it is above all a question of working out a "mode of education of a whole people" (NR 187): "To want to direct human creatures—others or oneself—towards the good" (NR 188).

What are the appropriate methods for leading human beings to the good? With respect to the political projects to be undertaken in post-war France, it makes the most sense to begin with the easiest one, namely, knowing how "to classify the means of education contained in public action" (NR 188). To do this, one needs to set aside the grossest means, namely, "fear and hope, brought about by threats and promises" or "[s]uggestion" (NR 188). These are means that are universally employed today, she thinks, and were brought to perfection by Hitler. So, it remains to examine the means that are too often ignored, such as "example," and the "modalities themselves of action, and those of organizations created for purposes of action" (NR 188). There is also another means that Weil wants to develop, one that we have already suggested: the "[e]xpression ... of some of the thoughts which, before being publicly expressed, were already in the hearts of the people, or in the hearts of certain active elements in the nation" (NR 188). Circumstances exist—war is certainly one of them—when "the march of public events occupies so much more important a place in the personal life of each of us than does the course of individual affairs, that a number of hidden thoughts and hidden needs of this sort are found to be the same with practically all the human beings which go to make up a people" (NR

190). There is a sort of implicit "general will" engendered by the march of public events. Because they are not bound by interest groups, or political parties, and are detached from the collective passions that one can never get to come together,[15] these needs and thoughts can be found to be identical, something which is impossible in the circumstances that normally determine collective thinking and feeling. It is this novel situation in which the minds who furnish the possibility of a specific action find themselves, since all of them, having as their object the people, take it personally. "Thus, far from stifling the resources concealed in the depths of each mind, which is what all collective action, in the nature of things, inevitably does, … this type of action awakens them, stirs them up and stimulates their growth" (NR 190). There is a sort of "pastoral" technique here in this art of governing human beings by leading their souls[16] in such a way that each individual participates by oneself and for oneself in a certain collective result. It is a question, moreover, in *The Need for Roots*, of molding souls or of "refashioning the soul of the country" (NR 148).

How does one move from the principles of such a method to their application? With respect to the mission of the Free French in London, Weil writes that it should consist above all in making "use of words answering the secret thoughts and needs of the human beings composing the French people" (NR 197). To be capable of doing this, it is necessary to recognize "by signs, thoughts which go unexpressed" (NR 197), and knowing how in writing to express "delicate shades of meaning and complex relationships" (NR197). With respect to the modes of action which constitute the Resistance in France, Weil recommends the creation of an organization which would translate inspiration into words (NR 212). A method cannot do without language. In the matter of public action, it is necessary, after having recognized the mute aspirations and needs of the people, to translate them into clear ideas in a language which can become common property yet without losing its specificity. It is a question of translation, a type of method of "transposition" of truths

---

15. On the interpretation of the "general will" see "Note on the General Suppression of Political Parties" (OC V.1 400 ff.) ; APP).

16. See Michel Foucault, *Sécurité, Territoire, Population* (Paris. Ed. du Seuil-Gallimard, 2004), 154 as well as 196–197.

to which Weil was so attached.[17] It is necessary to be able, by this translation, to transpose without cheapening, without weakening. *The Need
for Roots* tries to elaborate the modalities of this method of translation,
of choosing "words likely to awaken an echo in the hearts of the French"
(NR 198).

It is necessary to figure this out while still respecting the tensions
between the demands "of the good, in the spiritual sense of the word"
and the necessary demands of "utility" that one has to take into account
relative to circumstances, all the while keeping in mind that only "what
is spiritually good is good in every respect, at all times, in all places,
under all circumstances." (NR 198). Wherefore one can draw this practical consequence: among the list of echoes that can be provoked in the
heart of the people "we must first of all choose everything which is
purely and genuinely good, without the slightest consideration for expe-
diency, applying no other test that that of genuineness; and we must let
them have all that very often, untiringly, using words that are as simple
and clear-cut as possible" (NR 199). In order to complete her examination of the necessary means to lead human beings to the good, Weil argues that it is necessary to pay attention to education, whether that of
children or adults or individuals or a whole people. Education ought to
give birth to motives that are capable of furnishing action with "an indispensable amount of energy" for effective execution (NR 188). The
London notebook talks about a method for analysis: "first establish theoretically the list of possible motives for a particular action, in the light
of its originating idea" (FLN 347). Weil affirms the unity and the universality of this method: "*Analysis of good and evil by motives.* Apply this
method *in every sphere.* A universal method of discrimination for educating oneself, and others, and a whole people" (FLN 347). From this
general analysis flow a method determined to better human beings by
"modifying the conceptions in such a way as to bring the purest motives
into play" (NR 249). To this end, in order to appreciate something, it is
necessary "to discern the proportion of good contained, not in the thing
itself, but in the motives for the effort which has produced it. For the
amount of good in the thing itself is the same as the amount of good in

17. See Robert Chenavier, "Se Mettre dans la troisiéme dimension: Une théorie du
transfert chez Simone Weil" in *Simone Weil: Réception et transposition*, Robert Chenavier
and Thomas Pavel eds. (Paris: editions Classiques Garnier, 2019), 65–79.

the motive behind it, neither more nor less" (NR 249). That comment clearly defines the importance of action and what is essential in it. "Discerning the good in the thing itself" is the most powerful tool—even more powerful than words—for molding souls. In effect, being incited "only becomes real to the mind when it has brought about an action performed by the body" (NR 201). It is necessary to transform force and desire by attention taken at the highest level. It is a question of directing well one's vital energy, of avoiding brutality, or of squandering that energy. In order to do that, one has to act on motives. Let us note that the expression "molding souls" evokes the direction of conscience that Weil talks about in respect to the "true mission" of the Free French in London, which is a "spiritual mission before being a military and political one." Such a mission is a matter of being "a director of conscience on a national plane." (NR 213), and it squares up exactly with the problem of finding a method of how to breathe an inspiration into a people.

A Method in Action in Work

In the realm of social activities, there is then a question of applying a principle that she defines in this way: "The completely precise representation of the supernatural destiny of each social function alone gives a norm for our will to reform things" (LPW 141). If it is easy to distinguish the forms of activity that keep attention from being oriented towards God—and which for this reason, ought to be abolished—it is not always easy to define each activity's specific link to the supernatural. Certain practical problems arise when it is a question of examining the conditions of imbuing a spirituality in the quite different milieux of the peasantry, the intellectuals, and the workers. That is a matter of defining a "spirituality for each job" (OC VI.4 82) and finding a symbolism appropriate to each of these professions. When Weil speaks of symbolism here, she characteristically brings in the notion of a profession or job in its particularity rather than "work" as an overarching function. There is a spirituality of work, but there is also a symbolism of the specific work that people do, and the former goes hand in hand with the latter.

> As a stage on the way, it is a good thing that in any activity there should be a part of the soul that remains withdrawn and

concentrated in God, but it is not the end of the way. A very different relation is needed between worldly activity and the spiritual part of the soul. Every worldly activity should be so performed that there appears in it the meaning with which God created it. (FLN 268)

In "Christianity and the Life of the Fields" notably, Weil sets out the principles for a spiritual inspiration that would pervade the milieu of the peasantry. She observes that "Christianity will never impregnate society until each social category has its own specific, unique, and inimitable link with Christ" (OC IV.1 269). The idea comes up again in *The Need for Roots*:

> For example, surely, there is no reason why a peasant engaged in sowing shouldn't have at the back of his mind, without shaping words—even unspoken ones—on the one hand certain similes drawn by Christ, such as: "Unless the seed die ...,"[18] "The seed is the Word of God ...,"[19] 'The grain of mustard seed ... which is the least of all seeds ..." and on the other hand, the double mechanism of growth; the one whereby the seed, by consuming itself and with the aid of bacteria, reaches the surface of the soil; and the other whereby solar energy pours down in rays of light, is captured by the green colouring matter of the plant stalk, and rises upward in an irresistible ascending movement.[20] (NR 94)

Weil goes on to argue: "[t]he analogy which makes the mechanism of this world a reflection of the supernatural mechanism ... then becomes luminously clear" (NR 96). Agricultural work is the activity in which it is easiest to transform daily life into a "metaphor of divine significance" (OC IV.1 265). Working the soil permits the purely human to find poetry of a "metaphor that is real"[21] (FLN 207) in the fullness of attention

---

18. John 12.24. This is a frequent citation of Weil, notably in the *Notebooks*. See also "Christianity and the Life of the Fields" OC IV.1 264–265.

19. Matthew 13:3–9; Mark 4:3–9; Luke 8:4–8. See "Christianity and the Life of the Fields" OC IV.1 264.

20. See "Pensées sans ordre concernant l'amour de Dieu" OC.1 284, and OC VI.3 308.

21. Rolf Kühn early on pointed to the importance of this notion in his article "Le monde comme texte," in *Revue des sciences philosophiques et théologiques*, October 1980, 522, 528–529.

to the task to be accomplished, without discursive reasoning. References abound, in "Christianity and the Life of the Fields" most notably, to the symbolism of seeds, labor, or the harvest. One can find references to vineyard work, the planting of trees, to the cultivation of wheat, to the raising of animals, or to fishing. All the tasks described in these examples give a place to a precise representation of a symbol that evokes a virtue and a form of spiritual attention. Think back only to the characteristic example of the seed she gives in the citation from *The Need for Roots* above and how she develops it in "The First Condition for the Work of a Free Person." "In one's own room, in envisioning a new and truthful birth, one must stop to think of the need for a moral death, and to read or repeat to oneself the words about a seed only bearing fruit by first dying." Moreover, for the one who is in the middle of sowing, Weil observes that he can "turn his attention to this truth without the aid of any word through his own gestures and the sight of the grain that is being buried in the ground.": "[i]f he doesn't reason about it, if he just looks at it, the attention that he pays to the accomplishment of his task is not impeded but brought to the highest degree of intensity" (LPW 136–137). This intuitive attention in work is not a disposition of the mind that precedes or accompanies the activity, but a disposition of the whole being. This makes work into the equivalent of art, into poetry insofar as it is an "emotional knowledge"[22] of "the universe as a metaphor" (OCVI.4 126), and finally, an equivalent of prayer. If the universe is "a real metaphor," it is in the reality of necessary relations in which one ought to read their supernatural meaning, which is to say, their "infinitely more real than nature" (SWW 101), than its reality as a web of intellectually conceived necessities. According to Weil, the metaphor takes the form of a non-verbal schematization, namely, that of work, that directs the intuitive attention, attention which does not wait for discursive reason to take up. This non-verbal schematization leads to a new, poetic level elevated above the *logos*. At this superior level, one discovers the unity of mind that comes from the highest form of attention, from the body in its fluidity, and from the world in its experienced reality.

---

22. This expression comes from the linguist Georges Mounin, *La Communication poétique* (Paris: Gallimard, 1969), 114. It links to the interpretation that Weil wants to give at the beginning of "Christianity and the Life of the Fields": by "the association of appropriate ideas, deep at the center of the mind, by intense emotions." (OC IV.1, 264).

What, then, about spiritually inspiring the working classes? Weil well knew that in these milieux there was a question of a "'worker's culture,"[23] although, she observes, "[o]thers used to say there was no such thing as working class or non-working class culture, but just plain culture" (NR 65). The unfortunate consequence of this last observation, she thinks, has been to apply a conception to "the most intelligent workmen and the ones most anxious to learn as is reserved for semi-imbecile boys' in a *lycée*" (NR 65). One of the obstacles to a worker's culture is material, such as a lack of time and energy. The second obstacle is a "certain disposition of feeling" that belongs to the worker's condition. "Consequently, there is something outlandish about what has been elaborated by other people and for other people" (NR 67). It is important, in applying a method, to know that to each condition "corresponds a certain particular disposition of feeling" (NR 67), and that the state of one's feeling can hinder the truth's circulation. The remedy for this is to make an "effort of translation." That does not mean "vulgarisation." "It isn't a question of taking truths—of already far too poor a quality—contained in the culture of the intellectuals, and then degrading them, mutilating them, and destroying all their flavour; but simply of expressing them, in all their fullness, in a language which, to use Pascal's expression, makes them perceptible to the heart,[24] "for the benefit of people whose feelings have been shaped by working-class conditions" (NR 67). "To breathe an inspiration into individuals, it does not suffice to use words that only appeal to their reason, there needs to be an appeal to the feelings capable of reinforcing in the heart of each one the inspiration that one wants to descend into it. At the center of this elaboration of the method, there is an "art of transposing truths," which is "one of the most essential and the least known" arts, but also one of the most difficult. "What makes it difficult is that, in order to practise it, one has to have placed oneself at the centre of a truth and possessed it in all its nakedness, behind the particular form in which it happens to have found expression" (NR 67–68). This art does not belong to any particular realm of knowledge, or

---

23. Weil herself was personally involved in this by virtue of the courses she taught at The Worker's Exchange at Saint-Étienne. She taught French, political economy, and she spoke on Marxism. (See OC II.1 68–84, 90–94, 314–317, and 329–333).

24. Blaise Pascal, *Pensées*, in Œuvres *complètes* (Paris: ed. du Seuil, 1963), frag. 424; 552.

faith. It concerns the totality of thought and experience: philosophy, science, religion, and even action.

Relative to action, especially the action of work, what Weil here calls "culture" needs to be found by fully attending to the whole, completed task. It should not be divided into pieces. Certainly, from 1931 on, she had observed that it is necessary to give to workers the power of using language so that one might weaken "the domination of those who know how to use words over those who know how to use things" (OC II.1, 69). However, the most important conquest of a revolution should be the abolition of "the degrading division between intellectual work and manual labor," an abolition that it is absolutely necessary "to prepare for now" (Ibid.). It is a question of creating conditions "for the union of intellectual work and manual labor while seizing for workers, inasmuch as it is possible, the intimate relation that exists between work and the theoretical knowledge of every kind that humanity has acquired over the ages" (OC II.1 69–70). It is necessary that in the activity itself, that in each moment of work there be present "the knowledge of all human efforts (theoretical and technical) which have rendered and that now render it possible" (OC VI.1 131). The worker is above all to assimilate such knowledge that, as *The Need for Roots* stresses, "everything that belongs to standard Science ... derived principally from an analogical method, consisting in transporting into the realm of nature the relations which govern human labour. Consequently, it is far more a natural concern of the workers, if one know how to present it to them properly, than it is of secondary schoolboys" (NR 70). One clearly sees by this specific application of method that one brings about cultural inspiration in work.

Ultimately, work is a model of spiritual virtue. In her earliest writings Weil thought out some of the moral functioning of a profession, while developing the idea that, by a profession, morality takes on its sense by a relation to society.[25] Later on, she sought to define a spirituality of work, maintaining that it is by a job that spirituality has its sense in a civilization imbued by the supernatural. Such a sketch of a spirituality of work is not a mere pious meditation, meant to offer commodious images and representations; rather, it is meant to order life to the supernatural. Jobs are conceived as "conditions of life favorable to the highest opera-

---

25. See OC I, 27 and 273–274.

tions of the mind, that the worker will develop by his daily labor."[26] Here is where the most difficult problems arise. How can a spirituality of work be transposed onto the conditions of work in the industrial age, an age which is so destructive of the work done by the artisan or the worker? With respect to the question of giving inspiration to work in the industrial milieu, it appears that the method needed to do so has to be invented. Weil imagined some concrete solutions which could help to determine more general methodological considerations in *The Need for Roots*. It will help to recall briefly some of what these concrete investigations are.

The Eucharist, for example, is a special symbol for the producer of wheat, for the winemaker, and for the making of bread. For the peasant it is easy to understand how a human being becomes, thanks to one's work, this wheat or this grape by which he or she receives in person the body and blood of Christ when he goes to church.[27] However, for a worker who works in a steel factory, the relation to the Eucharist is not at all evident. However, "becoming matter" applies to him just as much as it does to the others, and so it is necessary to find a symbolism that fits the worker's condition. Can one discover any symbols which, in any exactness, lend themselves to the factory worker, and even more particularly to this kind of job? Weil sketches out two symbols in view of this, that of the Cross, and that of rhythm. Let us consider these briefly in order to illustrate again her concern for the concrete in using any method.

The Unity of Method, Inspiration, and Perception

In "The Love of God and Affliction," Weil clearly tells us in just what sense the symbol of the Cross is a universal symbol. The Cross is "necessity itself put into contact" with all the levels of our being, "with our

---

26. Mario Miegge, *Vocation et travail: Essai sur l'éthique puritaine* (Geneva: ed. Labor et Fides, 1989), 79.

27. "The priest has the privilege of offering on the altar the flesh and blood of Christ. But the peasant has a privilege no less sublime. His flesh and his blood, sacrificed in the course of endless hours of labor, passing into the wheat and the grapes, themselves become the blood and flesh of Christ" (OC IV.1 266).

physical sensibility by its evocation of physical pain and with supernatural love by the presence of God" (SWW 68). Contact with necessity, we should not forget, defines reality.[28] To the degree where "Necessity is the supreme criterion in all logic," and to the degree where it alone puts "the mind into contact with the truth" (OC VI.4 166), work occupies a privileged place among the activities that have the Cross of Christ as their truth. It offers precisely the whole range of contacts with necessity on all the levels of our being, from physical sensibility (by physical suffering) up to what is highest in ourselves (our orientation towards supernatural love); and for all the in-between parts there is the experience of the equilibrium of necessary relations from beauty of love, to the perfect obedience of necessity of the universe sensed as something else than as a violence done to the flesh and to the carnal part of the soul. In this way, the symbolism of the Cross, "could be an inexhaustible inspiration" (LPW 137) making all its value available to the worker. For example: "The body of Christ was a very light weight, but, because of the distance between the earth and the sky, it makes for a counterweight to the universe" (LPW 137). Just as God was able to raise up the world thanks to the fulcrum which is the Incarnation, "every human being who perfectly obeys God constitutes such a fulcrum," for "he is but an infinitely small force in relation to the universe, but by obedience, the point of application of this force is transported out into heaven" (OC IV.2 298). There can therefore exist in work the fullness of an equilibrium experienced by the effectiveness of an infinitesimal point, outside the world, but which acts in this world. It is necessary to understand that all the problems posed by the introduction of a method to breathe a supernatural inspiration into an activity come back to finding intermediaries that allow that activity to be oriented towards a unity holding together elements which are otherwise so far apart. At spirituality's high level, it is necessary to find intermediaries which will permit separate elements to be oriented towards a unity, "outside the world," all the while maintaining the worldly tension between them.

How does an attentive individual find, for example, an analogy which would allow him to realize the unity of understanding and perception, of the discursive and the intuitive? At this level, the best example of an integration capable of maintaining a unity with the necessary tension

---

28. "Reality = contact with a necessity" (OC VI.3 403 FLN 88).

between the terms is offered by music, thanks to rhythm, which unifies "the fast and the slow." "During the slow movement one continues to follow at the same time the fast movement, where they are put into a simple relation" (OC VI.3). It is this simplicity of relation that is necessary to discover in work, so that higher, intuitive attention may be possible. One needs to discover in the set of the worker's movements, the secret of rhythm, which give to the spectator "the impression of slowness, even through extreme rapidity" (OC II.2 296).

Rhythm, from this point of view, is the best illustration there is of a "composition on several planes, [which] is perhaps the key to all the arts" (OC VI.1 232). "A poet, in the arrangement of words and in the choice of each word, must simultaneously bear in mind matters on at least five or six different planes of composition" (NR 214). What is it that gives unity to the rules of versification according to the poem's form, to the grammatical and logical coordination of the words, to the rhythm, "formed by pauses, stops, duration of each syllable and of each group of syllables"? It is a "unique intuition for beauty" (NR 214). At this level, and at this level only, it is possible to comprehend that "[i]inspiration is a tension on the part of the soul's faculties which renders possible the indispensable degree of concentration required for composition on … multiple plane[s]" (Ibid.). Certainly, art is at a higher level. Nevertheless, other activities, in their own realm, can illustrate this conjunction of inspiration and method. Weil gives the example "of the union between the real sailor … and his boat, such that each order he gives comes from inspiration, without hesitation or uncertainty. This presupposes *a regime of attention* that is very different, both from reflection, and from concentrated work" (OC II.2 267). Such a union is the "condition of full happiness," Weil adds, for "it alone makes work into the equivalent of art" (OC.II.2 268). What are the conditions that might exist for such a union between the worker and his machine?

Of course, inspiration is, in a sense, "what *method* cannot give any account of"[29] (OC V.1 110). In effect, method supposes that thought is able to find universal relations of a sort between phenomena so that we are able to apply procedures that will give us results. In method, as in

---

29. "*Genius* can be defined by considerations of this type, all of them involve intuition, inspiration, etc. (as regards everything that is not accounted for by *method*.)" (OC VI.1 110) (FLN 37).

technique, there is an "adaptation of means to ends" (OC VI.3 278). For "authentic art is a finality without an end," which means that "authentic artistic technique is … transcendent technique," and this technique is "something other than inspiration" (Ibid.). One can say that in art, in a certain way, "there is only inspiration … for non-transcendent technique should not play any role,"[30] but one can say at the same time that "there is only technique, for the inspiration is in the technique" (OC VI.3 278). It is from the "transcendent technique," however, which is to say that which, in creating, comes from the genius that gives us rules of art in the place of following rules—as Kant has shown.

These principles, applied to work, signify that method can be called transcendent when inspiration has rendered the body penetrable by the mind, in an ensemble of coordinated movements that give the impression of being entirely natural. Then, in a sense, nothing is methodical, *apparently*, for method is overshadowed by inspiration. Yet, on the other hand everything is method, for the body is informed by the mind, but in such a way that it gives the impression that it is acting in immediacy—that is to say, precisely by inspiration, or by a spiritual sense that pervades it. Inspiration joined to method in work offers a model of what can be bodily aptitude joined to thinking that is capable of grasping intelligible relations. Such a conjunction would simply be *virtuosity*, an alliance of mastery and grace.

If a method that is at one and the same time both unitary and diversified in its applications could be realized, then workers and intellectuals could meet, "without any inequality, at the highest point, that of the fullness of attention that is the fullness of prayer" (LPW 139). The unity of a method does not prevent one from recognizing the same truth at different levels, it "does not prevent equality" (LPW 139). On the contrary, it assures a real equality between active individuals in different realms.

At the most elevated point and the most ideal one of her reflection on the material and social means of making work a spiritual activity, comes the need to conceive of new machines. The results of this research, which she began in 1935–36, are taken up again in *The Need for Roots*. Among the factors in reforming the means of production, the technical factor is

---

30. Non-transcendent technique does not play any role in the business of adapting means to end.

particularly important: "Speaking in general terms, a reform of an infinitely great social importance than all the measures arrayed under the title of Socialism would be a transformation in the very conception of technical research"[31] (NR 56). For example, "the relative ease with which energy can be transmitted in the form of electricity certainly makes a high degree of decentralization possible" (NR 55–56). With respect to the machines, they are still not even yet at the point where there is any real transformation of the means of production, "but the examples provided by adjustable automatic machines already in use would no doubt make it possible to effect such a transformation by dint of an effort, if the effort could only be made" (NR 56). After her experience in working in the factories, Weil remembered the interest that she had in the researches of the engineer, Jacques Lafitte.[32] She wrote to him in 1936: "It is necessary to have ... automatic and flexible machines. The type of machines that you call 'reflexive' allows us to envision such a possibility, it seems to me" (CO 259). What Weil holds out for, with respect to these "reflexive" machines, is the possibility that they offer, and that simply automatic ones do not, of introducing flexibility. The notion of flexibility witnesses to the possibility of the machine being modified according to variations coming from reflective and thought out activity, and exercised by the worker. The flexible machine would permit the perfecting of activity that depends on tools, while coming up with a technical object that is at one and the same time modifiable by a worker, and self-modifying. Human activity would be enriched by a relative reduction of operations due to the machine's capacity of modifying its own functioning in relation to its perception of the variations in the flux of the human activity that works the machine. The flexible machine would then be at one and the same time a tool which arms the human body, an instrument of perception, and a technical object capable of regulating its own functioning after receiving human input. Machines have, in history, congealed method in the technical objects, while separating out the thinking and perceiving individual.[33] A new way of thinking could be

---

31. See "Reflections on the Causes of Liberty" (OCII.2 108) as well as the response to Alain's letter, SL 3–6.

32. J. Lafitte is the author of *Réflexions sur la science des machines* (1932) (Paris: Vrin, 1972).

33. Among the procedures that are offered to the human being to produce more with less effort there is "the substitution of dead work for living work." It consists in "giving

associated with a new way of perceiving, even in a mode of production that depends on machines. That is, in the case that these machines are invented by the one who actually produces, and not by the laws that establish objective relations between things.

A Method for Reading the Past

How does one conceive, in these conditions, the education of a whole people? This conception, Weil answers, "should be that of a civilization." She goes on: "An educational method which is not inspired by the conception of a certain form of human perfection is not worth very much" (NR 216).

> It must not be sought in the past, which only contains imperfect models;[34] far less still in our dreams of the future, which are necessarily as mediocre as we ourselves are, and consequently vastly inferior to the past. The inspiration for such an education must be sought, like the method itself, among the truths eternally inscribed in the nature of things. (NR 216)

Let us observe that, in this realm more than in the others, the principles and applications of method have to be "invented."[35] Weil is not the sort of backwards-looking author that she is sometimes described as, one who looks for solutions to present problems by a return to the past. The past is a source of inspiration, but making the effort "of thinking out fundamental notions as if they were new things" is necessary, and "we today cannot stand aside from it, without creating a catastrophe" (OC VI.1 389). In her London writings, Weil several times appeals to "a creativity within the social fabric, an eruption of new inventions" (SWW 129).

---

over to matter what seems to be the role of human effort" (OC II.2 41). "Machinisme" is a step in this substitution. The last step comes with automation, where the principle "reside in the possibility of giving over to the machine not only an self-repeating operations, but also a bunch of varied operations" (OC II.2 42).

34. One should keep this passage in mind if one tries to invoke, without any accuracy, Simone Weil's "love of the past."

35. Weil often exhorts her reader in the London writings to "invention." See for example, "Are We Struggling for Justice?" (OC VI.1 246, 248), "The Legitimacy of a Provisional Government," (OC VI.1, 386 and 389) and "Essential Ideas for a New Constitution" (OC VI.1 429). In *The Need for Roots* see notably NR 216.

If it is not necessary to turn towards a past where one only finds the imperfect, it is also not necessary to look into the history that has been written by the conquerors, as she put it. In an attempt to construct a history of sovereignty, *The Need for Roots* elaborates a counter-history,[36] which extends from Greco-Roman antiquity up to the Third Republic, passing through the history of the monarchy and its degradation as well as through the birth of the State and its authority, illustrated by Louis XIV and Richelieu. The point of this counter-history is to reveal what the powerful have hidden, and to make new persons appear, namely, the conquered and those whom academic history has called the "barbarians." This counter-history, where Weil gives us an original reading of the past, has present goals: "In this almost desperate situation, all we can look to for encouragement here below is in those historical atolls of the living past left upon the surface of the earth" (NR 51). In trying to pry from the past some "signs," some "small significant things," some "survivals," or some "some still glowing embers" one can make an image of what would have been an authentic civilization appear, which is not a matter of opposing an imaginary history to the real one, but of showing that we can put our steps back into the traces of authentic civilizations. The originality of this method of reading the past is sensed in Weil's interpretation of inspired civilizations—Greece, India, Occitania. For example, Weil looked behind even Plato's work to find a Pythagorean inspiration, a mystical one, according to her. She argues that "Plato, in his age, was a survival of an already far distant past" (NR 293). With respect to the Greek Stoics, there was a "flame from a still-living spark belonging to that same past" (NR 293). She admits, of course, that there is something hypothetical about this past when she affirms, for example, that we badly understand the penal character of work in the *Genesis* story, saying that it is necessary to admit that "[i]t is more likely that it was handed down by some very ancient civilization in which physical labour was honoured above every other activity" (NR 292). She is always looking under what history has transmitted to us for some kind of trace, invisible to the inattentive mind, for an inspiration. This is not backward looking. With respect to the past, it is necessary to seek out what is eternally and

---

36. This counter-history was used by Weil before *The Need for Roots* in her articles on Hitlerism and ancient Rome and in her essays on Occitania (OC II.3, 168–219, OC IV.2 403–424).

universal of value. In place of "lov[ing] the historical wrapper of the past" (NR 230) we ought to look for what can inspire the education of a whole people "among the truths eternally truths inscribed in the nature of things" (NR 216) sometimes in a subtle way,[37] but nevertheless always valuable.

One will not understand the effort of invention of a spiritual politics in *The Need for Roots* if one has not kept in mind these elements of Weil's counter-history, which, upon first reading, can be very disconcerting. It is on the basis of this reconstruction of the past that Weil tries to give to spirituality its proper function, namely, "of suffuse[ing] with its light all of secular life, public or private, without ever in any way dominating it"[38] (NR 118). Weil studied these inspired civilizations in her unique perspective, less as a history to be known through the course of its temporal events than as "a model" to imitate, being understood, as Plato did, as a "model that always signifies inspiration" (OC VI. 3 50) (NB 374). It is a question of imitating the model in order to create the conditions which will allow an authentic and eternal inspiration to descend. Here is where all the interest in method appears. Spiritual discernment is a rare thing;[39] one cannot hope that someday a society of sages and saints will arise. Failing that, spiritual discernment is then a human means of finding some higher principles that are capable of guiding us towards a renewal of civilization, and the means to that is a type of history that is written as a counter-history. It is a question of rejecting every notion of a progress that ends up invalidating the past; it is necessary that a counter history refuses both a theodicy and a view of providential design that is supposed to have been realized, despite all appearances to the contrary, claiming that good comes out of evil.[40] A counter-history, paradoxically,

---

37. Weil thus observes that with regard to France's history, that "it is necessary to love the mute part, the anonymous, the lost" (OC V.2 297).

38. In the *Notebooks*, the warning is equally explicit: "Social problem. To keep to a minimum the indispensable supernatural part in order to give breathing space to social life. All that tends to increase it is bad" (OC VI.2 418) (NB 296).

39. "Some do not have any faith; others have faith only in a single religion and do not give other religions any sort of attention except that which one gives give to strange marine life. Still others believe themselves capable of impartiality because they have a vague religiosity that they indifferently spin out no matter where" (OC IV.1 316).

40. Christine Ann Evans has well demonstrated how Weil opposed both usages in the history of France: one which, from Léon Blum to Charles de Gaulle, passing by Marc Bloch, tried in its interpretation of the debacle of 1940 to "safeguard a certain version of

denies temporal values which do nothing. What is valuable remains outside time, like a Platonic Idea. Time and history alter, corrupt, and destroy the Good more often than they realize it. Such is the revision of the
historic method proposed and practiced in *The Need for Roots*. For example, Weil recognizes that a civilization such as that of twelfth-century
Toulouse has not left many traces; the song of the crusader against the
Albigensians, "some troubadour songs, some rare texts about the Cathars and some marvelous churches" (OC IV.2 405). The historian is
powerless here. However, if one looks into these vestiges that remain
alive despite their near destruction by armed violence, one will discern
an authentic civilization, "romanesque civilization," a "true Christian
civilization," as opposed to the "totalitarian spirituality" of the Gothic
Middle Ages (OCIV.2 419). The application of a method of mental ex-
perimentation allows us to put forward a Christian civilization that
"would only have been possible if the Roman conception of enslaving
people's minds adopted by the Church had been cast aside"[41] (NR 294).

One will find another example, one that is significant for the way in
which it shows how a counter-history is capable of revealing the sources
of actual evils in the reversal of the pair "civilization" and "barbarism."
"The barbarians, in their plunderings, have never committed more than
limited evils.... Only an extremely civilized state, but civilized with low
values ... like Rome, can bring about to those they menace and those
whom they subdue this moral decomposition that ... breaks ... defini-
tively the continuity in the spiritual life" (OC II.3 224). Thus she guesses
that Christianity could never have become "the principle of an original
civilization until after the fortunate invasion of those who are called barbarians" (OC II.3 209). It is "the barbarian heritage ... mingled with the
Christian spirit," but "between the spirit of Rome and that of Christ

---

the telling of French history," which was a matter of "the holy history of the Republic"
where a sense of French history dominated, through defeats and mistakes, by the immen-
sity of its merits and virtues. The other is the one told by the ideologues of Vichy and all
the adversaries of the Republic who wanted to dismantle this version of history, to liqui-
date the past, and make of the debacle a blow of expected grace, the foundation of a
"national revolution." ("La débâcle vue pas Simone Weil et ses contemporains" *Cahiers
Simone Weil*, vol. XXXIV, no. 2 (Juin 2011), 167–182).

41. Weil asked herself, for example, what would have happened if the Occitanian
civilization had survived: it would have, perhaps with time, "reached a degree of spiritual
liberty and fecundity as elevated as that of ancient Greece, if only it wasn't killed" (OC
IV.2 407–408).

there has never been any fusion" (NR 141). From this Weil draws out a counter-history of the Church. The pagan virtue of patriotism found in ancient Rome was passed on but never baptized,[42] but the Church needed, for reasons of temporal domination, the Roman conception of God, and it is the power of the Church that, by the crusade against the Albigensians, demolished forever a conception of the world which gave hope for an authentic Christian civilization.[43] This helps us to understand something characteristic about the Weilian method: the Church's past screens out the authentic inspiration of a civilization whose traces only exist among the heretics.

Conclusion

In conclusion, let us observe that ever since *Reflections on the Causes of Liberty and Social Oppression*, Weil made a distinction between "methodical ... action" and "action in accordance with method":

> The difference is capital; for he who applies method has no need to conceive it in his mind at the moment he is applying it. Indeed, if it is a question of something complicated, he is unable to, even should he have elaborated it himself; for the attention, always forced to concentrate itself on the actual moment of execution, cannot embrace at the same time the series of relationships on which execution as a whole depends. (OL 92)

Method ought not to be confused with an abstract schema applicable under the form of a simple execution, which would make it a "formula resulting from mere routine" (OL92). *The Need for Roots* offers a range of suggestion relative to the *invention* of a method which may be at one and the same time unique and universal without being a recipe; a method whose principle does not yield a routine and uniform application but an adaptation proper to each realm and each level: education,

---

42. See OC.V.2 141.

43. There should have been a Christian civilization. We see promises of it appearing in the eleventh and twelfth centuries. The countries of the south of the Loire, which were the principal places of this shining, were inspired with both Christian and ancient spirituality. (OC V.2 361).

action, and knowledge, whether that is scientific or supernatural. This is
what Weil wants to say in a formula that we have already cited that con-
tradicts only in appearance the idea of a unique and universal method:
"The method merely differs according to the different sphere" (NR 186).
This observation means that is no domain that is beyond method: "Everything in creation is dependent on method" (NR 186). It is necessary
in each case to test both logical mastery and inspiration. All method is
above all a *tension* between distant and even incompatible elements. The
differences and the contradictions exist for the discursive faculties, for
the intelligence, but using the different and the contradictory well raises
the mind and confirms its mastery of the real.

In the end, Weil stresses the importance of method in studying the
manifestations of the supernatural here below, at the level of human society,[44] at the "points of intersection between this world and the next"
(NR 186). Speaking truly, "from remote antiquity, long before Christianity, right up to the latter half of the Renaissance, it was always universally
recognized that there is a method to be followed in spiritual matters and
in everything connected with the soul's welfare" (NR 186). It is only
since human beings began exercising a more and more methodical and
effective hold on matter, thanks to the physical sciences, that they have
come to believe "by way of contrast, that the things of the soul are either
arbitrary or else bound up with some form of magic, with the immediate
efficacy of intentions and words" (NR 186). Yet, "it isn't this way at all"
Weil contests. Notably, "those who believe that the supernatural, by definition, operates in a random way and is beyond all study, misunderstand
it just as those who deny its reality" (OC V.1 609). There is nothing in
reality, natural or supernatural, where there is a "loosening of the chains
of necessity" (OC VI.4 83). It is quite the contrary, for "the logic of supernatural reason is more rigorous than that of natural reason" (OC VI.1
139). Thus "the authentic mystics, like St. John of the Cross, describe the
operation of grace on the soul with the precision of a chemist or a geol-
ogist" (OC V.1 609). So, Weil stakes out an essential and urgent task for
herself: "Make a logic of the absurd. Define as far as possible the criterion of the true and false in the transcendent realm where contradiction
has its place, the realm of mystery. It is necessary that there be more

---

44. See below, note 47.

rigor in this realm than in mathematics. A new rigor that our time has no idea of" (OC VI.4 87).

Natural reality, the supernatural, the points of intersection between this world and the other one, the mechanisms that determine the things of the soul—nothing escapes this method. Wouldn't it be "quite strange" that the order "of material things," because it is manifestly more accessible to a method, the scientific method to be precise, "were to reflect more of divine wisdom than that of spiritual things"? (NR 187). By elaborating a logic of the supernatural one would realize that the contrary is true. More generally, is there only a reason for one of the realms or levels of the real and the other escapes the divine wisdom? What is at stake in the invention of a method and its right use is major, and it is that of how to read the order of the world in its relation to a reality situated outside the world. It is a question of the order of the world. "All that differs is the type of concentration demanded, according to whether one tries to conceive the necessary relations which go to make it up or to contemplate its splendour" (NR 291). For science, just as for art, "the order of the world is the same as the beauty of the world" (NR 291), for there is a beauty in necessary relations.[45] With respect to the ensemble of things which constitute this world, and together with the reality outside this world, and the points of intersection between them, it is necessary to say: "It is one and the same thing, which with respect to God is eternal Wisdom; with respect to the universe, perfect obedience; with respect to our love, beauty; with respect to our intelligence, balance of necessary relations; with respect to our flesh, brute force"[46] (NR 291). We have lost this unity. We need to restore it, with the means of our own time, most notably science. For science is "an effort to take in the order of the universe, it follows that it is a contact of human thought with eternal necessity" (OC V.2 390). We have forgotten what the pre-Christian ancients

---

45. Weil gives as an example of supreme beauty "the effect of gravity on sea waves as they flow in ever-changing folds, or the almost eternal folds of the mountains" (SWW 50). She argues that "[t]he sea is not less beautiful in our eyes because we know that ships are sometimes wrecked.... If it altered the movement of its waves to spare a ship it would be a creature gifted with discernment and choice, and not this fluid perfectly obedient to every external pressure. It is perfect obedience which makes the sea's beauty" (SWW 50).

46. One should compare this very dense passage with "The Love of God and Affliction" (OC. IV.1 354 and 363).

knew, namely, that "inert matter, by its submission to necessity, gives human beings the example of obedience to God" (OC V.2 390).

Finally, the search for a method has but a single goal: "To allow us to embrace in a single act of mind science as the investigation of the beauty of the world, art as the imitation of the beauty of the world, justice as the equivalent of the beauty of the world in human matters, and love towards God in that he is the author of the beauty of the world"[47] (OC.V.2 390). Method needs to set as its task giving life back to this unity lost for so long. That is to say, that only the invention of a method can save us:

> It is unfortunate for us that this problem, in regard to which, unless I am wrong, we have nothing we can look to for guidance, should be precisely the one that requires today the most urgent solution on our part, under pain not so much of disappearing altogether as of never having really existed. (NR 187)

Translated by Eric O. Springsted

---

47. Without forgetting that a "science of religions" itself—something that has not yet begun—would reveal a similar method, in the measure where it is a question of the "science of the supernatural in its diverse manifestations across diverse human societies." (OC VI.2 323). This science would have for its object the points of intersection between the supernatural reality and that of this world. *The Need for Roots* realizes in part this project, with respect to French society, and it is not an accident if Weil's essay tells us something about the use of this method in all realms.

CHAPTER 7

What Is Greatness?—
On *Reading* the Past

Ronald K. L. Collins

Imposing one's will on time, people, or even nature itself is the mark of greatness. That dictum, exalted by many historians in various ways, is the problem with both our notions of greatness and our conceptions of history. For Simone Weil, it equated greatness with its opposite—a *false* sense of reality, one beholden to a grandiose sense of State (NR 114) and self. Moreover, that mindset was willfully oblivious to the workings of the world and the sufferings and sanctity of those in it.

The notion of greatness preoccupied Weil's thought in *The Need for Roots* (NR 97, 167, 171–172, 216, 217, 223–225, 230, 235, 252, 253, 257), among other places. It was also a notion linked to her more general concerns about language, about ways of using "words to answer ... the secret thoughts and needs of ... human beings" (NR 194). Likewise, her notion of history was concerned with how we comprehend the past with due attention to its evils as well as its cultural and spiritual values (NR 51, 52, 221–222, 228–229).

For Weil, the question of greatness was also part of a larger argument about what prevents us from becoming a worthy civilization, which pointed to a related argument about how to *inspire* a people. Moreover, to understand Weil's idea of the growing of roots it is useful to have some grasp of just how she conceived of greatness and history. As we will see

in the next two chapters (on method and the spirit of truth), by analyzing her notions of greatness and history we stand to get a clearer picture
of Weil's vision for a reconstituted France, one in which rootedness
might return, at least in some forms.

Introduction

The fall of France, between early May and late June of 1940, incensed
Weil. She viewed the collapse "as an act of negligence, an abdication on
the part of the entire nation—the culmination of a long process of de-
cay."[1] As she wrote in a 1942 letter to Jean Wahl: "I was dismayed … by
the news of the armistice.… There was a collective act of cowardice and
treason, namely the armistice; and the whole nation bears responsibility
for it" (SL 157, 158). And while in London in 1943 she reflected again on
the matter: "The macabre comedy that put an end to the Third Republic
took place in Vichy in July, and the abolition of the government did not
cause a tinge of regret, pain, or anger in the hearts of the French.…
There was total indifference."[2]

France's fall, however, did have one redemptive aspect: it pointed to
the possibility of a reconstituted nation. That prospect opened an inspirational door for Weil, one that led to what became *The Need for Roots*.
For France to reconstitute itself, what would be required? Culturally,
politically, and spiritually speaking, what did that presuppose? What
were the lessons of history, properly understood, and what did they
teach the French about their nation's future identity?[3] To answer such
questions, Weil had to address several other ones, including issues related to France's own idea of its greatness and history. And it was just
that idea that Weil thought was false and contaminated, and dangerously
so. But why? After all, if France survived the Nazis, could it not then
reclaim its greatness and thereby once again celebrate its history? For
Weil, that was the problem, one she hoped to remedy.

---

1. Athanasios Moulakis, *Simone Weil and the Politics of Self-Denial*, Ruth Hein, trans.
(Columbia, MO: University of Missouri Press, 1998), 178–179 (citing EL 60).

2. *Ibid.*, 180 (citing EL 60).

3. See Christine Ann Evans, "The Nature of Narrative in Simone Weil's Vision of
History: The Need for New Historical Roots," in John Dunaway & Eric Springsted, eds.,
The Beauty That Saves (Macon: GA: Mercer University Press, 1996), 56.

"The Most Serious Defect"

"Our conception of greatness is the most serious defect of all, and the one which we are least conscious that it is a defect: at least a defect in ourselves" (NR 217). At first blush it seems odd: Weil's linking of a "conception of greatness" to "ourselves." By "ourselves," however, she may well have been referring to France. That is, she was raising the issue of the French conception of greatness. This claim might, of course, be generalized more broadly, but in the first place it is France. In context, the French had long thought of themselves as the "great" victors. But when the Vichy government came to power, the tables were turned—it was so un-French and so un-glorious. But, she goes on, the French think of themselves as always being the victors. So, when the Germans took over, everybody just figured they had made a mistake about which side was which, and so, thinking that France never loses, they easily took the side of the Germans. That said, let us inquire further into this "most serious defect" and what it means.

There is a passage in *The Need for Roots* in which Weil associates the quest for greatness with Adolf Hitler, albeit the man in his youth: "Let us imagine for a moment [a] wretched, uprooted youth wandering about in the streets of Vienna, [with] a thirst for greatness. It well became him to [have] a thirst for greatness. Was it his fault if he was unable to perceive any form of greatness except the criminal form?" (NR 223). Note that while young Hitler is described as "wretched," Weil raises a question as to his culpability. Why?

On the one hand, this drive for greatness, of the utterly ruthless variety, might be explained by Hitler's youthful fascination with a "tenth-rate" biography of Sulla, a Roman general who won the first large-scale civil war in Roman history (NR 223). On the other hand, note the association of greatness with war *and* with what the latter implies in Weilian thinking. That something is *force*, a key concept in Weil's philosophy. "Force is not a machine for automatically creating justice," Weil wrote, though even force is subject to the laws of limit (NR 284, 288–290). "It is a blind mechanism which produces indiscriminately and impartially just or unjust results, but, by all laws of probability, nearly always unjust ones" (NR 240).

Force is a multifaceted concept that operates within a wide range: from the murderous dehumanizing power waged in war to that subjugation exercised over others in the collective, political, and economic spheres. Think of it as a mode of social domination, a relationship with others defined by the invocation of authority without meaningful consent. There is no consent because we do not *read* others as humans and thus do not treat them as such. Rather, by nature, force governs the relational dynamic. For Weil, force was the key criterion by which we measure and admire greatness.

Where force is the domain the *other* ceases to be a person and instead is treated as a thing, a way to acquire power and pleasure. What matters is what is *perceived* rather than the actual person. When linked to force, perception thus has a transformative psychological power insofar as it trades the reality of a living person for that of an exploited image of that person, one that can be manipulated and even murdered. In the process, people become one's personal property. As discussed in Chapter 1 of this book, our power over others is thus seen as a right; hence, we have no obligation to treat them as persons worthy of our attention and respect. Owing to the "empire of force" (IC 53),[4] Weil "strove to find strategies, [both practical and philosophical,] by which such destructive readings [of people] could be resisted or reversed."[5] In important part, that explains some of her main concerns about how greatness and history are perceived.

Weil's conception of *false* greatness was also informed by her views of the *collective* and how it shapes the minds of the multitude (NR 25–26, 63, 190). At the same time in 1943 when she was busy crafting what would become *The Need for Roots*, Weil warned of the danger of collective influence, what she labeled "the social poison [that] permeates all men's thoughts without exception" (OL 180–182, 192).[6] Fragments from her London writings of this time reveal, quite clearly, the link Weil saw between force and the collective (OL, 165). It is precisely that link that will also figure into her analysis of the traditional ideas of greatness.

Mindful of such matters, consider the following passage: "Our conception of greatness is the very one which has inspired Hitler's whole

---

4. See E. Jane Doering, *Simone Weil and the Specter of Self-Perpetuating Force* (Notre Dame, IN: University of Notre Dame Press, 2010), 41–68.

5. Alexander Irwin, *Saints of the Impossible: Bataille, Weil, and the Politics of the Sacred* (Minneapolis: MN: University of Minnesota Press, 2002), 42.

6. In her "Theoretical Picture of a Free Society" Weil had earlier expressed concerns about the collective and its influence on people. See e.g., OL 97, 98, 145.

life. When we denounce it without the remotest recognition of its application to ourselves, the angels must either cry or laugh" (NR 217). Judged by what Weil says here, the evil that is truly Hitler is not aberrational. Rather, and as Larry Schmidt pointed out earlier, "Weil argued that Hitler's emergence as a national leader should be considered as continuous (and consistent) with the values of Western civilization" (Chapter 5). "The appetite for power, even for universal power," wrote Weil, "is only insane when there is no possibility of indulging it."[7] But that possibility had long been alive and well in Europe. Moreover, the way Hitler rose to power was with the endorsement of the collective, whose propaganda he promulgated, and they perpetuated (NR 223). His "greatness" inspired them; it was a horrific example of ill-conceived greatness. To believe otherwise, to think that the traditional idea of greatness (the same idea that made France "great") could be separated from force leaves the angels with no alternative but to "cry or laugh."

It is important to appreciate the radicality of Weil's thought here. What is at play in Weil's philosophical enterprise is nothing short of the "total transformation" (NR 224) of our notions of greatness and the utter "disruption" of how we comprehend history.[8] Whereas historians claim to seek objectivity—a claim Weil contested—her theory of history, by contrast, had a normative side. It injected *morality* into the conceptual equation. Her mission was to create "a central place of moral analysis in historiography."[9] The latter exemplified her transition from a critical notion of greatness (false greatness, that is) to her embrace of a transformative understanding of greatness, one with spiritual import.

Furthermore, Weil's realist notion of history was not one of God triumphing over evil, or righteousness prevailing over wickedness, or one that chronologically progresses toward enlightenment or greater humanity.[10] She was too sober (nay cynical?[11]) to place any stock in such

7. Quoted in Simone Pétrement, *Simone Weil: A Life* (New York: Pantheon Books, 1976), 511.

8. Bennett Gilbert, "Simone Weil's Philosophy of History," *Journal of the Philosophy of History*, vol. 13 (2019), 66, 71, 72.

9. *Ibid.*, 68.

10. "We must get rid of our superstition of chronology in order to find Eternity" (LP 29).

11. "Some commentators have argued that such a pervasive, undifferentiated notion of force must lead to a paralyzing cynicism, if not to a kind of paranoia." Irwin, *Saints of the Impossible*, 57.

wishful, though commonplace, thinking. To rewrite history required *re-thinking* how we live in history, how we exist in the face of the forces that define it, and what we as a nation aspire towards. True to Weil's philosophical penchant, this was another way of saying that thought must work in tandem with action, and vice-versa—philosophy requires labor!

With that primer (philosophical, psychological, political, anthropological, and scientific) on the pursuit of greatness, let us unravel some basic ideas about greatness writ large, especially when it is grounded in force. Once we have explored that domain, we will be better situated to comprehend Weil's critique of greatness and her reconceptualization of history. We may then consider how all this fits into the larger scheme of her thought as set out in *The Need for Roots*.

On Greatness:
Contexts and Categories

In her *Notebooks* Weil referred to the "The Valiant Little Tailor" (N, 23; SWW, 83). Early on, this Grimm brothers' fairy tale provided a lens through which to view greatness. The little tailor is a story of false greatness, both as perceived by the tailor and those who came to venerate him. When some flies swarmed onto his jam the tailor became enraged and swatted them, killing seven in a single swoop. Delighted by his feat, he said to himself: "You're quite a man!... The entire city should know about this!" To that end, he made a belt to memorialize his greatness; on it he inscribed the words "Seven at One Blow." He then went out into the world to seek his fame. Owing to others misreading his words (i.e., "seven *men* at one blow") and his subsequent trickery, he came to be seen as great. Weil viewed this tale as an example of how greatness is what we admire—and how we foolishly admire the wrong things. But how does this happen? To answer that question, it may be useful to frame what follows by way of an overview of how we think of *greatness* itself.

Context: The idea and language of greatness move in time—present and past tenses. When the notion of greatness finds expression in real time it may be akin to *popularity*, though it is more than that. While both terms involve some fostering of popular favor, the way we often speak of greatness suggests that it has a wider and more serious connotation.

Thus, while the actor Zarah Leander (1907–1981) was wildly popular in Nazi Germany between 1936 and 1943, no one would give up their life for her as they did for the Führer.

Categories. We might also think of greatness in terms of the class or category of persons to which the term is applied. For example: Plato was a great philosopher, or Michelangelo's Sistine Chapel (aka the "Great Chapel") was a great artistic achievement, or Caligula was a great leader, or Diego Maradona is the greatest soccer player of all time.

Power: The Caligula example suggests the importance of *conquest*, *power*, and *dominion* in the political realm. "The unhappy peoples of the European continent," Weil wrote, "are in need of greatness even more than that of bread, and there are only two sorts of greatness: true greatness, which is of a spiritual order, and the old, old lie of world conquest. Conquest is an *ersatz* of greatness" (NR 97). By Weil's calculus, the France of her day would "have to choose between attachment to her [colonial] empire and the need once more to have a soul" (SWC 124). That is, "she must choose between a soul and the Roman … sense of greatness" (NR 145–146).

The Nation State: The idea of greatness is often thought of in *national* terms. At the outset, it would be helpful to note Weil's assessment:

- "To posit one's country as an absolute value that cannot be defiled by evil is manifestly absurd."
- To speak in terms of "'eternal France' is "a sort of blasphemy."
- More importantly, a "nation is a fact, and a fact is not an absolute value." Though there may be things of value in a state, the State qua State is not absolute.
- By definition, she added, it is a domain where "good and evil are always mingled with one another" (NR 130).

Given that, while a nation-state may lay claim to greatness, it does so in oppressive ways. For example, some would herald nineteenth-century Britain, where the new industrialism gave birth to venture capitalism, as a great nation. The same might be said of the United States and its unrestrained version of capitalism, dating from its eighteenth-century birth through its twenty-first-century manifestation. Though she clearly had serious reservations about the grandiose promises of Marxism, Weil was horrified by the excesses of capitalism: "Capitalism and totalitarianism form part of [the] progressive development of uprooting" (N, II, 575). The question of capitalism also gives rise to the notion of *entrepreneurial greatness*. Take the fifteenth-century Portuguese entrepreneurs who made trading in slaves both a business and the key element of economic progress[12] or the nineteenth-century "robber barons"[13] of the "Gilded Age," those who traded in unchecked greed, corruption, and monopoly.

What is at issue here is the relationship between greatness and *oppression*. When a leader, nation, or economic system pursues power in furtherance of some grand objective, what are the human costs of such pursuits? What are the costs of the vestiges of exploitation? This holds as true for ruthless despotism, illusory Marxism, and runaway capitalism. For Weil, oppression did more than rule a person; it transformed that person into an object, a subhuman thing. To place greatness on the altar of human suffering is to commit a crime against humankind.

Measuring Greatness: From Critical to Transformative Notions

In some important respects, Weil is the critic par excellence of modernity. Her outsider perspective is well at work in *The Need for Roots* and informs much of her thinking on greatness, albeit *false* greatness. Thus, J.P. Little has recently observed: "Most of Simone Weil's reflections on [greatness] turn the notion of greatness on its head, to such an extent that in history, religion, politics, where greatness is recognized in a 'normal' sense, this is taken as proof by Simone Weil that the phenomenon at issue is in fact suspect, if not completely debased."[14] But why?

Think of what she is saying: the "normal" is "debased." And this is so across a wide spectrum, from religion to politics, and from history to science. The problem is where we default; that is, we live and operate within the realm of *necessity* where the laws of *force* often triumph over

---

12. See Howard W. French, *Born in Blackness: Africa, Africans, and the Making of the Modern World, 1471 to the Second World War* (New York: Liveright, 2021), 66–110.

13. See Matthew Josephson, *The Robber Barons: The Classic Account of the Influential Capitalists Who Transformed America's Future* (New York: Harvest Book, 1962).

14. J.P. Little, "Weil's Single-Minded Commitment to Truth: A Q & A Interview with J. P. Little," *Attention*, no. 2 https://attentionsw.org/weils-single-minded-commitment-to-truth-a-q-a-interview-with-j-p-little/.

justice. Of course, if one were to say that "Joseph Stalin and Adolf Hitler[15] were great men" (or Idi Amin and Muammar Gaddafi), there might be some legitimate pause. That pause suggests there is something awkward about speaking thusly; yet we do speak that way. Even so, that linguistic hesitation indicates that there is a *conceptual* problem here. That problem in turn points to a *normative* one, namely, that something is disquieting about equating greatness with evil. Then again, what if upon closer examination we came to realize that what disquiets us is the predictable outcome of our own collective will?—that evil originates not merely with evil men but with those who make their evil possible. Of course, in speaking of greatness the mind may skip over the moral problem of placing greatness and evil in the same conceptual camp. Here again, that may well prove to be predictable. Nonetheless, that leap troubled Simone Weil, if only because how we speak influences how we think.

What is also at play here is a *sociology of evil* (NR 203, 240). That is, how does evil, when executed on a grand scale, come into existence? Furthermore, the *psychology of evil* (NR 223) is inexorably linked to the latter insofar as it takes its mental cue from it in pursuit of a kind of greatness tied to evil. This evil flattens all states of the psyche "without concern for value, as if good and evil were external to them, as if the effort towards the good could be absent at any moment from the thought of a human being" (LPW 154; SNL 168). Perhaps this is what Weil was driving at when she wrote: "Let us imagine for a moment that [a] wretched, uprooted youth wandering about in the streets a Vienna, [had] a thirst for greatness. Was it his fault if he was unable to perceive any form of greatness except the criminal form?" (NR 223). Notice that she asks: *Was it his fault?* To raise the question is to suggest a connection between the psychology of evil and the sociology of evil—a behaviorist sort of connection as to how language, and its influence, operate at a collective plane in ways that shape individual thought and action.

Plato's metaphor of the "Great Beast" (*Republic*, bk VI, 493-a-b; NB, II, 481) speaks to that question, of how the words and will of the multitude come to invite the acts of those who seek power and greatness by

---

15. Hitler is mentioned by name no fewer than 37 times in *The Need for Roots*. See also Weil's "Observations Concerning the Essay on Hitler," and her "Reflections on the Origins of Hitlerism" (SE 89–140) and Pétrement, *Simone Weil*, 511.

whatever means. Consideration of that relationship, a complex one, re-surfaces time and again in Weil's writings. This is all the more important when one realizes that the young man to whom she was referring as that "uprooted youth" was Adolf Hitler. As the last quote reveals, Hitler's evil was too often tied to conceptions of greatness. Again Weil:

> People talk about punishing Hitler. But he cannot be pun-ished. He desired one thing alone, and he has it; to play a part in History. He can be killed, tortured, imprisoned, humiliated, [but] History will always be there to shield his spirit from all the ravages of suffering and death.... [F]or the idolizer of His-tory, everything connected with History must be good [mean-ing desirable]. (NR 224)

True, a strongman may be judged mercilessly in time, but historians nonetheless give him a place, even a large one, in the annals of history.

* * * *

"How can we be great if we can't even be good?"[16] A trial lawyer might respond to Professor Wampole's question by saying: "Madame assumes facts not in evidence." In other words, her question presupposes a con-nection between greatness and goodness. But what if one were to chal-lenge that assumption, or even deny it? Surely, much in our common language links greatness with evil. Likewise, many a historian has seen fit to declare evil rulers to be great men. To begin to answer Wampole's question, one must ask another one: Why is greatness valued?

Admiration is one answer. Thus, we deem the likes of Rosa Parks or Nelson Mandela great because we admire them; their humanity inspires us, and it awakens a spirit of justice within us. But there are other rea-sons why traditional notions of greatness are routinely valued, as in the case of Winston Churchill. Quite apart from whether he is admired, he is considered great because he did extraordinary things in exceptionally difficult circumstances. To that point, consider the case of Friedrich Ni-etzsche. Even if one deemed the man and his philosophy evil, it would be difficult to imagine any list of "great philosophers" that excluded Ni-etzsche, at least as he is accepted today. Something of the same could be

---

16. Christine Wampole, "Simone Weil for Americans," *Los Angeles Review of Books* (April 26, 2021).

said of the likes of Caligula (the demigod of antiquity) and Stalin (an infamous figure of modernity). That we do not admire them would not, if only as a matter of common language and historical practice, disqualify them from being deemed great.

To continue: If Weil's objective was to delink the idea of greatness from evil and/or collective idolatry, and instead link it with justice and something *spiritually* transformative, then what word would one use in referring to the Caligulas and Stalins of the past? If we infused the word "greatness" with some negative connotation, would that be enough to defeat that criminal "thirst" that so concerned Weil? Consider this: Even if the young Hitler was fully aware that Caligula and Cortés were murderous, greedy, and evil, might he nonetheless desire such "greatness"? If the answer is yes, that may have much to do with the ego, the human desire to be *widely noticed* and *widely remembered* for bold acts, even if evil. Here, unlike Plato's *Republic* (Bk. II, 352a–362a), what is sought is not the appearance of justice but precisely its opposite, the appearance of evil, albeit actualized today in the person of Vladimir Putin. Of course, when the collective legitimates such evil, it thereby normalizes it and thereafter glorifies it. Thus operates the psychology of evil. That psychology works in a two-dimensional way: on the one hand, there is the desire for fame and collective approval in one's lifetime, and on the other hand, there is the desire for posthumous remembrance be it good or evil. In both instances, of course, it is the ego that must be placated first and foremost.

＊ ＊ ＊ ＊

The idea that the crown of greatness could attach to evils of momentous enormity and that historians could thereby legitimate them by that conceptual standard infuriated Weil. Greatness and evil ought not to be synonymous; the linking of the two ought not "escape the scrutiny of the mind. If they escape such scrutiny, how could they be scrutinized, however hard one were to try?" (NR 219). Hence, any attempt to remedy this problem required a significant reconsideration of how we speak and think about greatness—a *transformative* change. That call for a change in thinking was integral to Weil's "method for breathing … inspiration" (NR 185) into the souls of those fighting for France and its future. As with so much else in her thought, hers was a radical idea but one with a powerful critique of accepted conventions combined with an aspirational counter-objective.

"Greatness," when associated, as it often is, with power in the political realm comes at a certain price even before the heavy hand of oppression presents itself. The price is winning the support of some critical mass of the public, by whatever means. As Hitler once told a British correspondent in June of 1934: "At the risk of appearing to talk nonsense, I tell you that the National Socialist movement will go on for 1,000 years! ... Don't forget how people laughed at me 15 years ago when I declared that one day I would govern Germany. They laugh now, just as foolishly, when I declare that I shall remain in power!"[17] That movement took time and propaganda to build; it took appealing to the masses, albeit in the basest of forms.

Greatness Unbound?

"More!" That could be the mantra of modernity, at the very least in advanced capitalist nations. In matters both political and personal, there can never be enough ... power, money, land, leisure, consumption, or scientific invention. *"Modern life is given over to excess"* is how Weil characterized it. "Everything is steeped in it," she added—"there is no more equilibrium anywhere" (FLN 50). In the political domain, greatness is often associated with this principle of excess; it energizes the pursuit of power. Thus, the more power one amasses, the greater the likelihood that a person will be deemed great. The same holds true for conquering or colonizing nations. Such power implies sovereignty over others, the ability to dominate them even without their free and knowing consent. When that occurs, when force reigns, the relationship (between individuals, a ruler and the ruled, and between nations) is altered dramatically, so much so that we deem it authoritarian—that is to say unjust. One reason it is so is because the balance of power has become imbalanced.

---

17. "Germany, Second Revolution," *Time*, (July 1934), reproduced in "Hitler Caricature," *Chicago Sentinel* (1934). In a 2023 paper delivered at the American Weil Association's annual colloquy, Mac Loftin tellingly observed: "The French might look in horror on Hitler's conquest of Europe, but as soon as they turn their eyes to the past, to Alexander the Great or Christopher Columbus, or as soon as they look abroad to their own colonies, suddenly they bow down in servile admiration to men of conquest and domination. Weil bitterly jokes that Hitler might actually be the most morally upright European—he shares everybody else's idea of greatness, but unlike everybody else he has the courage to try and achieve it" (unpublished paper).

A real (or just) balance of power is rooted in the notion of equality in which there is a certain *equilibrium* of power (SNL 79).

The idea of equilibrium is key to Weil's political and spiritual thinking; it constitutes what she deemed a just balance (NB 202). The wills of two persons or two nations do not coincide where there is an imbalance of power, as between the strong and the weak. Thus, when the Athenians gave the Melians (allies of Sparta) a choice between submission or destruction, the edict was "natural" in the sense that since there was no equality (albeit no proportion) there could be no justice between them (IC 174). Part of this proportionality formula of justice is the idea of *consent*, which defines the relationship between individuals. The more consent is absent, the more unjust a regime or ruler will be out of balance. Hence, the measure is both the means and ends; it represents that division of power, that organization of the social *order*, upon which justice depends. Force, by stark contrast, transforms that order; it redefines the relations between persons; it thus yields to no measure other than greater force. When force delimits the relational equation, there is no longer a connection between humans, there is only the strong treating the weak as inert matter. Power, thus exercised, does not attempt to understand or even recognize the existence of others save for their ability to serve power. Slavery—supreme servitude—exemplifies this. Inextricably connected to this concept is the perception of people as subhuman and even expendable after their servitude has performed its purpose—mass-scale annihilation thus becomes a predictable result along with the centuries of monetary profit grounded in such evils.

To return more directly to the notion of greatness: when Caligula and Hitler are deemed great when school children learn this, a profound injustice is committed. Such a notion "contains little or no awareness of limits and seeks to expand domination as far as possible."[18] A tyrant, intoxicated with his power, knows no limit, seeks no limit, and thereby acts as if this illusion of absolute power rendered him God-like. By his gauge, neither the laws of the land nor the laws of necessity constrain him—*more* is his mantra.

Weil read Hitler's *Mein Kampf* (1925–26), a work she quoted from in *The Need for Roots*:

---

18. Vance G. Morgan, *Weaving the World Simone Weil on Science, Mathematics, and Love* (Notre Dame, IN: University of Notre Dame Press, 2005), 189.

"Man must never fall into the air of believing himself to be the lord and master of creation.... He will then feel that in a world in which planets and suns follow circular trajectories, moons revolve around planets, and force reigns everywhere and supreme over weakness, which it either compels to serve it docilely or else crushes out of existence, Man cannot be subject to special laws of his own." (NR 237)

To be sure this was a curious passage coming from the pen of Hitler (then 36). On the one hand, he seemed to grasp "in faultless fashion" (NR 237) the rule and role of force in human affairs; he appeared to appreciate the absurdity of thinking that a political philosophy could be premised on some science of ruling not subject to force and necessity. On the other hand, Hitler's idea of a chosen race, replete with its chosen lands, was his mechanism for attempting to create "special laws of his own" by which to lord over the world. Thus, his "brief moment of intellectual courage and perspicacity" ended when he selected "as his machine the notion of a chosen race, a race destined to make everything bow before it" (NR 240).[19] This was, after all, the rebirth of the ethos of Roman rulers. And that ethos knew no limits; it fed on seizing ever more power in its quest for greatness.

The demand for "more"—what Weil termed an "appetite for power" (SE, 184)—runs in philosophical tandem with the illusion that one can *will* one's thirst for power over the world; that the will to power can by its very force reign over all contingent matter and therefore be immune, or largely so, from the exigencies of the world. "I exist, therefore I control," might be the imperative. Weil's 1939 account of Hitler speaks to this:

> Hitler ... governs a country which is strained to full pitch; his will is fiery, unflagging, pitiless, and closed to considerations of humanity; his imagination plays with grandiose historical visions of the future, in a Wagnerian style; and he is a natural gambler. He is therefore clearly not the man to refrain from exploiting to the full any possibilities that are open to him; he will be influenced neither by reasonable proposals nor by threats. Only a short time ago the idea of achieving universal

---

19. In that sense, Hitler was a "demonic genius" (OC, IV, 1, 93).

domination must have seemed to him merely an abstract one ... [b]ut today ... there is an actual possibility of universal domination and therefore Hitler, too, must necessarily see it as an actual possibility. (SE 184–185)

Notice the reference to the nation being "strained to full pitch." It is wildly out of balance; it is nearly beyond the time of its continued existence. And yet, soldiers and citizens submit to the will of a madman elated by operatic "Wagnerian" illusions and "grandiose historical visions of the future." If we pause here we can discern that essential to Hitler's will to power, as Weil portrayed it, was a play to the future, an attempt to be glorified because of his conquests, no matter how vile they were. To which it should be replied: this is no more than wishful thinking, assuming it is thinking at all. "Even if all we wished for were to happen," Wittgenstein once counseled, "still this would only be a favour granted by fate, so to speak: for there is no *logical* connection between the will and the world, which would guarantee it, and the supposed physical connection itself is surely not something we could will."[20] The modesty of mind suggested by Wittgenstein's admonition is foreign to the mindset of notions of greatness divorced from reality, detached from any idea of measure.

Similarly, in late winter of 2022, Vladimir Putin directed some 190,000 Russian military personnel (land and sea) to first threaten and then savagely attack the people of Ukraine. This unprovoked assault was accompanied by predictable threats from Putin: "No matter who tries to stand in our way ... they must know that Russia will respond immediately, and the consequences will be such as you have never seen in your entire history," he said. And as if to up the aggressive ante, he added: "Today's Russia remains one of the most powerful nuclear states."[21] On the financial front, the then-global chief investment officer at Credit Suisse declared that he believed "that Russia's invasion of Ukraine marks nothing less than a shift away from the largely US/Western-dominated

20. Ludwig Wittgenstein, *Tractatus Logico-Philosophicus*, translated by C. K. Ogden (New York: Dover Publications, 471st ed., 1998), 6.374.
21. Neel Dhanesha, "How to think about the risk of nuclear war, according to 3 experts," *Vox* (Feb. 25, 2022).

world order that has prevailed since the fall of the Berlin Wall."[22] In troubling ways, it was reminiscent of September 1, 1939, when the German army under Hitler launched an invasion of Poland. Here again, power, greed, and the quest for "greatness" informed Putin's actions—it was a case of history repeating itself.

For all his barbarous successes, failure was the final measure of Hitler's fame. And yet the mantle of "greatness" attaches, if only by the magnitude of his mark, to his name in the history books … and perhaps to Putin's too. Why? Let us continue to explore yet other answers and what they reveal.

War and Colonialism:
The Price of Greatness

The Principle of Continual War: "The constant sight of gladiators in combat made the Romans extremely fierce. It was observed that Claudius became more inclined to shed blood by seeing spectacles of this kind." So wrote Montesquieu.[23] Had Hitler read Montesquieu's *Considerations on the Causes of the Greatness of the Romans and their Decline* (1734, 1748), he would have been quite enamored with the "greatness" that was Rome and that of its various tyrants. For in *Considerations* there is a certain pseudo-political "realism" at work, one that praised conquest over virtue. Whatever one makes of the historical accuracy and comprehensiveness of Weil's portrayals of the Roman empire, Montesquieu's account is one that in some notable ways comports with her objections to that empire. In his introduction to *Considerations*, David Lowenthal sketches the mindset that informed Montesquieu's conception of greatness and how it was linked to the history of Rome: "By deciding to concentrate on the theme of Rome's greatness or power, Montesquieu already shows that he has decided the crucial philosophical question against Plato and Aristotle and in favor of Machiavelli."[24]

---

22. Julia Horowitz, "The invasion of Ukraine changed everything for Wall Street," *CNN Business* (Feb. 27, 2022).

23. Montesquieu, *Considerations on the Causes of the Greatness of the Romans and Their Decline*, ed. and trans. by David Lowenthal (Indianapolis: Hackett Publishing Co., 1999), 28, 136.

24. *Ibid.*, 6.

Such "realism," as Weil well understood, came with its costs, which included the evils that accompany the pursuit of power. Thus, the true realism of war means understanding precisely what that entails and not romanticizing it. Consider Hernando Cortés, the "great" *conquistador* who in the early sixteenth century launched the Spanish colonization of the Americas.[25] This war effort first instilled terrifying fear in the Aztecs, and when that proved inadequate Cortés and his men (aided by indigenous terrified Tlaxcalans) embarked upon a murderous campaign that led to the enslavement of indigenous survivors. This murderous uprooting of the Aztecs and much of their culture exemplified part of what so troubled Weil, especially because France had its own oppressive hand in the conquering and colonizing campaigns of history.

Contrary to how they are too often historically recounted, certain concepts of greatness can be morally hollow. There is no moral imperative; there is mainly the power principle and the ability to maintain and perpetuate it. As Weil put it: "All the absurdities that make history seem like a long delirium are rooted in one essential absurdity, that of the nature of power."[26] Where that is the conceptual and linguistic touchstone, it makes sense to speak of the greatness of the Roman Empire or even that of Joseph Stalin and his "great purges."

* * * *

As for the French of her time, Weil's Roanne lectures (1933–1934) and later writings (1936–1943) reveal a preoccupation with the question of the cost France paid for its greatness when it came to the colonization and the oppression of Arabs, Indochinese, and other colonial peoples.[27] Thus, France's "greatness" and the history designed to support it vexed Weil, both as a philosophical and patriotic matter. In J.P. Little's words:

> Simone Weil saw with horror and dismay—at a distance—the brutality of practices in force in the 1930s, in Indochina, the necessary uprooting through colonization of indigenous peo-

---

25. See Matthew Restall, *When Montezuma Met Cortés: The True Story of the Meeting that Changed History* (New York: Ecco, 2018).

26. Quoted in Jacques Cabaud, *Simone Weil: A Fellowship in Love* (New York: Channel Press, 1964), 159 (see SE 168).

27. J.P. Little, ed. & trans., *Simone Weil on Colonialism: An Ethic of the Other* (Lanham, MD, 2003), 5.

ples in vast areas of the globe, and came to the conclusion that
"the uprooted uproot." She devoted most of the latter years of
her short life militating for an end to barbarous practices, but
also for a structural way forward that would put an end to the
hierarchical relationship between peoples.[28]

What this meant for a post-war France of the kind envisioned in *The
Need for Roots* was that the Free French must, in Weil's words, "choose
between a soul and the Roman ... sense of greatness" (NR 145–146). To
make such a choice meant attempting to repair the wrongs of colonization. While she painted with a broad conceptual brush, any just remedy
required a meaningful measure of *independence*: "The essential [thing]
is to find a solution by which those [colonized] nations that are not nations, and which find themselves in certain respects dependent on certain organized states, are sufficiently independent in other respects to
feel themselves free. For freedom, like happiness," she added, "is defined
first and foremost by the feeling that one possesses it" (SWC 117). That
notion of freedom, of course, could not be the product of propaganda
(which is a lie masquerading as truth) or even any bureaucratic directive
(which is no substitute for real justice). Rather, what must be done is the
creation of a new political and social order ordained not to repeat the
injustices of the past and likewise to usher in a regime attentive to what
is sacred in every human being. What that meant was eschewing the
"greatness" that was France and also renouncing the history that glorified that history, while at the same time attempting to rediscover what
was lost to war and colonization.

Important as the power dynamic, as exemplified by colonialism, is to
Weil's understanding of greatness, it is insufficient to explain the full
depth of the problem. Why? The reason is that the history of the conquered, if truly recounted, might nonetheless reveal the evils of force,
albeit operating at the microcosmic political level. After all, the vices of
the collective can also exist in a village community as in a nation-state.
Instead of aligning greatness with a Roman emperor or a French gover-
nor, for example, one can imagine followers of a small and powerless
religious sect worshiping the "greatness" of their leaders. Admittedly, the
scale may enter into the conceptual equation insofar as such problems

---

28. "Weil's Single-Minded Commitment to Truth."

may be less likely and less severe in smaller communities or cultures. Hence, Weil's attraction to such communities is evidenced by the farm work she did while laboring in Gustave Thibon's vineyards. Still, the problem of the collective, about which Weil wrote extensively, does not disappear over time.

To remedy that problem Weil urged that a people must be *rooted* in a culture in which the idea of the collective was reconceptualized[29] to give breathing space for a "notion of a vital milieu" (Chapter 2). This new "philosophy of a public life" is what Weil was getting at when she spoke of the need for a certain continuity with the past, a certain vital link to one's customs and culture—a place to call *home* in the highest sense of the word. It is a "community which preserves in living shape certain particular treasures of the past and certain particular expectations for the future" (NR 40). Colonialism ended that continuity such that even its history was largely lost.

History Falsified:
The Limitations of the Historical Record

Historians have long prided themselves on being objective, on presenting us with dates and data. Though Weil's theory of history was of an entirely different order, she doubted that historians could tell "the whole truth" if only because so much of it died with the death of the conquered, the subjugated, and the oppressed (this is part of the focus of her play *Venice Saved*). The domain of injustice cannot be divorced from the realm of human affairs, properly understood. In their quest for documented facts, historians overlook that, or they picture history as a work in human *progress*. But such detachment does not make up for the absence of a moral perspective, one attentive to the cause-and-effect workings of force in all things political and social.

Notable Passage: "History is founded upon documents. The professional historian won't allow himself to form hypotheses which do not rest upon something. That seems to be very reasonable, but in reality, it

---

29. In Chapter 2 (note 22) Emmanuel Gabellieri identifies four types of collectivity.

is far from being so. For, since there are holes in documents,[30] a balanced judgment requires [those] hypotheses which haven't any basis should be present to the mind, provided they be there in that capacity, and that there be several of them in connection with each particular point" (NR 221–222). Here again, there is a lot to unpack—as so often before, Weil left much work to be done on our own.

To investigate the meaning of those words requires a certain way of looking at history, a *philosophy of history* if you will, or as Robert Chenavier has labeled it, a "counter-history" (Chapter 8). Though history may be founded on documents, they are often woefully inadequate. Why? Weil's answer: such a view of history demands "a subordination of the mind to documents" (NR 222). Here the problem may be said to be at least threefold: (i) even if documents were foundational, the determinative presupposition is that *all* the relevant documents exist and/or have been discovered; (ii) that documents *alone* define history; and (iii) and most importantly, the documents are *biased*: "History ... is nothing but a compilation of the depositions made by assassins with respect to their victims and themselves" (NR 222). By that did Weil mean *all* history or rather certain kinds of history?

We live in the present, yet we also live in the light of the past as well as in its dark shadows. Thus viewed, justice and history are integrally related. The idea of thinking "historically" may well discount that idea. Why? The answer has to do with how we *think* of history. On this score Weil was bold: "History is a tissue of base and cruel acts in the midst of which a few drops of purity sparkle at long intervals" (NR 229). Here again: does she mean to say this is true of *all* history?

While the *surviving* documents may tell the story of certain historical details, they leave much out and often fail to capture the *spirit* of the time and the cultural experiences of those who lived then. Owing to that, the conquers and their heirs tend to absolve themselves of their wrongdoing

---

30. See Simone Weil, *Lectures on Philosophy*, intro. by Peter Winch & trans. by Hugh Price (New York: Cambridge University Press, 1978), 140. ("Generally speaking, history is scientific when it depends on documents whose accuracy is not questioned. But, as things are, it is difficult to find out the truth. There are distortions due to corruptions in the text, to prejudice, etc. There are periods of which we can know next to nothing (Egypt), others about which there is no shortage of documents and information which contradict each other. One has to take into account falsifications, to study the life of the writer, his passions, his interests, etc.").

by erasing it from the pages of written history. When one reflects on the matter, there is a certain hubris at work in the idea that historians can actually capture history, both as recorded and as lived; this is especially so in the case of the conquered and/or oppressed. But if their working hypothesis is that recorded history as discovered and presented represents the essence of history, then the defining element of their endeavor is fatally flawed. This brings us to our third concern, the one about the "depositions made by assassins." Case in point: During his Nuremberg trial, Hermann Göring (then president of the Reichstag) spoke brazenly: "The victor will always be the judge."[31] Perhaps that is another way of saying that "history is written by the victors." By that measure what we are left with is, in Chenavier's words, a "history of sovereignty" (Chapter 8). Think of that, the link between sovereignty and how history is recorded. To be sovereign is to be supreme, and that supremacy governs how the events of the past are chronicled.

Only that which has life can have a history. There is no history of nothing. By that logic, when life ceases, its history often ceases. What remains is memory. But when memory is erased the past of the living dies with them. The evil of murder, oppression, and suppression is then twofold: first, it halts the life process and thus ends the prospect of its future, and then it destroys the memorial record of what life had been lived and how it had been lived. The same holds true for a sect, town, or even a civilization.

In *The Need for Roots* and elsewhere, it is precisely that problem that Simone Weil addressed as a philosophical matter, one inextricably contrary to her notion of justice. This is so not only due to the bias that the victor imprints on the historical record, but also because of the obliteration of the culture and history of the defeated (thus, Weil could never forgive the Church for the destructive crusades it waged against the Cathars,[32] SE, 35–38).[33] As Toril Moi has duly noted: "To conquer a people

---

31. Quoted in Joe Julius Heydecker & Johannes Leeb, *The Nuremberg Trial: A History of Nazi Germany as Revealed Through the Testimony at Nuremburg*, trans. by R. A. Downie (Madison, WI: Greenwood Press, 1975), 84.

32. See Cabaud, *Simone Weil*, 218–224. Moreover, the regime that forged the Roman Empire was, by Weil's measure, "the deadliest phenomenon to be found in history. It killed and even almost destroyed all trace of several civilizations" (SE 76).

33. According to a noted Cathar scholar, "Weil's claim that the Cathars, although little was known about them, were 'in some way the heirs of Platonic thought' shows both

is to destroy its traditions, which means destroying both its past and its future. And since history is written by the victors, these peoples will be eradicated from the historical record."[34] Hence, the "holes" in the documents. This respect for documents as revered by professional historians does "not incline their minds towards [the needed] exercise. What is called the historical spirit doesn't pierce through the paper to discover real flesh and blood" (NR 222).

Recorded history has long been the province of those in power; those whose "greatness" first thrusts them into the historical limelight and then darkens the history of the powerless. Neither most historians nor those who cling to their words appreciate the importance of "read[ing] between the lines" (NR 222) so as to reveal what has been lost *because* of history. Ironically, history tethered to documents and traditional notions of greatness often distorts and eradicates the actual history of civilizations, cultures, and human beings.

Translated into Weilian terminology: force largely governs the human social experience; it is the cause and effect of many human affairs. "Weil's writings on force," it has been observed, "mark the crossroads of her political thought, her mystical teachings, and her lived experience of the ambiguity of embodiment."[35] Given that, such a focus would naturally figure into her thinking on greatness and history. To hold to that focus, ad infinitum is to deny any real recognition of some kind of meaningful justice, past or present. In that respect, Weil's philosophy of history might be viewed as a moral counter designed to "disrupt" history[36] as traditionally understood. As Bennett Gilbert has observed: "One of the most striking things in this line of thought for the philosophy of history is the suggestion that the historian acting on Weil's moral

---

in its cavalier disregard for evidence and [in] its vagueness that her approach was fundamentally unhistorical." Malcolm Barber, *The Cathars: Dualist Heretics in Languedoc in the High Middle Ages* (New York: Routledge, 2nd ed., 2017), 243 (endnote omitted). See also David McLellan, *Utopian Pessimist: The Life and Thought of Simone Weil* (New York: Poseidon Press, 1990), 16–17 ("her history teacher saw her as 'an intelligent girl who visibly feels herself to be above history.'") (citing Pétrement) and 151–152 (arguing that Weil's "historical scholarship" re the Old Testament seems "far-fetched").

34. Toril Moi, "I Came with a Sword," *London Review of Books*, vol. 43, no. 13 (July 1, 2021).

35. Irwin, *Saints of the Impossible, op cit,* 41.

36. See "Simone Weil's Philosophy of History," 66, 71, 72, 78.

prescription, *steps outside of history*, even as she is writing it and *participating in it.*"[37]

Understanding the bias of recorded history, recovering the spirit of unrecorded history, and then grasping how our notions of greatness figure into the picture were a few of the challenges Weil presented to her Free French colleagues as they pondered the future of a newly constituted France.

History and the Human Dimension

"Without history there can be no sense of patriotism. We have only to look at the United States to see what it is to have people deprived of the time-dimension" (NR 229). When Weil penned those words, segregation and Jim Crow prejudice were alive and well in the United States. And this was true even *during* the war when the very future of the United States was uncertain and when men and women of color were giving their all-too-human best for the United States. By Weil's measure, such wartime demands for racial fairness were to be expected given that Black Americans had been "deprived of the time-dimension."

But what exactly does that mean? What does it mean to be deprived of the time-dimension? Such questions are, of course, linked to patriotism, to devotion to one's nation. To be sure, Black Americans who served in the war were patriotic in a variety of ways. But their patriotism was of a different kind; it was a devotion colored by the history of slavery and the uprooting of peoples from their motherlands and cultures.[38] Thus, their patriotism must be viewed through the lens of devotion to the cause of a more just America, an America committed to *transforming* itself. But such a transformation seems Sisyphean.

When you tear a people from their land, when you rip them from loved ones, and when you uproot them from their culture, when all of that occurs with the vilest kinds of brutality, you steal their past from them. You deprive them of that time that was once theirs. History, after all, requires some real and even ongoing ties to the past. When those ties perish, the very idea of history perishes with them. And when a people's

---

37. *Ibid.*, 78 (note omitted and itals. added).
38. See French, *Born in Blackness*, 411–421.

history is silenced by the worst kinds of subjugation, there is no record of greatness if only because there can be no greatness among slaves. There is only subordination and the history that is associated with it.

Where subordination is the yardstick, the testimony of "the greater part of what little there is remains hidden" (NR 229). History neither records the life stories of the voiceless nor remembers the contributions of the anonymous—they both vanish with few or no memories left for posterity. If some notion of *perpetuity* is a vital part of living, then the denial of the perpetuation of one's cultural history represents a collective evil committed against the victims of such denials. For those victims, the very idea of greatness is difficult to conceive because the evidence of their ancestors' greatness was wiped out of existence.

"Love of one's country," Weil counseled, "is pure so long as it is ... a man's love for the harmony which knits together the collective body of citizens, and not participation of the Great Beast for itself" (NB, II, 618). That knit is not woven when colonialism and racism not only obliterate the past cultures of people of color but compound the cultural and spiritual sin by perpetuating the vestiges of subjugation[39] in both economic and legal terms—and this while also expecting the allegiance of the oppressed even when so much in their daily lives is foreign to them. That some may seek refuge in the marketplace of money is less a sign of accommodation than an indication of desperation.

* * * *

The problems of misguided patriotism[40] notwithstanding, Weil did value, and valued greatly, the importance of *rootedness* and the pride that comes with a *certain* kind of love of one's nation and its cultural and spiritual heritage (Chapter 4). But patriotism of the kind she valued was tied to "some higher good" (NR 211), the pursuit of which gave one more of an objective perspective—the very kind that allowed (and even demanded) criticism of one's own and one's "great" leaders. The patriotism of the collective was antithetical to Weil's notion of rootedness. When allegiance to the state or a leader moves from conditional loyalty

---

39. See Scott B. Ritner, "A Critique of Greatness," *Theory & Event*, vol. 26, no.2 (April 2023), pp. 345–367.

40. See Richard Rees, *Simone Weil: A Sketch for a Portrait* (Carbondale, IL: Southern University Press, 1966), 129–133.

to absolute loyalty, it becomes a form of idolatry: "The real sin of idolatry is always committed on behalf of something similar to the State" (NR 115). Hence, the patriot's cry: My country right or wrong.

The question, then, is this: How does one remain rooted in one's heritage and at the same time respect all those others who are foreign to it? Though there is a line between pride and prejudice, when is that line breached? One answer concerns the mass of the group in question, both its geographic mass and the size of its population. As suggested in Part II of *The Need for Roots*, the transition from the countryside to towns to the nation-state (and all that such transitions bring with them) increases the likelihood of uprootedness and likewise renders patriotism ever more suspect (SWC 115). As commonly and historically understood, the measure of greatness is gauged by the mass of *territories, wealth, industrial production*, and the might of *military forces*. By that measure, such greatness and the patriotism associated with it would be contrary to the pursuit of that "higher good" that is so central to Weil's vision (see Chapter 4).

A nation is thus deemed "great" by its size and conquests along with the "efficiency" of its economic system. And such a nation may organize its constitutional and legal system in ways that enhance the economic *rights* of those who benefit most from its yield. But, in Weil's eyes, such a regime enjoys its success on the backs of the conquered, the oppressed, and the neglected. The excesses of American capitalism, dependent as they were on a false and exploitative conception of progress, concerned Weil considerably. The cultural and spiritual annihilation of Europe, she believed, was threatened not only by Nazism and Fascism but also, and especially in the long run, by the increasing "Americanization" of the world—she tagged it "a very grave danger" (SWC 105, 113, 114). That "patriotism" should pledge itself to such a cause was more than regrettable; it was immoral.

A Radical Idea: Greater than "Great"

When viewing the matter from Weil's conceptual perch, one begins to get a better sense of the real radicality of what she is asking of us and how we think about greatness. That is, she urges us to conceptualize greatness free of ego, *sans cérémonie*. How is that even possible? If, for example, one were to act according to a Gandhian creed, but did so for social approval (either in this life or posthumously), then the desired objective would not be goodness itself but the *appearance* of it—again, this is the riddle presented in Book II of Plato's *Republic*. Though Weil might deem such actions to be great *on some lower level*, they would not be great on the *transcendent level* of which she wrote in her report for the Free French and her later essays. And then there is this: "The contemporary form of true greatness lies in a civilization founded upon the spirituality of work" (NR 97) (Chapter 9). Such a conception of *true* greatness, however, was rife with risk. "But one can only lay hold of such a conception," Weil stressed, "in fear and trembling. How can one touch it without soiling it, turning it into a lie? Our age is so poisoned by lies that it converts everything it touches into a lie" (NR 97).

If such is Weil's notion of greatness, or at least an approximation of it, then true greatness is nearly impossible. If greatness in the social context is to be measured by concern and care for others—one divorced from a will for power, a desire for conquest, or any expectation of collective praise—and if it is oriented to a transcendent "reality outside the world" (SE, 220), then who can lay claim to greatness? Answer: Weil's idea is aspirational, even if not collectively realizable.[41] Such inspiration can, nonetheless, move us ever closer to the ideal. For France in 1943 looking towards a Weilian future meant forsaking that greatness that attached to its colonization of so many peoples. Any such attempted resolution would be thwarted by "the ignorance in France concerning the facts of the situation" (SWC, 71). But this is to cast the range of options in an either-or sort of way. That is, to assert, as Weil did, a hierarchy in values is not to say that all our thoughts, actions, and the language we employ relative to them need to operate at that highest of planes.[42] A valid critique of the status quo, after all, does not lose its currency owing to the difficulty of alternative options. While this may not satisfy the pragmatist, it does nonetheless retain its moral legitimacy as evidenced by the

---

41. See Christine Ann Evans, "The Nature of Narrative in Simone Weil's Vision of History," 67–68.

42. Consider Eric Springsted, "The Language of the Inner Life," in Sophie Bourgault and Julie Daigle, eds., *Simone Weil, Beyond Ideology?* (Switzerland: Palgrave Macmillan, 2019), 26.

city in words created in Plato's *Republic* or the society envisioned in Rousseau's *Discourses*. Moreover, as Benjamin P. Davis has observed, "we can learn how to struggle: to implicate ourselves in our country's violence and to own up to the predominance of colonial force as it informs who we take ourselves to be. The alternative is to avoid reality, to hold fast to the colonially framed and ideologically informed claim that there are prestigious spheres outside of politics."[43]

* * * *

In so many ways, Weil's reflections on history and greatness point to the need for a "critical survey of our civilization," which though perhaps "impossible" is nonetheless "no reason for not undertaking it" (FLN 45). To that end, the "temporary laying low of France as a nation gives her the opportunity of becoming … an inspiration" (NR 195). Was Weil trying to say that owing to Germany's dominance, France had lost its "greatness" (i.e., of its own dominance), which allowed it to aspire to true greatness and thus become "an inspiration"? In this moment of weakness (albeit with the possibility of the "defeat of her enemies"), France could work towards a government "based entirely on free consent," instead of one "based on physical power" (NR 196). For the French people and their leaders, this meant: (1) moving away from colonial power and all that was associated with it; (2) repudiating the "glorious history" of conquest; (3) establishing a social order based on *obligations* stemming from "a passionate interest in human beings" (NR 196) rather than one grounded in an exploitative notion of rights (NR 1–6); and (4) instituting a method of "using words" to adequately and honestly reflect such aspirations (NR 197–199). If the Free French could move towards such goals it might rediscover its genius and then spread this inspiration "throughout the world" (NR 196).

---

43. Benjamin P. Davis, "The Colonial Frame: Judith Butler and Simone Weil on Force and Grief," in Bourgault and Daigle, eds., *Simone Weil, Beyond Ideology?*, 140.

Reflections and Intimations:
Orientation Towards the Eternal

In what ways might it be said that Weil's ideas about greatness and history were *transformative*, at least by conventional notions of those ideas? The following points may help to guide our thinking in response to this question:

- There was a *moral* component to her thinking; that is, neither greatness nor history could be considered in a morally free way;
- questions of greatness and notions of history must include a critical evaluation of the ruinous role of *force* in the affairs of humankind;
- history is more than selectively recorded data pertaining mainly to the *conquests of the powerful*;
- both history and greatness must have some *human focus*, lest they compound those evils already committed;
- greatness must be understood not in terms of power but rather in terms of the *pursuit of the good*;
- *preserving history*, properly understood, is essential lest a people become uprooted; and
- in its purest form, history has a *transcendent* spiritual element in it, something beyond the repetitive laws of force that rule matter and the affairs of people.

In *The Need for Roots*, as elsewhere, Simone Weil often painted with a broad conceptual brush. This may be due, in part, to the fact that her 1943 unfinished report was written at an unwavering pace—within a few months with little rewriting. Hence, questions arise when one digs deeper when one questions her own questions. This is not to devalue her analysis but rather to place it in its proper context.[44]

Recall that Weil's critique of greatness and history presupposes a "total transformation" (NR 224) of how we think and speak about such

---

44. Re the questions raised herein, consider R. G. Collingwood's *The Idea of History* (New York: Oxford University Press, 1946).

matters.[45] From the perspective of her "meta-politics" or her "'metapolitical' plane" as Emmanuel Gabellieri has described it (Chapter 2), her ideal notion of history proves to be both sensible in its critique of conventional history and aspirational in its transcendent capacity. That transformation is revolutionary, as Thucydides wrote and Weil echoed, in both a personal and political sense given that "everyone commands wherever he has the power to do so" (EHP 303). In other words, if that transformation is to be effective, it requires some *inner* change within the soul. One cannot, after all, escape the "most serious defect of all" (NR 217) simply by venturing to reword history or tagging a new name onto greatness, or idly vowing to forsake power. To be transformative requires some meaningful alteration within the inner self—admittedly, an almost "impossible" undertaking but one that should be attempted (FLN 45). This holds true for those who write and read history. Likewise, for those who aspire to greatness as well as those who revere it. The same holds true for those who live within history in the making. By this measure, Weil sought to bridge theory and practice, philosophy and spirituality, along with sociology and psychology.

* * * *

Let us close, if only briefly, with some pertinent entries from Weil's *Notebooks*, entries chock full of implications of the kind that widen the lens of the mind. For example: "Time in its course wears away and destroys what is temporal.... Thus there is more of eternity in the past than in the present.... The value of history rightly understood is comparable to that of a recollection in Proust. In this way, the past offers us something which is at the same time real and better than ourselves, which is able to draw us upwards, a thing which the future never does" (NB, II, 444).

Note that time does not erode everything, but only the temporal. There is, in Weil's mind, some residue that is beyond temporal. True, but only if there is some constant in the past, something that even in Heraclitus' domain remains fixed, something unchanging. On one plane, the past is just that; it is that which is lost to time, save for memory (rightly grasped). Yet for Weil, there is also something in the past that is beyond time and thus not framed by it. History, rightly understood, is transcen-

---

45. Consider French, *Born in Blackness*, 12–13 (noting the need to rewrite everything from school lessons to historical texts to the way a society views its heritage).

dent—such history is impregnated with the eternal. All other forms of history are cabined by the realities of this world. That is what the historian must capture; that is a key component of her study. Contact with that "something" is made indirectly, in a Proustian sort of way. Thus, the essence of the past is recalled, albeit involuntarily, when something in it triggers something in the soul—i.e., intimations of justice or beauty as revealed in a past culture's customs or art or in the lives of certain spiritually exceptional people (again, this is a theme in her *Venice Saved* play).

And then there is this equally rich passage: "there is a right and a wrong way of making use of history. We can either seek something to exalt the imagination; or else we can seek therein something that is purer than ourselves" (NB, II, 444). History as recounted in the political and social realms is cabined in the temporal; it mirrors the practices of force, that is, what is worst in humans. It equates power with greatness of the kind that leads people (like Donald Trump and his followers) to believe that they can circumvent the realities that govern their lives.

Moreover, "[t]here is a sort of phagocytosis in the soul; everything which belongs to the temporal in us secretes lies in order not to die and in proportion to the danger of death. This is why there is no veritable love of truth without a total, unreserved consent to death. The Cross of Christ is the only gateway to knowledge" (NB, II, 444). Here Weil draws on a biological reference ("phagocytosis") to illustrate her point. The process to which she refers involves a type of cell within the body capable of engulfing and absorbing bacteria. Phagocytosis is thus a sort of cleansing process. The temporal (the workings of this world and humans in it) is infected with "bacteria" that contaminate the sacred within us.

Finally, this: The kind of *eternal history* of which Weil wrote was "a reality ... absolutely beyond our reach. We cannot take a single step towards it but can only orient our minds so as to receive an emanation from it" (LPW 78; SNL 121). Hence, knowledge of such history is gleaned from "emanations." This Weilian "orientation" occurs when the eternal within the soul is aligned (by love, beauty, joy, justice, or affliction) with God. This "balance" between the two is an instance of "eternity allow[ing] itself to be present through time"; or to put it another way, of glimpsing at "eternity through the veil of time" (LPW 154; OS-NLG 168). Notice that this turn towards eternity is not direct; it perceives God *through* a shroud, which allows recognition of the eternal while at the same time concealing it.

* * * *

As we have seen, so much of what is set out in *The Need for Roots* and other works centers around *method* (Chapter 6) about new ways of *reading* the universe and understanding truth (Chapter 8). As with her reflections on history and greatness, her methods (properly understood) awaken within us something that is transcendent (Chapter 9) and thus truly inspirational.

CHAPTER 8

The Spirit of Truth:
Science and Providence

Eric O. Springsted

After considering what constitutes "greatness," Weil turns to a long discussion of science that evolves at its tail end into a concern about the religious doctrine of Providence. It begins by Weil declaring, "The modern conception of science is responsible, as is that of history and that of art, for the monstrous conditions under which we live, and will, in its turn, have to be transformed, before we can hope to see the dawn of a better civilization" (NR 235).

A determined argument runs through these pages. Its lines are not always clear, though; many of Weil's illustrations and side comments are more extensive than the time she spends directly on her chief points. However, what goes into those chief points are often considerations that she has spent extensive time on in previous essays. These especially include ones written in Marseilles, particularly those on science,[1] the Greeks, and the important last section on the love of the beauty of the

---

1. Most notably, "At the Price of an Infinite Error: The Scientific Image, Ancient and Modern" (LPW 155–198), "The Pythagorean Doctrine" (IC 151–201), and "Divine Love in Creation" (IC 89–105). For a thorough examination of Weil on science, see Vance Morgan, *Weaving the World: Simone Weil on Science, Mathematics, and Love* (Notre Dame: University of Notre Dame Press, 2005). Morgan accurately notes that Weil's concerns with science go all the way back to her diploma essay, *Science et Perception dans Descartes*, of 1929.

world in "The Forms of the Implicit Love of God" (WG 81–142). Thus, this section on science, probably more than any other in *The Need for Roots*, excepting what she writes on the spirituality of labor, draws upon earlier work which can be used to understand it. What is equally important, though, for understanding this section's contribution to *The Need for Roots* is to see how it fills out her concern for the human "need for order" that is first raised in the beginning of *The Need for Roots* (NR 10–12). In order to make clear what her argument is and what its contribution to *The Need for Roots* is, I will first summarize it, and then turn to a discussion of its chief points.

The Argument

The discussion of science and Providence follows that of the question "what is true greatness?," the first of the obstacles separating us from a worthy civilization. More broadly, the discussion of these obstacles is a topic in the second half of *The Need for Roots* within her larger concern for how we can find an inspiring education. That, she thinks, is a task that is ultimately a matter of finding inspiration in the truths "eternally inscribed in the nature of things" (NR 216). The treatment of science and Providence is in good part meant to get explicitly at what it means to say we are to find truths that are eternally inscribed in the nature of things.

At first, however, her introduction of science appears to fail to keep her promise to discuss the second of the four obstacles that separate us from a worthy civilization, namely, "the degradation of the sentiment of justice" (NR 216). Clearly, though, she has not forgotten, for this "degradation of the sentiment of justice" is precisely what she means to get at when talking about science. Science, she claims, "constitutes our only claim to be proud of ourselves as Westerners, men of the white race, modern men" (NR 235). We question everything, but give unbridled authority to science. But what do we get from science? Quoting Hitler from *Mein Kampf*, who claims that "'force reigns everywhere and supreme over weakness, which it either compels to serve it docilely or else crushes out of existence'" (NR 237), she claims that the idea that force reigns supreme, is the "only conclusion that can reasonably be drawn from the conception of the world contained in our science" (NR 237–238). Clearly, she is now dealing with the second obstacle. Contemporary science's conception of the world has given us a world where force reigns supreme, and justice is not a part of the world as science presents it to us. This is, indeed, a degradation of the sense of justice. What we need, therefore, is to see something else besides force at work in the universe.

Weil briefly defends this big claim, noting how utilitarianism, economic liberalism, and Marxism[2] all are attempts to show how force can or does produce justice. She will have none of it. "Force is not a machine for automatically creating justice. It is a blind mechanism which produces indiscriminately and impartially just or unjust results, but, by all the laws of probability, nearly always unjust ones" (NR 240). As she adamantly notes throughout her writings, there is a distance between Necessity and the Good, and one cannot cross from Necessity to the Good without bridges.

Are we then stuck with having to face the idea that the world's reality is strictly composed of force, and that justice has no place in it? Weil does not think so at all, for justice is inerasable from the human heart, and has a reality in the world. So, if science only gives us force, then it is science that is wrong. At least, modern science is wrong. The Greeks thought of things differently, for they regarded science, the knowledge of the world, as a religious subject, worthy of religious contemplation.

The science of the Greeks, however, was forgotten for nearly a thousand years (NR 243),[3] and when it was rediscovered, its spirit was not recovered. Weil does not spend much time defending this here, but the claim is not particularly contentious. Modern science, beginning with Galileo and continuing through Descartes and Newton on through our own age, gained the immense analytic and predictive power it did precisely because it limited itself to working only on what was describable by mathematics. It excluded final causes, such as the good for which anything came about, and it excluded secondary qualities from consideration, the qualities that are dependent upon human perception, such as color, feel, etc. It was left with the easily mathematized primary qualities of mass and extension. In short, and this is Weil's point and a concern in all her writings on science, the life world of the human being

---

2. On Marxism, see especially, "Is There a Marxist Doctrine?" in OL 169–195.

3. Weil does not seem to think that Aristotelian science, which reigned over the last five hundred of these years is worthy of the name "science."

became irrelevant to the world science then gave us. What that meant, she continues, is that religion and science were split. Believers now feel that they are not entirely in line with truth, and atheists feel entirely justified and superior because of science. This is our situation.

The question is one of truth. But that is a complex problem. Even though justice is at stake, which is a problem that science has created for us, the issue cannot be dismissed by saying that religion has been right all along. It is not a matter of pitting one against the other. The problem, according to Weil, is that there is a question on both sides about their relation to truth. Both need what she calls "a spirit of truth," for both often miss it. Even if religion is itself inerasable from the human heart, too often, it has justified itself by what she calls "pink pills," by which she means justifying religion simply by its social utility, or through its consolations.

This notion of the spirit of truth leads into and surrounds the heart of Weil's thinking in this section of *The Need for Roots*. This is also where it is easy to miss where Weil is going, as she adds a number of provocative side discussions from here on about both religion and science and the mistakes they make, and their motives, which are at the root of these mistakes, and of how we see both science and religion.

When she introduces the notion of the "spirit of truth." Weil wants her reader to think about motives, and wants one to understand that the truth is not going to be realized unless a thinker is motivated by a love of the good. That requires the purest motives, ones where utility and benefit, and any sort of self-interest need to be set aside. But what is that? What does that mean? It is about more than knowledge. It is a matter of the truth about something we love; having pure motives is to accept that truth, adjusting our own being in accordance with it. But *what* is that we should love? Weil says simply, it is reality. While this central point of her argument will need much further discussion, which she doesn't give here, it might simply be said that what she is pointing out is not vacuous. What she thinks we need to love is things as they are. Science, of course, claims that it is just giving us the facts, so it is doing just this. But, she rightly notes, modern science from the beginning has bracketed the question of good and evil, so the "just the facts" stance hardly encompasses reality. It pretends to do so only by begging the question. In order to concentrate on what is central to her case, we will leave aside her criticisms of what motivates scientists for the moment. Suffice it to note, here, her suggestion that even those scientists who claim to be purely interested in theory fail to be motivated by a love of reality. While they say they only care about things as they are, what they don't think about is what that means for "human destiny." Not only has something very important been put to the side, their indifference treats human beings like ants viewed from above, and lets scientists play the role of gods.

Some additional specificity is needed, though, about the idea of loving reality. In good part, it is a matter of motive. One does not love reality as reality unless one is willing to accept it, no matter which way it cuts, even if it undercuts a prized belief or theory or project. But what is its object? Loving reality can be claimed by just about anybody. What is it then that one is to study and contemplate to get a better sense of justice? Weil argues that it is the beauty of the world. For her that is more than an aesthetic category. Where it becomes a genuine object of thought, study, analysis, *and* contemplation, is that, according to her, the beauty of the world is the order of the world. Here is where science and religion can unite.

The beauty of the world as it plays out for scientists is a matter of studying the order of the world. They don't actually study force as such, she notes—what force is in itself is a black box. What they do study are the patterns that the mind finds in the universe. Thus, she argues, the point of science is to unite one's mind, one's thinking, with the mysterious wisdom inscribed in the universe. Put that way, one can see why she thinks that there shouldn't be any opposition between science and religious contemplation. Rather than fully explicating that most important point, however, she concentrates on how science and religion continue to be kept apart. It is at this point that she starts to consider Providence.

Providence should be considered as impersonal, she thinks, and says that the Bible often represents it this way (NR 259–260). Her suggestion involves a certain amount of conceptual complexity, for she wants to give us an account wherein somehow the patterns that the mind finds in the workings of the world reflect, and, indeed, involve God's goodness. This goodness is not, she is careful to point out, a matter of miracles, i.e., good things happening at helpful times by God's direct intervention, nor, as we shall see, even a matter of asserting that good things outweigh bad things in number and quality. It is, instead, that the workings of the universe involve what she calls a "supernatural mechanics." To see the deep workings of the world and what they mean requires patience, and the long view. The goodness is seen in the beauty of the whole; that allows one to have a conception of the world that is both scientifically rigorous, but not reductionistic, and that sees the world as a place where justice reigns supreme. So, here is where we can find inspiration.

For this to happen, however, Weil thinks religious people need to start thinking more about the sort of impersonal Providence that she is talking about, and less about the personal Providence that consists in fortunate interventions in the world, violations of the created order. That conception of Providence she thinks simply portrays God as the cosmic equivalent of a Roman emperor who treats his creatures as slaves, subject to an arbitrary will. It is the religious counterpart to the scientific conception of force as ruling the world. This interventionist view of Providence clearly runs counter to scientific thinking.

This also suggests that religion needs to adjust itself so that we might have a different inspiration than we have been using. Were we to be able to think with reverence about the goodness of the workings of the world as a whole, which beauty reveals, we would have a way to access it. This allows her then, with respect to science, on the other hand, to recall the all-important sense of how the order of the world works. That order is a matter of how force, and brute necessity, are kept within limits, as the Pythagoreans, and then Plato, conceived. It is a matter of seeing then, that force is not supreme, but obeys a higher law, not by virtue of being dominated by a greater force, but by a principle of love and harmony, that, in the words of Plato, persuades necessity. If this is so, then there is, indeed, something more real than force in the universe, and there is something inspiring that we can look to in building communities.

We can now turn to the particulars of her argument.

The Order of the World and the Beauty of the World

At the beginning of *The Need for Roots*, Weil says of two distinct needs of the soul, the need for roots and the need for order, that they are "first" (order) or "the most important" (roots). In giving priority to these two needs, Weil is laying out the heart of her entire enterprise in the book, and she keeps her eye on it throughout. The two needs are correlated. The need for order touches on the soul's eternal destiny. It is, as it were, a need for Being, or better yet, the Good that is beyond Being. The need for roots is a need for a history that we can inherit and live, and that lets us draw sustenance in communal life from the eternal.[4] Knowing this allows us to see the significance of the arguments about the problem of greatness and then about science. The argument about the problem of greatness is an argument about how we are to think about our history in order to have the roots she thinks we need. The argument about science and Providence is its correlate. It gives us a sense of what thinking an eternal order means, about what we need in it, and how we have missed having it.

In order then to make sense of Weil's argument about science and Providence, we first need to turn to the order of the world and its relation to Beauty.

What, then, is the need for order? When she introduces this need in the beginning of *The Need for Roots*, Weil talks about it as a matter of social order, an order that keeps our obligations from conflicting. In carrying out obligations in one area we need to make sure that we do not, because of our particular social organization, have to violate or ignore other imperative obligations (NR 10). For example, a society in which generosity to others is made difficult or impossible because there is no way to be generous to others and at the same time to care for our own families adequately would embody a social order that defeats moral identity. It makes us choose between obligations.

It is easy to see why order is such an important need. It is also one that can be very difficult to imagine being easily met in the full range of complex and concrete circumstances in which it has to be played out. "When duty descends to the level of facts, so many independent relationships are brought into play that incompatibility seems far more likely than compatibility" (NR 11). However, Weil goes on significantly, we do have the example of the universe, which has a fixed order, and a balance among its parts, even though there is a nearly infinite number of mechanical actions going on all at once; yet, all those independent actions "concur so as to produce an order that, in the midst of variations, remain

---

4. On this issue and for an extended analysis of the relation between the two needs, see "The Need for Order and the Need for Roots: To Being through History" in Eric O. Springsted, *Simone Weil for the Twenty-First Century* (Notre Dame, IN, University of Notre Dame Press, 2021), 159–174.

fixed" (NR 11). Why is she so confident about this? Not just that we have not descended into chaos. It is the beauty of the world, a sense that "behind it [is] the presence of a something akin to that wisdom we should like to possess to slake our thirst for good"(NR 11).

Beauty is not something inherent in matter itself. It "is a relationship of the world to our sensibility" (WG 164). Beauty is a part of the human life-world and links it to the order of the world as whole. If there are other beings, Weil comments, who have different sensibilities, we must have faith that they, too, would find the world beautiful, but we would likely not know how. So, what kind of relation is this relation of the world to our sensibility? What do we sense because of it? Something distinctive and unique; in being struck by the beauty of the world, we are struck by a sense of finality, of completion, perfection, and even of purity. We take joy in it, even though it has suffering within it. Weil does not treat beauty as a matter of pleasure or emotion, although surely the emotion of joy would attend it. It is above all a sense of transcendence.[5] This sense of transcendence does not come from a calculation that good outweighs evil in the world, or any other calculation that puts together finite parts, which can never give a sense of the whole. It is a sense of completion and goodness of the whole as a whole, something that is a gift laid on the parts, giving them a sense that they do not possess simply as material forces. Weil says this is not pantheism; the world itself is not divine. It is something added from a God outside.

Weil is not the only thinker to talk about this intuition. It is frequently found in thinkers in the Platonic tradition, such as Plato, Plotinus, and Augustine. Weil admits that it is an intuition, and even if it is one that appears consistently in human experience, it may well be one that not everybody has.[6] It cannot be proved. But that is of the essence of a sense of transcendence. It cannot be reduced to its parts or made out as a sum

---

5. "Beauty—the manifest presence of reality; of a transcendent reality. But that is implied. Reality is only transcendent" (NB 361).

6. "One can never find enough visible finality in the world to prove that it is analogous to an object made with a view to a certain end. It is even manifest that this is not the case. Yet the analogy between the world and a work of art has its experimental verification in the very feeling itself of the beauty of the world, for the beautiful is the only source of the sense of beauty. This verification is valid only for those who have experienced that feeling, but those who have never felt it, and who are doubtless very rare, cannot perhaps be brought to God by any path" (IC 90). Weil rather closely reproduces Kant here in how she employs the grammar of "the beautiful," although she puts it to a much more pointed

of them. However, if one has this sense, it gives one a certain perspective on the various parts. They, in some way, can be seen to contribute to the whole, and the beauty of the whole can be found to be present in them. The goodness that beauty signals is something that one can thus continue to think, even in the parts, and even when the parts do not themselves seem to be good. Within the whole, even these seemingly deficient parts play a role. It is for this reason that Weil is able to talk about the "spiritual mechanics" of the universe. The universe is not a machine for grinding out good things, especially when we want or need them, as everybody well knows. Yet, somehow even in the midst of suffering, because of this sense of beauty and finality, hope remains. One can then think of life as an apprenticeship that brings one to a full love of the world, and appreciation of its goodness. She points out that one can't prove that the world was made with purpose. But because of its beauty, one is entitled to think that purpose is somehow interwoven in the world's mechanical workings (IC 90).

What ought to strike us is that this sense of transcendence and goodness comes from contemplating what is essentially matter and force. What that tokens is that matter and force are not all that there is to the world we live in. There is something else, an outside grace that permeates otherwise mindless necessity. As a result, Beauty gives us a sense of the universe as "our country here below" (WG 178); it is the "sensible image of good" (NB 246). We do not feel that justice, which is so important to us, is alien to the world in which we live. It is not an accident, nor is it merely something that we impose. Sartre once declared that human beings are an accident vomited up by nature. That is to say, nature is purposeless, and since we seek purpose, we are accidents and do not find ourselves at home in nature. Weil maintains the opposite. We are creatures of purpose, and the created world underpins that. "Beauty is a providential dispensation by which truth and justice, while still unrecognized, call silently for our attention. Beauty is really, as Plato says, an incarnation of God" (FLN 341).

---

use that is unique to her. See Immanuel Kant, *The Critique of Judgement*, trans. James Creed Meredith (Oxford: Oxford University Press, 1952).

Justice and Necessity

Weil thinks that this intuition of the world order as something other than mere force has far-reaching effects in how we think about any number of things. It has, for example, a clear effect in how one can conceive the beauty that is found in art. Art can be and is produced for pleasure or for various effects. Sometimes that is manipulative, and we do not mind. But there is also art that imitates the beauty of the world and has its value in giving us a sense of finality and completeness. In the microcosm of a canvas, or a poem, or a musical composition, we get access to the larger sense of beauty (NR 11). But if in this way the incarnation of Wisdom in matter in the universe as a whole can also be incarnated in a much smaller bit of matter, so can this Wisdom inspire any number of human projects. It can, she thinks, inspire social order and give us a sense of true justice:

> By looking at the world with keener senses than [those of the great instigators of violence], we shall find a more powerful encouragement in the thought of how these innumerable blind forces are limited, made to balance one against the other, brought to form a united whole by something which we do not understand, but which we call beauty. (NR 11)

As such, beauty can inspire our efforts with respect to the social order.

Borrowing from the Greeks, Weil develops a detailed understanding of physical phenomena and of creation that runs over into her understanding of justice, a sort of phenomenology of the relation between necessity and goodness. In both Plato's *Timaeus*, which she treats in the essay "Divine Love in Creation" (IC 89–105), and in his *Philebus*, creation comes about by taking the infinite, the *apeiron*, i.e., that which is without limits, and then something giving it limit, *peras*. For example, in the *Timaeus* (52-b), Plato talks of a primal necessity (*ananke*). This is not matter, as matter has form and can be described. Necessity cannot, but can only be assumed by a sort of "bastard reasoning." Necessity is something more like a receptacle, a passiveness upon which form is impressed. Once it receives form, or, rather, the forms of what material things there are, the creator can then further order these forms in relation to each other, creating a harmonious whole, a whole that in its order can be seen as admitting purpose, beauty, and goodness, all of which comes from its transcendent creator. Similarly, in *Philebus* (16-b), Plato talks of "the realities called eternal [which] derive from the one and the many, and carry, implanted within them, the determinate (*peras*) and the indeterminate (*apeiron*)."[7] In Weil's understanding, this is "not the union of the limited and the limitless, but what is much more beautiful: the union of that which limits and the non-limited. That which limits is God" (IC 100). So, God in giving form to the formless and ordering it effects the beauty of the world. Consequently, the world, which, even though it is full of all sorts of extremes, is "nevertheless continually bound up with, and in submission to, an absolutely unalterable order" (IC 101). That order witnesses to the Wisdom that shaped it. She writes:

> Brute force is not sovereign in this world. It is by nature blind and indeterminate. What is sovereign in this world is determinateness, limit. Eternal Wisdom imprisons this universe in a network, a web of determinations. The universe accepts passively. The brute force of matter, which appears to us sovereign, is nothing else in reality but perfect obedience. (NR 282)[8]

This union of the limited and unlimited is a key to human justice.[9] The human soul errs and brings in injustice when it gives into the unlimited—desires that are unlimited are unordered. Weil's important essay "The Iliad: Poem of Force" is a study of the destructiveness and madness of human endeavor, namely in war, when one believes that one possesses force and refuses limits. But when the human soul limits itself, and reins in force accordingly, it becomes capable of justice, and of living with others. In the essay "Are We Struggling for Justice?" (SWW 120–131) also written while Weil was in London, she argues that justice consists in seeking the consent of others in our projects, in restraining our-

---

7. Plato, *Philebus*, 16b. This is a translation of Weil's translation at IC 155.

8. While she utterly ignores Aristotelian science, there does seem to be in Aristotle's four causes (material, efficient, formal, and final) a hint or remembrance of the idea of the unlimited and the limited, as they, at the very least, allow many of the distinctions that the unlimited/limited schema calls for.

9. For a succinct and insightful treatment of this link, see Lawrence Schmidt, "The Language of Limitation as the Key to Simone Weil's Understanding of Beauty and Justice." *Attention*, no. 2 (Aug. 18, 2021): https://attentionsw.org/the-language-of-limitation-as-the-key-to-simone-weils-understanding-of-beauty-and-justice/.

selves from just extending whatever power we have. It is a matter of limiting ourselves in the presence of others, and in that limitation bringing ourselves into a harmony with the lives of others. This limitation in seeking the consent of others is at the heart of what obligations are about. As Lawrence Schmidt puts it, "Justice ... moves us as human beings to accept obligation and limit in the relationship to another individual and to the collectivities that from the context of our social relations."[10] In doing this, we order our lives in imitation of the beauty of the world. More importantly, we imitate the creator, who orders necessity, as Plato says, not by violence, but by persuasion. In doing so, we seek a goodness that dwells outside the world. We do not escape from the world, rather, in moral action, we incarnate the eternal goodness and wisdom, imitating God's own self-emptying (*kenosis*).

Necessity

Understanding the relation of the unlimited and the limited helps us also to understand just what Weil means by "necessity," a concept that she uses constantly throughout her writings. It is especially important with respect to what she thinks science involves. Having some clear sense of it is therefore important to bridge the distance between her accounts of creation given above and her critique of science.

Weil uses "necessity" in at least three different ways.[11] These different ways involve both subjective and objective factors and constitute an epistemological hierarchy. In the first place, "necessity" is the realm of brute fact. It is simply what we encounter in living in the world. It is our encounter with force. It is also the reality of the world that straightens us up when we engage in fantasies about our various projects. Subjectively, in relation to our sensibility, it is simply pleasure and pain. A person who lives at this level does not live morally on a level beyond the reign of force, and is one who finds the good simply to be one's own pleasure and

---

10. Schmidt, "The Language of Limitation."

11. For a detailed analysis of "necessity" in Weil and its relation to Plato's and the Pythagoreans' accounts of creation and its ordering, see Eric O. Springsted, "Divine Necessity: Weilian and Platonic Conceptions," in Diogenes Allen and Eric O. Springsted, *Spirit, Nature, and Community: Issues in the Thought of Simone Weil* (Albany, NY: State University of New York Press, 1994), 33–52.

ability to realize one's own projects. At this level, human life is itself devoid of purpose and essentially soulless. In this vein, Weil says that "[t] hose whom we call criminals are only tiles blown off a roof by the wind and falling at random. Their only fault is the initial choice by which they became those tiles" (SNL 177).

But human beings are something more than that. They can also *think* necessity under the description of mathematics, which necessity allows when it is shaped by imposed limits. So the human mind can see the events and things of necessity as ordered, and in strict relations that are quite thinkable. She points out that "Necessity always appears to us as an ensemble of laws of variation, determined by fixed relationships and invariants. Reality for the human mind is contact with necessity" (IC 178). This is the realm of science, for science deals with necessity as it discovers order in it. In that regard, as already noted, it is not just dealing with force, it is working on a different level. It sees order, and insofar as it can conceive that order, it can also consent to it and accept it as reality. One can contemplate it. This gives humans a sort of liberty, for we are not just the victims of what happens, we, as the Stoics knew, have dignity and agency in accepting the world as it is. We have risen above brute force, even though we have not left our very physicality. Weil says:

> This liberty is not actual in him except when he conceives of force as necessity, that is to say, when he contemplates it. He is not free to consent to force as such. The slave who sees the lash lifted above him does not consent, nor refuses his consent, he trembles. And yet under the name of necessity it is indeed to brute force that man consents, and when he consents to it is indeed to a lash. (IC 182)

This is a chastened sort of liberty, for it is the freedom of the one who knows that one is not an exception to the universe's laws. It involves the sort of wisdom and humility that comes from realizing the reality of the impersonalism of nature. That is a sort of wisdom that science can teach us.

But that is not all. Necessity as "an ensemble of the laws of variation" has the order it does because force has been given limits. So, at another level, necessity is not just this order, it is this order because it obeys a yet higher law. Necessity is, at this higher level, the obedience of matter to God. Beauty is what leads us to believe that necessity obeys something higher. It is therefore imperative to seek something more beyond the mathematical descriptions of physical reality. Then we can do more than simply consent to reality. We can love it as God's will.

It is because of these three senses of "necessity" that Weil can conclude her argument about science in *The Need for Roots* this way: "It is one and the same thing, which with respect to God is eternal Wisdom; with respect to the universe, perfect obedience; with respect to our love, beauty; with respect to our intelligence, balance of necessary relations; with respect to our flesh, brute force" (NR 291).

The Scientific Image of the Universe

Science is possible at the second level of necessity, for it studies the order of the universe. Indeed, science gives us the order of the universe as ordered force. Specifically, Weil understands it to be a matter of studying equilibrium and change. Equilibrium is a matter of limits; change is the rupture of equilibrium. But changes, when linked to all other changes in the universe, when ordered and given limits, compensate each other. That mutual compensation "makes all disequilibria an image of equilibrium, all changes an image of the motionless, and time an image of eternity"(SNL 79).

Weil is not a naive realist about science. Science for her does not simply discover and organize facts, and its history is not the ongoing fine tuning of what facts there are. Rather, science gives us an image of this equilibrium. It constructs this image, and over the course of the history of science it has done so in a number of different ways.[12] Almost always, the exception being contemporary science, it has done so by presenting this image under two considerations of the human life-world, which is to say, the world of the thinker who is thinking about the order of the world. In the first place, the image, while pertaining to the universe as a whole, is presented on a human scale so that its enormity does not overwhelm the mind, nor its fine details verge into the indiscernible (SNL 80). In doing so, the human life-world is integral to the image and is

---

12. In this regard, Weil's claims bear some analogy to Thomas Kuhn's notion of "paradigm shifts" in science in his *The Structure of Scientific Revolutions* (Chicago: University of Chicago Press, 2nd ed., 1986).

included in it, at least implicitly. Second, in doing this, the purpose, model, and principle of each of these images "is the relation between some aspiration of human thought and the effective conditions for realizing it; they reconstruct the whole universe according to this relation and try to decipher it in and through the world of appearances" (SNL 44). One cannot just make up a true image of the world at will. Nevertheless, Weil thinks, and she is not at odds with contemporary philosophy of science on this, that there can be as "many different systems of knowledge as there are relations of this kind conceivable by man between an aspiration and the conditions for fulfilling it, and the value of each system is, precisely, the value of the relation which constitutes its principle, and neither more nor less" (SNL 45).

One can see Weil's point in her presentation of Greek science and also in her discussion of classical science, that is, the science that reigned from Galileo to Newton up until quantum theory in the twentieth century. It is a point, as we shall see below, that is at the heart of her criticism of contemporary science. In Greek science, at least the science of the Pythagoreans and the Greek mathematicians such as Eudoxus and Archimedes, geometry was at its center, and at the center of its concern with geometry was a concern for equilibrium and balance. A thousand years later these conceptions gave way to the mechanics of classical science. But, Weil argues, Greek science was something more than just this. The concern for balance and equilibrium, while a concern for the physics of using levers and of circular motion, was a concern for a moral sense of equilibrium and balance as well (LPW 166). The physics did not dictate a set of morals, but its concepts have "all sorts of resonances and more than one meaning" (LPW 166). In this case, the aspiration of human thought that Greek science centered itself around is the human aspiration for justice and beauty and for something of the transcendent. The geometrical concepts of Greek science, such as equilibrium, harmony, proportion, and the like, therefore spilled over into Greek art and moral thinking. Greek science was a witness to the transcendent Good that gave limit to the unlimited world of force.

Classical science, once it shed itself of Aristotelian biologism and deductive method, inherited Greek science. But it also changed the root relation between human aspiration and the conditions for realizing that aspiration. Now the aspiration was for domination over the world, and the mechanics proposed for realizing this was taken from human labor.

The equations for energy are rooted in the idea of how much energy is required in, say, the work of lifting a stone to a certain height. In this regard, classical science still retained in its image of the universe something of the human life-world. But, Weil critically points out, this is a world of the slave and any aspiration to the good, except domination over nature, is absent. "In such a picture of the world, the good is everywhere absent, absent to the point that one will not even find a hint of its absence; for even the term of the relation that one is forced to suppress, the term that concerns the human, is entirely foreign to the good" (LPW 167). As a result, the beautiful is not a matter for consideration in classical physics. Insightfully, noting how artists regarded Newtonian physics, Weil observes that Keats and Goethe both hated Newton (LPW 167). One can add Blake's depiction of Newton drawing diagrams at the bottom of the sea of materialism. Thus, already in classical physics, we see Weil's central criticism that science has left us with nothing but force.

It is even worse with respect to contemporary physics which begins in Einstein, but it is especially so in quantum theory. Weil notes that contemporary physics is classical science after something has been taken away from it. What is that? The "analogy between the laws of nature and the conditions of work" (LPW 173). Not only has the good been left aside, chance now rules. Moreover, the physics of atoms, which is a central concern of contemporary physics, bears no relation to the physics of observable phenomena. Atoms are not really small billiard balls that function according to Newtonian mechanics the way that billiard balls do. They operate in very different ways, and, according to quantum physics, probability rules. So the human life-world is thoroughly excised for the image of the world that contemporary science produces.

While Weil complains about the absurdity of the world of physics—it just is not conceivable using natural language, although its results always get translated back into and explained by natural language—this does not mean that physics is a random and irrational exercise. Physics can easily be done, and is done, by mathematics. But this is not the geometry-based mathematics of Greek science, which are rooted in the phenomenal world; it is the mathematics of algebra, which involve symbols that can be mysterious and untranslatable into the human world. (Try making sense here of imaginary numbers such as the square root of -2.) For virtually all of her intellectual life, Weil was critical of algebra for just this reason, and voiced that concern both to her brother, the great mathematician André Weil, and to her teacher, Alain (SL 3–5; 112–126). In one variant of the essay "At the Price of an Infinite Error: The Scientific Image Ancient and Modern," Weil hints at a likeness of contemporary science to magic. Both involve an aspiration to power over nature, and both appeal for their efficacity to rites and symbols that are not fully understood (SNL 44).

While there is considerably more detail to Weil's case against contemporary science in the essay "At the Price of an Infinite Error: The Scientific Image Ancient and Modern," enough has now been said to understand just what her case is in *The Need for Roots*. At its center is the claim that contemporary and classical science, in the image of the universe that they have forged, fail to consider the human aspiration for good, or even the beauty of the world, which suggests that there is a good beyond force that limits it, and that lets the order of the universe be some sort of model for human projects.

Why does this matter? According to Weil, it matters because, while science has become more or less equated with the truth (usually more and not less), though the truth it presents is a truncated one for the human life-world, it does not include any consideration of transcending good. The good, for Weil, is *not* provable by science and can never be as such. But in considering the world as beautiful, which it can be considered as when seen as an ordered whole, science can and ought to point to a transcending good. It needs to do so, but its pointing cannot be a matter of positive knowledge, of facts. If it tries to do so, it quickly appears ridiculous, just as when in the Middle Ages Bernardin de Saint-Pierre, so convinced of the harmony of nature down to the smallest detail, declared that melons were meant to be eaten *en famille*, because they had stripes on the outside that indicated the pieces that they should be cut into (NR 277). But it can show an ability to generate some kind of metaphor and some analogies that can inspire art and morals. A world that in its scientific representation has no substance other than force cannot do that. There is no music of the spheres in such a world. In this sense, science, which is often portrayed as the greatest endeavor and achievement of the human mind, does not really hold in itself anything that ought to satisfy the human desire for goodness and beauty. If it doesn't, then the attraction and authority of science rests less on a truth that is loved and that bears contemplation, and more on its technological successes, its factual discoveries, and a sort of utilitarian and pragmatic understanding of truth. And in that, it also gives us an unfortunate model of what thought is about and for what it can be used.

Is Weil's Case Relevant?

What can we make of Weil's contentions about science and the role that it plays, or ought to play, in culture?

This is not an easy question to work through thoroughly. On the one hand, no physicist is likely to miss a beat in continuing his or her work because of Weil's critique of modern science. It is no more likely that, due to her criticism, scientists are going to rethink science and provide a different image of the universe than they currently do, or even worry much about such an image. This is all the more the case eighty years after she wrote that criticism. In fact, many of her own criticisms point in the direction of the extreme unlikelihood that this would happen. Yet, on the other hand, there is still something compelling about her case. Many of its particular criticisms and details are defensible and probative, and even echoed by others. Alfred North Whitehead and Edmund Husserl also argued that quantum theory was incomprehensible and failed to touch the human life-world, and that science had become lost in abstractions. So did Einstein, who famously complained of the image of chance that quantum theory presented us with, by saying that "God (*der Alte*) does not play dice with the universe." Her criticisms of the inability of scientists to change direction and consider alternative theories and images, and of how they live in an insular village, have parallels in the work of both Thomas Kuhn[13] and Paul Feyerabend.[14] And, as already noted, there is a certain parallel that can be drawn between Kuhn's work on how scientists work within paradigms and how it takes a revolution to change them, and Weil's writing of the history of science as a matter of shifts within the scientific image of the universe. That gives some reasonable sense to her call for rethinking the contemporary image, or lack thereof.

With respect to her larger case, Weil is quite right in her concern about science's lack of consideration of the good, and failure to incorporate some sense of it. Her considerations of the beauty of the world as an intuitive sense that there is something beyond force, some larger sense of purpose and coherence, some creating goodness, are striking. Such a sense is universal in world cultures, or nearly so. It certainly has played

---

13. See Kuhn, *The Structure of Scientific Revolutions*.
14. See Paul Feyerabend, *Against Method*, fourth edition (New York: Verso, 2010).

a role in Western thinking about God, including by philosophers and theologians such as Plato, Plotinus, Augustine, Aquinas, Bonaventure, and Nicholas of Cusa, to list just a few. The idea haunted Kant who certainly influenced Weil. But this is just where there is also the most difficulty, at least philosophically. Why should we, especially at this stage in the history of science, think that science should see as any part of its remit a consideration of a transcendent good, when science's job and method is to consider only empirical realities? Most scientists would not think that it is their job to think about anything beyond this at all.

Consider here Rush Rhees' comments on Weil's thinking about science, and Vance Morgan's assessment of them. Rhees, who was best known for his associations with Ludwig Wittgenstein, was deeply interested in Weil. He was most appreciative of her, but he also puzzled over some of her distinctive thinking in philosophy. Her views on science especially baffled him. Often, he worried, she constructed grand parallels based on a few common words that may well have had no common meaning. "Beauty" is one of those words. It may well mean different things in different contexts, and the beauty of a mathematical proof may well have nothing in common with the beauty of a Bach cello suite, much less the beauty of the universe. Asking science, therefore, to do all that Weil seems to want it to do, thus seems misplaced, and overly rationalistic. Why should we think that there could be an overarching image of the universe that is translatable into art and morals? Yet, Rhees also has a lurking suspicion that there is something profound in what Weil says. He just can't figure out what it is. Whatever it is, it seems to be on another plane, that of a *religious* insight.[15] In treating Rhees' comments, Vance Morgan suggests that perhaps it is Rhees who is stuck within a framework here that dictates what science is, whereas Weil is trying to challenge that framework, and trying to put things on a different foundational level. If Rhees sees science and religion as separate, Weil wants to gain a perspective in which they somehow overlap, or can be brought to bear on each other.[16]

Morgan's comments seem right. When he calls Weil's view, contra Rhees', "metaphysical," what I take him to mean is something that she

---

15. See Rush Rhees, *Discussions of Simone Weil*, D. Z. Phillips and Mario von der Ruhr, eds. (Albany, NY: State University of New York Press, 1999), especially 85–105.

16. See Morgan, *Weaving the World*, 80–89.

had maintained from the time of her 1934 essay "Reflections concerning the Causes of Liberty and Social Oppression" (OL 36–117). She had since then always believed that there is a "compact between the mind and the universe," so that some kind of representation of the universe is possible, although it can never be exhaustive, and is bought, as she says, "at the price of an infinite error." This is to say, it always has to leave something out. But what is just as important is that Weil thinks that there are so many different layers of meaning and value and that they cannot be reduced to just one. Her different senses of necessity noted above give an obvious proof that she thought this way. What she wants of science is some kind of recognition of this. She thinks that the ancient Greeks recognized it, and responded appropriately in their science and art. But, as a practical matter of her recommending, and even begging, that we need to change and develop a different sort of science now, as she does in *The Need for Roots*, this challenge is just the problem. It is hard to see how it can actually be responded to, or what it is asking for in present circumstances.

A good part of the difficulty in seeing the problem, I think, lies with Weil's continuing insistence on a universal method, a rigorous method to boot, something which Robert Chenavier has treated extensively in his essay on method (Chapter 6). It is hard when one hears this term not to think about contemporary scientific method, which more than anything else defines contemporary science and is imperious in its breadth. However, she does not want *this* method at all, and her later philosophy renounces it in words and in practice. The method she *now* wants is quite different. It includes, as Chenavier shows, these things: the need to use beauty as a clue to truth, a distinctive reading of history, and a demand to recognize and coordinate different levels. This new method apparently requires an inescapable subjective element.

Unfortunately, Weil does not spell out what this method should be, nor what makes it "rigorous." One wonders, therefore, what sense "method" even has left here. Weil herself only dropped hints about her desired method, and those are mainly seen in the resulting examples of her own distinctive approach. Perhaps, then, some other word than "method" should be found to describe what she was after. But, even if this is the case, we do not have to throw up our hands here quite yet. There is a core element in her call for a science that would take into consideration an overarching good that is important and deserves further reflection. As far as Weil is concerned, contemporary science, even when it is only implicitly so, is flattening with respect to our thinking about value. It does not provide an intellectual bridge or mid-point between the human and the eternal. Weil wants us to take a different kind of look at things. What kind of look is this? Peter Winch suggests what it is. If Greek science represents an escape from the limitation of looking at the world from a particular point of view, and gives us a multi-leveled representation of the universe, Winch argues that this is not all there is in her admiration of the Greek project. He argues:

> There is an aspect of her thinking about this which is particularly important, but also very easy to miss. It is not *merely* that Greek science is being said to seek a representation which will show the harmony and proportion between the elements with which it explicitly deals.... Her thought is *also* that the whole enterprise reflects in itself the incommensurability between the limited spatio-temporal character of human beings and their urge to understand the nature of the universe in which they exist.[17]

This is to say, the representation goes hand-in-hand itself with an inner aspiration to understand, and to put oneself in relation to, the universe, a rather humble one given our limitations. Winch thinks that this incommensurability between the individual thinker and the universal whole is experienced in the perception of beauty.[18] We see in it something awesome, something purer and better than us. That perception is something that we cannot simply stand outside of. It involves us, and it involves us in the lives of others, raising the question of moral harmony. This is what Weil wants to stress, and it is where questions of justice can arise.

This is where Weil's thinking about science and the order of the world inescapably verges into religious and moral questions. The representation of the universe as she wants it requires a sort of contemplation, and contemplation in this setting is not just merely "thinking about." Con-

---

17. Peter Winch, *Simone Weil: "The Just Balance"* (Cambridge: Cambridge University Press, 1989), 142.

18. To Winch's point, see her comment: "The beautiful goes beyond our intelligence, and yet every beautiful thing presents us with something to be understood, not only in itself but in our own destiny" (FLN 75).

templation involves a certain way of acting and being-towards-something. It requires a sort of restraint from possessing and dominating in favor of just looking, and of letting things exist. This is her point in talking about the beauty of the world as an implicit form of the love of God (WG 158–181). So, her whole case is not really understood until we see the importance of *contemplating* beauty. It is not just that modern science does not represent the world accurately, the very practice of modern science is too often at odds with a practice that is anything like a contemplative one. This, I suggest, is where Weil's recommendations have their real relevance: not in trying to get another representation of the universe *per se* (a conceptual map of the universe), but in getting us to contemplate the world, instead of simply solving the physical questions that the universe might pose to us, or trying to master the world. Morals and knowledge of the world are not separate.

There need not be a conflict between science and contemplation, although there usually is. It is not unusual for scientists to openly aver that they are struck by a sense of wonder, and that this has been important to them. It is an opening consideration that allows the possibility of some kind of dialogue between science and religion. But what all too often happens in that dialogue is that scientists want to continue invoking their sense of wonder while holding tightly onto scientific method, insisting that all work going forward needs to consider it or be done under its tutelage. The wonder then recedes and method takes over. At that point, religious questions to be considered comprehensible and solvable need to fit into this framework. What *then* happens is that questions of transcendence inevitably become naturalized. God, rather than being transcendent and eternal, gets treated as just a very large natural being, of lengthy duration. This can be seen, for example, in straightforward works such as Stephen Hawking's *A Brief History of Time* whenever Hawking considers a religious question, which is not often, or very penetrating when he does. It is even more obvious in aggressive works such as those by Richard Dawkins.[19] In the case of Dawkins, as Terry Eagleton once commented, his lack of understanding of talking about God is laughably obvious; his attempts to talk about God are as ham handed and fatuous as trying to insist that ballet steps are really just a botched attempt to catch a bus. For many scientists, then, the wonder stands

---

19. Richard Dawkins, *The God Delusion* (New York: Mariner Books, 2006).

oddly side by side with what too easily becomes a reductive approach to all questions.[20] Some, maybe even many, keep a sense of wonder and mystery somewhere in mind. But many more, and this is all too often the consensus of the scientific village, assume that a scientific education requires atheism, or, justifies it. It is at least considered an acceptable excuse for it. Many scientists confess that it is something that keeps them from being able to consider mystery. This is often a case of believing that there really is not any ultimate incommensurability between the limited nature of human beings and their attempts to understand the universe. They can do it, and they can master the problem. So wonder and adoration as life gripping surely are beside the point. A scientist can never give into them but must always press forward to give an explanation.

That is a *philosophical* judgment one way or the other. By itself, the scientific method or the current scientific image of the world self-admittedly does *not* consider the good. It has bracketed the question. To take on the position that because it does not consider the question that therefore the question itself is a non-starter is an error in logic and is question begging. So, if there is no image of the world forthcoming that might encourage science to take into consideration a more contemplative, and less problem solving-oriented approach, then perhaps the best recommendation one can make is to say that one needs continually and insistently to bear in mind that science as now practiced does *not* and *cannot* have anything to say about the good, or the beauty of the order of the world. Moreover, the scientific method should not be invoked with respect to questions of that sort. It is not and cannot be comprehensive as it stands, unless it reduces everything to one level. Here her critique is forceful.

Weil reminds us that the science of today does not and cannot think through questions about our destiny and any ultimate good. To think about the good that human beings aspire to then needs something other than science as we know it; it needs a different approach, a contemplative one, for example. One, of course, is not free to make up empirical facts to go along with it. But to take that kind of criticism of science seriously would be a start to thinking about the order of the world in a different way. It would at least leave the logical room to do so. But to find oneself

20. Terry Eagleton, "Lunging, Flailing, Mispunching, The God Delusion by Richard Dawkins," *London Review of Books*, vol. 28 no. 20, Oct. 19, 2006.

at home in that room may require another step, one into the religious. In that case, we are not entirely left with a meaningless universe. We still have in cultural memory the sort of harmony that Weil wanted to be contemplated. There are still religious symbols to be contemplated. There are still ways of talking to workers that can invoke a meaningful place in the world.[21]

The Question of Providence and Miracles

This, then brings us to Weil's discussion of miracles and Providence. Weil's first target here is a sense of miracle that is chiefly found in popular religion, especially Roman Catholicism. Miracles are direct interventions of God, perhaps done by a saint, prayed for by someone to somehow bring about a result that helps the one who is praying. The desired result might be a matter of healing; it could be a sign. As such, miracles can be described as a matter of a violation of the laws of nature. They are a direct intervention of God in the ongoings of the world, and done largely as a favor to the one who prays for a miracle. The intervention is required because, it seems to be believed, without it some important good will not occur. Weil is not wrong when she says that this makes God into a divine counterpart of the Roman emperor. In saying *that*, she also indicates just what sort of sense of miracle she has in mind and that she wants to correct.

Talking about miracles as a violation of the laws of nature (but, she says, we don't know what the laws of nature really are) is one possible way of talking about them. This is so especially if it is taken for granted that there are fixed laws of nature and they are the ones given by modern science, and that it would take a miracle to violate them. A more sophisticated position, though, such as one finds in Leibniz,[22] is slightly, but significantly different. Here miracles are acts of grace that bring about what nature by itself cannot and which are included in the very creation and fabric of the world to make it whole from the beginning. They in-

---

21. Such as in the essays "The First Condition for the Work of a Free Person" (LPW 131–144) and "Le christianisme et la vie des champs" (OC IV.1 263–271).

22. See, for example, Gottfried Wilhelm Leibniz, *Theodicy*, edited Diogenes Allen, E. M. Huggard, trans. (Indianapolis: Library of Liberal Arts, 1966).

clude Creation, and the Incarnation, both miracles that Weil herself believes, but does not bring into her discussion. This Leibnizian sense of miracle is probably closer to where she actually wants to go, as it allows for an integrated sense of nature and grace, which was Leibniz's life's goal. The world as we see it as a whole is a relation of nature and grace. Moreover, this sense of miracle does not preclude God's special providence which really should not be thrown out the window. So miracles are included in all that God has chosen to create. But most important in our context, this view also allows one to see what the point of miracles really is, which Weil gets right, namely that "[t]he exceptional character of the mighty acts [of Christ] had no other object than to draw attention. Once the attention has been drawn, there can be no other form of proof than beauty, purity, perfection" (NR 266). As she also puts it: "[W]hen a saint performs a miracle, what is good is the saintliness, not the miracle. A miracle is a physical phenomenon necessitating as one of its prerequisites a total abandonment of the soul either to good or to evil" (NR 263). The point of any miracle is to increase faith and holiness. It is not a favor granted to make one's life easier *simpliciter*. It is not an interruption, but a completion and perfection of nature, of necessity, and thereby allows nature and grace to work together. That is what Weil is after.

So, the real strength of her case is not in the battle with popular notions about miracles. It is her larger case, argued at length in her discussions of science, that the order of the world is not a matter of force and something neutral, with the good being a stranger to it. Rather, the world of nature as the human mind encounters it, is an ordered whole; it has limits transforming brute force, and these limits are imposed from the outside. They are a matter of grace. Thus we should avoid the Roman emperor model of God interfering in nature to make up its deficiencies, or what Dietrich Bonhoeffer called "the god of the gaps." This treats God as a divine plumber who fixes leaks in the plumbing system God invented. Her real case is a call within religion to treat the world of nature not as God's incomplete intention. It is to get religion to talk about the creation as something that involves within it God's ordering grace.

The strength—and ongoing relevance—of what she wants to argue in *The Need for Roots* in this section on Providence and miracles is to argue that religion needs to pay attention to the fact that nature is God's *creation*, and that as such it is not separate from God's grace or, in the case of human beings, their destiny. Rather, it is like a sacrament.[23] It involves both matter and the presence of God. Because it does, it demands contemplation, an attitude of looking and attention, and something deeper than problem solving.

Conclusion

At the center of Weil's discussion of science and providence is a long-held idea of hers on Creation. Creation is an ordering of brute force and necessity, turning it into an order of the world that is an integration of nature and grace, necessity, and goodness. Weil was always careful to make clear that it was an integration. The order of the world is not sacred, but, to the thinking human mind, in its beauty it hints at and reveals its divine source. In her readings of the ancient Greeks, Weil saw a possibility that science could make this somehow evident in a representation of the order of the world. Moreover, this representation called for a contemplative stance to the world that spilled over into morals, religion, and art. It was a key to having the sort of integrated culture, rooted in the eternal, that she called for in *The Need for Roots*. It would be a source for the ordering of human life that was responsive to the divine.

Her argument in *The Need for Roots* is a critique of both contemporary science and religion for failing to take this integration of nature and grace seriously, or, for forgetting it altogether. This failure consequently leaves us with a sense that force alone rules the universe, and with a religion that embraces less than the Creation, one that is sectioned off into private life. It leaves the motivation for science and its authority no longer in helping us to think about how to live, but in the power it gives us over nature. Science is treated as authoritative in part because of its inflated and unjustified claims to comprehensiveness, and in part simply because of its technological and commercial deliverances. That is no small thing, but it obscures a wider context of human life. This she wanted to reverse.

Weil's challenges to rethink science's representation of the universe are not likely to produce a new way of thinking about science. Other than giving a broad outline in a sketch for a new science (SNL 79–84),

---

23. See Springsted, *Simone Weil for the Twenty-First Century*, 105–118.

she herself did not give much of a sense of what that would even look like, other than pointing to how the ancients did it. Still, her arguments call on us to think about the issues in new and concentrated way. If we are not about to have new science, at least, until we have been newly inspired,[24] we can take science's authority for what it is, and understand far more critically what it decidedly is not, no matter what its pretensions. It has nothing to say about the good. We can then look at the Creation and order of the world in ways that are not constrained by the flattened picture of the world that scientific methods tend to lead to. That is not as detailed and methodically rigorous as Weil would have liked, but she may well have overextended her position in this regard. It may cause us, though, to take seriously that life is lived within a mystery, and that human thought and the order it gives to human communal life needs to depend on a beauty that transcends human thought itself. It may cause us to look for a gift and a goodness that can give sense and direction to our aspirations and our limits.

24. It is important to keep in mind that Weil is first looking for a way to inspire a people, and from that inspiration, things would, in time, change. She is not calling for a new France to invent a new science as soon as the Nazis were expelled.

CHAPTER 9

Work as the Spiritual Basis of Culture

Simone Kotva

The Critique of Working Conditions

Simone Weil carried on her search for a spiritual renewal of society
by criticizing extant modes of organized labor and suggesting detailed
plans for the total re-organization of working conditions, especially in
factories (a pressing concern following the French factory workers' occupation strike in 1936).[1] If Weil's remarks on politics in *The Need for
Roots* display a generalizing tendency, the same cannot be said of her
reflections on work: here Weil is remarkably detailed, and we find reflections not only on the meaning of labor but on the education of manual
laborers and the improvement of mechanical equipment. At the most
substantive level, Weil sought to show that only a philosophy based on
the critique of working conditions could understand the way in which
specific milieux constitute the individual. Hence, Weil not only reflects
philosophically on the nature of work, but attempted to expose the process of philosophical reflection to the realities of labor, and to do so from
the perspective of first-hand experience.

---

1. Michael Torigian, "The Occupation of the Factories: Paris 1936, Flint 1937," *Comparative Studies in Society and History*, vol. 41, no. 2 (1999): 324–47.

In *Need for Roots* Weil provides an example of what one commentator has called a "theological ontology of labor, linking divine and human work" in order "to draw some conclusions from this to apply to the practical problem of labor."[2] Weil proffers particular and explicit suggestions on the physical transformation of working-class conditions; these particular suggestions were developed alongside Weil's philosophy and her religious experiences and convictions. Her approach is more or less critical of society, and this is expressed by the utopian tone in which she chooses to write.[3] Work is inseparable from universal belonging and can only be realized in an equal society devoid of coercion, suppression, and domination. Thus, the critique of working conditions cannot be Marxist in the narrow sense of a strict empiricism, nor in any sense which would forsake those elements also essential for an adequate conception of "the soul" and which Weil considered to be intrinsically spiritual, such as "goodness," "truth," "beauty," and questions of morality:

> A civilization based upon the spirituality of work would give to Man [*sic*] the very strongest possible roots in the wide universe, and would consequently be the opposite of that state in which we find ourselves now, characterized by an almost total uprootedness. Such a civilization is, therefore, by its very nature, the object to which we should aspire as the antidote to our sufferings. (NR 98)

The "spirituality of work" is the question of what Weil calls "true greatness" (NR 97). True greatness is constructed on the basis not of achievement, glory, or recognition (even the recognition of friends and peers) but on the basis of pleasure, delight, and joy: "Nothing in the world can make up for the loss of joy in one's work" (NR 81).

Weil's passages on work in *Need for Roots* are focussed on in Part II, where she discusses "Uprootedness," or loss of a sense of belonging. The section titled "Uprootedness in the Towns" addresses factory work (NR 45–78). This part is the most detailed in scope and precision, while "Uprootedness in the Countryside" centers on farming communities and the

---

2. John Hughes, *The End of Work: Theological Critique of Capitalism* (Oxford: Blackwell, 2007), 7. Hughes is discussing a broader movement of theological writers reflecting on the nature of work at the opening of the twentieth century.

3. David McLellan, *Simone Weil: Utopian Pessimist* (Basingstoke: Palgrave Macmillan, 1989).

relationship between town and country (NR 78–97), areas where Weil had less personal experience. Her analyses deal with a wide array of topics, including technology, economics, and the education of workers, as well as consisting of reflections on cultural mentalities, the conflict between urban and rural communities of workers, and more general theoretical concerns. At the end of each of these sections are proposals for re-organizing working conditions in urbanized areas and in the countryside. The most famous of these is the "plan for re-establishing the working-class by the roots," which touches principally on working milieux in towns (NR 73–78). But her comments on work are not restricted to Part II, and the question of physical labor—its spiritual meaning and place in society—occupies her thought again and at length in the very final pages of the book.[4] In an important sense that will become clear as we proceed, the critique of working conditions is at the heart of *Need for Roots*.

Weil desired to experience something of the realities of manual labor for herself.[5] Barely a year into her first teaching position—at a girls' *lycée* in Roanne—Weil applied for leave of absence for the 1934–1935 academic year. She made arrangements with Auguste Detœuf (1883–1947), essayist and founder of the Alsthom factory (a plant that made electrical equipment for metro cars and trams), to be hired as an unskilled worker.[6] Her correspondence indicates the significance of this year for Weil, who wrote of it attentively and at length.[7] Later, in Marseille in 1940, while exiled from Paris during the Vichy regime, she requested that Father Perrin (1905–2002)[8] find her work as a farm hand. Perrin put her in touch with his friend Gustave Thibon (1903–2001), a self-taught philosopher and farmer in the *Ardèche*. From Thibon's farm Weil commuted to the grape harvest, where she worked for four weeks, eight hours a day,

---

4. E.g., NR 15–16 (working conditions), 29–31 (trade unions), 35–36 (the modern factory), 295–298 (general theory of physical labor). The final pages of *Need for Roots* are discussed at the end of this chapter.

5. George Abbott White, "Simone Weil's Work Experiences: From Wigan Pier to Chrystie Street," *CrossCurrents* vol. 31, no. 2 (summer, 1981): 129–62.

6. Detœuf was, at the time Weil contacted him, managing director of the company that then owned Alsthom (now Alstom SA). For Weil's letters to Detœuf, written in the summer following her factory year, see SL 55–69.

7. E.g., SL 14–71.

8. Perrin was a local Dominican priest working with Jewish refugees, who subsequently became Weil's informal spiritual director.

every day.[9] Weil draws heavily on both experiences in *Need for Roots*; they are also mentioned by T. S. Eliot, in his then widely noticed preface to the first edition of the English translation (NR xiii–xiv).

The critique of working conditions, moreover, occupied Weil's thought from an early age. From 1925–1928 she attended the Henri-IV Lycée, where she studied under Alain (Émile-Auguste Chartier, 1861–1951), a charismatic philosophy lecturer and also prolific public intellectual who wrote copiously on the division of labor and the tension between the proletariat and bourgeoisie.[10] In the 1920s, Alain stood for the school of French classical radicalism during the Third Republic (Jean-Jacques Rousseau and his thought above all), but also traditionalist currents, as opposed to the socialist agenda later espoused by the French Radical party (founded in 1901). From the 1900s onward, there had been a dispute between radicals and socialists over how to define the working classes. Alain questioned Marx's view of the proletariat as consisting of those bereft or dispossessed of property, arguing instead that the true proletariat were *"those who act and do*, primarily artisans, labourers who work with their hands and with simple machines and tools."[11] Weil then associated herself with the school of Alain, with developing a new account of work that would see the latter as a form of being,

---

9. Weil had initially intended for this experience to equal that of her "Factory year" in length. Simone Pétrement, *Simone Weil: A Life* (New York: Pantheon Books, 1976), 423 (letter to Gilbert Kahn). Recollections of Weil during her time in the *Ardèche* can be found in Joseph-Marie Perrin and Gustave Thibon, *Simone Weil as We Knew Her*, Emma Craufurd trans. (London: Routledge, 2003), 104–105. Thibon later went onto become a celebrated Catholic author and public intellectual.

10. Gilbert Kahn, "Simone Weil et Alain," *Cahiers Simone Weil*, vol. 14, no. 3 (1991): 206–12. On Alain and his influence on Weil's generation, see Jean-Francois Sirinelli, *Génération intellectuelles: Khâgneux et normaliens entre dans l'entre-deux-geurres* (Paris: Fayard, 1988), 427–496.

11. Ronald Howell, "The Philosopher Alain and French Classical Radicalism," *Political Research Quarterly*, vol. 18, no. 3 (1965): 594–614, at 612 (emphasis in original). The best summary of Alain's political thought, displaying his emphasis on individual liberty, is *Le citoyen contre les pouvoirs* ("The Citizen Against the Powers that Be") (Genève: Slatkine Reprints: 1979 [1926]). For a discussion, see the illuminating account by Raymond Aron, *Introduction à la philosophie politique* (Paris, 1997), 17, 27. Aron was, like Weil, a former pupil of Alain.

rather than as an occupation. Alain in turn praised Weil's early political essays for being written "as with a workman's pickaxe."[12]

Weil's writings on labour re-organization are uncompromising and embody much of the spirit and indeed the letter of French classical radicalism. The main analysis (contained in "Uprootedness in towns" and "Uprootedness in the countryside") is full of elliptical references to Alain's general philosophy and ideas regarding labor, such as the insufficiency of Marxism, the danger posed by collectives and big society thinking, and the obligation to provide for the worker's individual liberty.[13] The starting point is thus at once politically progressive and socially conservative, with Weil calling for the liberation of the working classes yet disparaging extant socialist imperatives and defending traditional values, such as family and private ownership. Over the course of these sections, Weil makes suggestions for a re-organization of working conditions which, according to her expression, would be "neither capitalist nor socialist" (NR 77). For example, instead of organizing working environments so as to promote the interests of competition (capitalism) or big industry (socialism), Weil suggests organizing factories in order to serve the needs of the individual worker, their family life, and their local community and environment. So, "[l]arge factories would be abolished" and all work would be outsourced to "an assembly shop connected with a number of little workshops, each containing one or more workmen [sic], dispersed throughout the country" (NR 73). Machines would be improved, but developed so as to increase the operator's autonomy, intellectual interest, and general well-being, rather than the rate of production. Machines would be multi-purpose and ergonomic, enabling independent and safe manufacture of a variety of goods in response to the fluctuations of demand—thus all workers would be "competent professionals" in charge of their own workshop (NR 58). Working days would be short, with ample time for leisure and socializing: thus, house-

---

12. In *La Table Ronde*, vol. 28 (1950), 47, quoted in Athanasios Moulakis, *Simone Weil and the Politics of Self-Denial*, Ruth Hein trans. (Columbia: University of Missouri Press, 1998). On Weil and Alain with regard to work, see Robert Chenavier, *Simone Weil: Une philosophie du travail* (Paris: Cerf, 2001). It should be pointed out that Weil's association with Alain was not an identification: "One day she told [Gilbert] Kahn that there was in Alain's thought a part that seemed integral to her beliefs and another part that she no longer accepted." Pétrement, *Simone Weil*, 414.

13. Moulakis, *Simone Weil*, 79–93.

hold economies and local demands, rather than top-down dictates, would guide the speed and rate of production. Education would consist of a mixture of classroom lectures and work placements, on the model of the apprenticeship (the decline of which Weil laments at length, NR 63). A tailor-built curriculum would consist of literature concerning "the human condition," as well as advanced classes in the natural sciences—the latter taught principally through a down-to-earth "analogical method" involving images from mechanics, since these would be most familiar and appropriate to the aspiring technician (NR 70).[14] When apprentices reached adolescence, they would be offered the opportunity to embark on a *Tour de France* of the nation's workshops, acquiring new skills and making useful contacts.

The account of farming life proceeds in the same manner, with a programmatic decentralizing assumed as the requisite for restoring autonomy to the individual agricultural labourer, together with an emphasis on curricula tailored to stimulate intellectual interest and pride in farming. In one place, Weil goes into great detail on how the "analogical method" already mentioned in relation to the education of factory workers would be adapted to farm work. Farmers' children should be taught the natural sciences on the model of biological rather than mechanical action, and thus photosynthesis should be the operative metaphor: "Everything connected with Science can be situated around this cycle, for the notion of energy is at the heart of everything. Were the thought of this cycle to sink deep into the minds of peasants, it would permeate their labour with poetry" (NR 87). A large part of an aspiring farmer's education would consist, additionally, of an immersion into the "folklore of all countries" and the parables of the New Testament (NR 91–93). The latter, Weil reasons, are mostly drawn from the agricultural year and eminently suited to an audience of farm laborers. Religious themes would be central but not restricted to Christianity, however; the aim would be to cultivate discussion "about no matter what genuine current of religious thought" (NR 93). Work would thus be inseparable from both intellectual and spiritual activities. As in the section on the re-organization of urban working conditions, the main concern is to think

---

14. On method and its meaning in Weil's philosophy, see Robert Chenavier's essay (Chapter 6) in this book. For Weil's early and detailed remarks on the "analogical method," see SL, 3–5 (letter to Alain).

not only of ways in which work may be made easier and less exhausting, but also to consider the factors necessary in order to create milieux where work would be experienced as pleasurable and above all as a source of spiritual nourishment.

The Philosophy of Action

Weil's understanding of work in *Need for Roots* is typical of the philosophy of action, a prevailing theory of freedom and social responsibility, developed by a number of writers in the 1890s largely on the basis of a French nineteenth-century current known as "spiritualism."[15] The philosophy of action had direct implications for Weil's conception of manual labor as "spiritual," and for how she conceives of "spirituality." Alain's teacher Jules Lagneau (1851–1894), was the most relevant spiritualist thinker influencing Weil; in addition, Henri Bergson (1859–1941) and Maurice Blondel (1861–1949) were all contemporaries of Alain whose work developed the philosophy of action. This influence proved far more important than the influence of Marxism.[16]

The issue that preoccupied these writers was how to harmonize freedom with necessity. The opposition between freedom and necessity that had prevailed ever since Descartes's *Meditations* was redefined fundamentally by the engagement of spiritualist philosophers during the second half of the nineteenth century. Put simply, Cartesian philosophy, especially as it had been revived under Victor Cousin (1792–1867) at the beginning of the century, stood for the reification of spirit and the debasing of matter, and for the identification of freedom with a form of activity that was mental rather than bodily. Cousin originally called this type of Cartesianism "spiritualism," following a pre-modern precedent; and it meant a valorization of intellectual effort and a complete disassociation of spiritual activity from the body.[17]

---

15. Jean-Louis Vieillard-Baron, *Le spiritualisme français* (Paris: Cerf, 2021).

16. Weil criticizes Bergson's philosophy in *Need for Roots* (NR 246, 256), but both philosophers were working within a shared tradition of ideas. On Weil and spiritualism, see Simone Kotva, *Effort and Grace: On the Spiritual Exercise of Philosophy* (London: Bloomsbury, 2020), viii–xii, 131–172. I return to Weil's critique of Bergson at the end of this chapter.

17. Vieillard-Baron, *Spiritualisme français*, 87–114.

In the 1860s a reaction to Cousin's spiritualism set in and an alternative definition was proposed by Félix Ravaisson (1813–1900). Ravaisson was supported by a group appalled by the prevailing nationalist philosophy, which they judged to be excessively idealist. Ravaisson thus defined his spiritualism as "positivist" and "realist," contrasting it to the idealism of Cousin's school, and put embodied action at the heart of spiritualist philosophy.[18] In the early 1890s, versions of Ravaisson's spiritualism reached their most explicit statement in several influential texts focussing on the theme of action,[19] among them Lagneau's "Simple notes pour un programme d'union et d'action" ("Brief Notes concerning a Programme for Union and Action,"1892). Lagneau's short manifesto applied the spiritualist philosophy of action to contemporary society.[20] The final section, "Notre action" ("Our Action"), is devoted to describing "a high spiritualism preached by example first, by action," an "active union," "without ulterior motive and without any mystery," which would provide "the living core of the future society" and "re-establish social harmony."[21] The manifesto explains what "action" is and how it will serve the purpose of creating "the material conditions of morality." "Action" is to be neither collective nor ideological but charitable ("a pure and active charity"); "action" will attend to the spiritual and moral needs of the individual in direct defiance of an "outer" society based on interest, competition, and legal justice. "Our rule," writes Lagneau, is "to combat false optimism, the low hope of a happiness that would come ready-made, the belief in salvation by science alone and by material civilisation, this vain figure of civilization—a precarious external arrangement that is a poor substitute for intimate agreement, the consent of souls."[22] After Lagneau's death in 1894, his ideas were iterated by Alain, who en-

---

18. Félix Ravaisson, *Rapport sur la philosophie en France au XIXème siècle* (Paris: Fayard, 1984 [1867]), 243.

19. Cf. Maurice Blondel, *Action: Essay on a Critique of Life and a Science of Practice*, Oliva Blanchette trans. (Notre Dame: Notre Dame University Press, 1984 [1893]); Henri Bergson, *Matter and Memory*, N. M. Paul and W. S. Palmer trans. (New York: Zone Books, 1991 [based on 5th ed. of 1908]).

20. Jules Lagneau, *Écrits de Jules Lagneau réunis par soins de ses disciples* (Paris: Sandre, 2006), 117–121.

21. Lagneau, *Écrits*, 121 (my translation).

22. Lagneau, *Écrits*, 120 (my translation).

couraged his students to read and reflect on Lagneau's philosophy of action.[23]

The philosophy of action is thus highly complex. On the one hand, it was a reaction to idealism, and an attempt to develop a more embodied account of freedom. On the other hand, in Lagneau's interpretation, it meant the adoption and development of new forms of social criticism in order to create universal fellowship. Weil was enthusiastic about the possibilities offered by both approaches, and her own "spirituality of work" represents yet another spiritualist interpretation of action. These notions appear early in her work, under many different labels.[24] They structure much of Weil's underlying thinking, in *Need for Roots*, about the nature and meaning of work.

Two of Weil's early definitions of work, written while she was still in close proximity to Alain and fresh from her first encounter with Lagneau's thought, are the most germinal for her later ideas. Her university dissertation, "Science and Perception in Descartes" (1929–1930), ends with a remarkable paean to the crafts of the pilot and agricultural laborer as models for scientific reason, while her "Factory Journal" (1934–1935) seeks to reclaim manual labor from the encroachments of big society. Her choice to focus on work—rather than on the more abstract notion of "action"—is a development of Lagneau's socially oriented spiritualism, and her interpretation of work is consistent with spiritualist ways of harmonizing freedom and necessity.[25]

Work re-unites the two substances prised apart by Cartesian metaphysics, Weil argues in her university dissertation. The body follows the commands of thought and yet perception is foundational to knowledge, and the method of philosophy is essentially a close study of sensations and their relationship to will—that is, philosophy is a study of work: "Only through the intermediary of the world, through the intermediary of work, do I reunite […] the two parts of myself, the one that undergoes and the one that acts" (FW 57). At the same time, Weil maintains that Descartes was right to recognize that there are two very different

---

23. Robert Bourgne, ed., *Colloque Alain—Jules Lagneau* (Paris: Le Vésinet, 1993).

24. Kotva, *Effort and Grace*, 131–172.

25. Chenavier argues that the preference for "work" over "action" is distinctive of Weil's thought. This preference is amplified in Weil's religious philosophy, where the analysis of work reflects the analysis of contemplation, and thus adjectives denoting passivity dominate (pre-eminently, "waiting"). See Chenavier, *Simone Weil*.

aspects to reality, the active (spiritual) and the passive (material). What, then, to make of work? Work cannot be defined as purely spiritual nor as purely material; rather than being an expression of either substance taken separately, work is the medium through which spirit and matter, or "the one who acts" and "the one who undergoes," combine. She expresses this by saying that in work, freedom and necessity are no longer in opposition:

> The great correlations that form the core of the doctrine become apparent; there is no longer any contradiction between freedom and necessity, idealism and realism. To no longer be brought up short by this last opposition it is enough to observe that the whole mind acts when thought is applied to an object (FW 87).

This theory of work is at one with the philosophy of spiritual action and the general trajectory of spiritualist thinking, and with spiritualist ways of harmonizing freedom and necessity—the realm of spirit with the sphere of matter—by insisting on the primacy of embodiment.[26] For Weil, the justification of her theory is thus to be found in the lived experience of work. If mind and body were truly separate, then how is it that physical tasks, such as sailing and tilling, are able to occupy a person's entire mental faculty? For "the whole mind acts when thought is applied to an object" (FW 63).

Weil rejects the view that work, or embodied action, is alien to intellectual effort or thought. The two are one: "the pilot who holds the tiller in the storm, the peasant who swings the scythe, knows himself [sic] and knows the world in the way meant by the statement 'I think, therefore I am' and the ideas that follow from it. Workers know everything" (FW 85). "[H]owever," she goes on, "when their work is done, they do not know that they had all the wisdom in their possession" (FW 85). Work-

---

26. Lissa McCullough, "Simone Weil's Phenomenology of the Body," *Comparative and Continental Philosophy*, vol. 4, no. 2 (2012), 195–218. Weil's essay is also typical in taking Descartes and Cartesian method as a touching stone. French spiritualism after Ravaisson rejected substance dualism while maintaining that reality was constitutive of two distinct perspectives or modalities—active and passive. Weil is working on the assumption that while Descartes was mistaken in the way he interpreted his study of reality, his method of studying reality, including his distinction between activity and passivity, was true.

ers are not elevated to scientists or philosophers in terms of a romanticized view of manual laborers; instead, "scientific" discoveries and "philosophical" insights are only achieved under conditions of work, that is, through the body. When scientific proofs and demonstrations about the world are referred to as isolated objects, they become detached from the simple perception through which "I touch the world directly" (FW 85). Science does not presuppose a distant view of matter, but always arises on the basis of a direct engagement with material forces and expresses the experience of that engagement. "Science so conceived [...] will add only one thing to the knowledge that is implicit in self-conscious work, namely, it will add the knowledge that that knowledge contains all there is to know, and that there is nothing else" (FW 86). If, for example, a worker experiences a direct contact with the universe in a simple perception, science will do nothing but break this sensation down into its component parts; it is not privy to occult knowledge hidden from the view of the ordinary person. To exist is to act. Thus, the spiritualist philosophy of action is Weil's criterion, in her 1929 dissertation, for what counts as work.

Weil therefore rejects the idea that the working-class needs to be liberated *from* work; instead, she sees work itself as the salvation to be sought by workers. For spiritualists like Lagneau, embodied action rather than intellectual effort represented true freedom, and Weil applies this reasoning also to physical work or labor (*travail, labeur*). If, in society, work is experienced as humiliating servitude, this cannot be the fault of work but must be the fault of society.[27] Weil develops this argument in her "Factory Journal," the principal source for Weil's remarks on the re-organization of urban working conditions in *Need for Roots*. This journal reflects material gathered between December 1934 and August 1935, when Weil kept a notebook recording her experience working in three different factories outside Paris. Here, we see Weil railing against the inhumane treatment of workers yet at the same time appreciating the thrill of physical labor and the satisfaction of a job well done. What she comes to dislike about factory life is less the work itself (though she also has, as we have already seen, ample criticisms of one-sided and monotonous labor) but the way in which the factories *qua* working environ-

---

27. Roy Pierce. "Sociology and Utopia: The Early Writings of Simone Weil," *Political Science Quarterly*, vol. 77, no. 4 (1962): 505–525.

ments subvert the pleasure of work, reducing what, in another setting, could be pleasant and convivial yet to a nightmare. External pressures imposed by speed, efficiency, and productivity, combined with fear of punishment, hunger, and malaise, make all other thinking impossible:

> The effect of exhaustion is to make me forget my real reasons for spending time in the factory [...] It's only on Saturday afternoon and Sunday that a few memories and shreds of ideas return to me, and I remember that I am *also* a thinking being. [...]
>
> Revolt is impossible, except for momentary flashes (I mean even as a feeling). [...] We are like horses who hurt themselves as soon as they pull on their bits—and we bow our heads. We even lose consciousness of the situation; we just submit. Any reawakening of thought is then painful. (FW 171)

This perspective reflects Weil's earlier argument in "Science and Perception in Descartes," but tackles it from the perspective of first-hand experience. In her university dissertation, Weil had written about how manual labor unites mind and body. That perspective, while not romantic, nonetheless paints work in rosy hues. What she experiences in the factory is the disjunction of mind and body: too exhausted to think straight, she is all body, and forgets "that I am *also* a thinking being" (FW 171). Her conclusion is that factory work forces a separation of a person into mind and body, compartmentalizing (as she will say later in *Need for Roots*) a person into a creature who toils on the one hand, and a creature who occasionally thinks, on the other. In order to work at the "uninterrupted tempo" required, Weil finds that she needs to repeat continually to herself the operations, "not so much to keep myself from making a blunder as to prevent myself from thinking, which is the condition for going fast" (FW, 185). The question is not whether physical labor debases the factory worker, but whether factories debase the spirit of physical labor.

It was Lagneau's socially oriented philosophy of action that gave Weil the philosophical tools with which to reflect on her experience of factory work in ways that contribute to the spiritualist task of harmonizing freedom and necessity, or mind and body. Factory work makes the free activity of a person impossible. Simply to exert oneself, with no space for thinking, is not to act as a free person. Only when the rhythm of physical labor is unhurried and relaxed enough to allow for thinking is it possible to speak of work, as opposed to slavery and the "bowing of the head." Weil traces the changing status of freedom and necessity among the types of work she encounters in the factories. Wherever speed is imposed, the feeling of slavery increases. This situation is most extreme in the worst-paid jobs where, in order to meet the "rate," the physical exertion required is so exhausting as to break the body prematurely; in addition, such work typically is performed by single workers in isolation from colleagues. By contrast, in shops where the work is better paid, tasks are generally less physically taxing, more collaborative, and, as a result, independence increases. In such shops, where Weil was allowed to work only infrequently, Weil observes people working together, discussing their craft, consulting complicated geometrical designs and generally working carefully and without haste, with time to socialize. Unhurried work thus decreases significantly the sense of enslavement and restores the feeling of autonomy. In a letter written in 1935, Weil cannot stress enough her belief that it is possible to experience perfect freedom in manual labor, even in the manual labor of the factory floor. "But that experience stands out as unique in my factory life," she comments (SL 21). This alternative working milieu is not the rule, and indeed, to model entire factories on it would be to undo their current form. In her "Factory Journal," the list of "changes to be desired" thus passes over in silence the question of salaries, hygiene, and living conditions and addresses instead the organisation of the factory floor and its layout, with the new order of machines organized so as to give "every worker a view of the entire process" (FW 194). The aim is to envisage not an alternative to manual labour, nor a better-paid version of extant factory work, but an organization of manual labour in which the needs of the body and of the mind were both satisfactorily met, where necessity and freedom could and would coincide.

A Changed System for the Concentration of Attention

The popular school's job is to give more dignity to work by infusing it with thought, and not to make of the working-man a thing divided up into compartments which sometimes works and sometimes thinks. Naturally, a peasant who is sowing has to be careful to cast the seed properly, and to be thinking about lessons learnt at school. But the object which engages our attention doesn't form the whole content of our thoughts. A happy young woman, expecting her first child, and busy sewing a layette, thinks about sewing it properly. But she never forgets for an instant the child she is carrying inside her. At precisely the same moment, somewhere in a prison workshop, a female convict is also sewing, thinking, too, about sewing properly, for she is afraid of being punished. One might imagine both women to be doing the same work at the same time, and having their attention absorbed by means of the same technical difficulties. And yet a whole gulf of difference lies between one occupation and the other. The whole social problem consists in making the workers pass from one to the other of these two occupational extremes. (NR 94–95)

In *Need for Roots*, Weil pictures the relationship of body to mind in work as a direct result of the concentration of attention. In the example given by Weil, and quoted above, we see how mind and body are compartmentalized and harmonized alternatively, depending on the form of attention; in turn, we are shown how attention is shaped by specific working conditions. The milieu of the female convict strains attention to focus on nothing but the work at hand, leaving the ability to think about other things difficult if not impossible. This is the forced separation of body from mind that Weil experienced during her time in the factories, and which is given here as the principal cause for workers' unhappiness. The milieu of the expectant mother, by contrast, relaxes the attention so that—while the mother remains absorbed fully in the task of sewing—she nonetheless is also able to be attentive to other things. This is the harmonizing of mind and body that Weil describes in her university dissertation from 1929, and which Weil, in this example, now situates in a domestic working environment free of fear. A civilization founded on the spiritual nature of work facilitates the harmonizing of mind and body by providing working environments in which attention is relaxed rather than strained. The guiding principle for reorganizing working conditions is thus, for Weil, the question of attention, rather than of production: "We must change the system concerning concentration of attention during working hours, the type of stimulants which make for the overcoming of laziness or exhaustion—and which at present are merely fear and extra pay" (NR 55).

As a factor in determining the efficiency of the worker's productivity, attention may refer to concentration, or the ability to focus on one task exclusively, but as receptivity to surroundings and extraneous thoughts, it must be considered as a form of receptiveness, in a way analogous to John of the Cross' understanding of attention as a "passive waiting" for God.[28] The notion of attention (*l'attention*) that would be at the same time a kind of waiting (*l'attente*) or expectancy is a key concept in Weil's religious philosophy, and it appears also in her discussion of work.[29] Manual labor, on Weil's description, also permits the mystical and ecstatic perceiving of God which is not associated with everyday physical activity, according to the conventional notion of the *vita contemplativa*. However, for Weil, attention in the realm of physical labor depends on the same qualities of openness and receptivity that Weil describes elsewhere as devotional practices. Weil does not say what this attention would be in terms of mysticism, spiritual exercises, and prayer. She simply divides the object of a worker's attention into two types: "this world," or the needs of the body, and "the world beyond," or the needs of the soul. The attention of the expectant mother, in this sense, combines both objects of attention into the same act, because the expectant mother is focussing on bodily needs (her baby's clothing) *and* on spiritual needs (love for her child). This perspective does not separate mind from body, but makes both "present and associated in the act of work, like the child about to be born in the making of the layette" (NR 95). In Weil's philosophy of work, the mind is counted as absorbed when in standard psychological terms it would be counted as being in a state of light trance. The attention of a worker is judged not only in relation to their rate of productivity, but also in relation to their degree of inactivity, relaxation, and free association. To be attentive while also paying attention is, for example, the activity we perform when having an insight or idea while doing a familiar task that has nothing at all (or nothing necessarily) to

---

28. *The Collected Works of St. John of the Cross*, ed. and trans. Kieran Kavanaugh and Otilio Rodriguez (Washington, D.C.: Institute of Carmelite Studies, 3rd ed., 1991), 102 ("Ascent to Mount Carmel," 2.13.4). See Kotva, *Effort and Grace*, 151–2, 157.

29. E.g., WG 49–60, 125–129. On the role of attention, see Lissa McCullough, *The Religious Philosophy of Simone Weil: An Introduction* (London: I. B. Tauris, 2014), 28–36.

do with the task. In the realm of manual labor, attention is for Weil what contemplation is for the mystic.[30]

Weil's sections on work in *Need for Roots* are devoted mainly to suggesting methods for transforming working conditions in light of the thesis that an imbalance in the system of the concentration of attention has deprived work of dignity and meaning. There will always be need for a farmer sowing a field to focus on the task at hand and not on something else, however,

> there is no reason why a peasant engaged in sowing shouldn't have at the back of his [*sic*] mind, without shaping words — even unspoken ones — on the one hand certain similes drawn by Christ, such as "Unless the seed die ...", "The seed is the word of God ...", "The grain of mustard seed ... which is the least of all seeds ...", and on the other hand the double mechanism of growth; the one whereby the seed, by consuming itself and with the aid of bacteria, reaches the surface of the soil; and the other whereby solar energy pours down in rays of light, is captured by the green colouring matter of the plant-stalk, and rises upward in an irresistible ascending movement. (NR 94)

The wordless association taking place in the back of the farmer's mind as they sow a field constitutes the supernatural object of attention. The natural object of attention, by contrast, is the field: the soil, the seeds, the equipment. Weil's point is that these two objects of attention — the wordless association on the one hand, and the field on the other — should not be separable, because in the life of a worker who works without being motivated by fear of punishment, they are never thus. This harmonizing of mind and body would be made possible by the special curriculum, already mentioned. The notion of an effortless association of ideas, in the midst of effort, is only really possible "by a habit impressed upon the mind and connecting these thoughts with the work movements" (NR 95). By "a habit impressed upon the mind" Weil does not intend education in the conventional sense. We have already seen her emphasize apprenticeship and work placements. Actual school

---

30. On the unity of work and contemplation, see Emmanuel Gabellieri, Être *et don: Simone Weil et la philosophie* (Peeters: Louvain, 2003), 83–104.

hours should be kept to a minimum; not, however, in order to reduce mental work, but rather to increase it by allowing mental reflection to combine seamlessly with bodily work. Years of singing and reciting gospel parables to the rhythm of the scythe and the plough is what will enable, in Weil's argument, the farmer to become conscious of the knowledge their work already (and unconsciously) allows them to possess. Conversely, Weil implies that any form of intellectual instruction will merely cast light on rather than add anything essential to the knowledge gained through physical labor. This notion will be discussed again by Weil at the end of *Need for Roots*.

The meaning of attention here is most clearly explicated at the level of paradox, ecstasy, and revelation. A farmer who is sowing a field while also exulting, wordlessly, at the direct contact with reality their actions entail, is both paying attention to the field and being attentive to something in excess of the field; performing a voluntary action and allowing an involuntary activity quite beyond their control to seize hold of their being. Marxism, to Weil's mind, implies that material conditions are significant for work, but the definition it gives of materiality is reductive. Thus, the free association of the attention that is accessible to the worker but imperceptible to the onlooker is made to seem irrelevant. Weil connects the ways in which work appears intelligible through material relations to illusions regarding religion. She notes that at the 1937 International Exhibition a French country village was displayed without a church at its center.[31] Traditional working milieux that are reproduced according to prevailing materialist standards mistakenly appear as intelligible, both in terms of the modes of production and in terms of value. For instance, the activity of sowing may appear intelligible, with a clear purpose and meaning (to grow more corn, feed the farmer and their family, and so on), but in spiritual terms those material forces alone are not what might inspire joy in the farmer. By giving attention in work a dual object, Weil sought to avoid the reintroduction of a mind-body dualism into discussions of work and the illusion that work was entirely intelligible through either a materialist or an idealist lens.

---

31. The choice to display a village without a church was the subject of controversy and newspapers published several petitions voicing outrage. Shanny Peer, *France on Display: Peasants, Provincials, and Folklore in the 1937 Paris World's Fair* (Albany, NY: State University of New York Press, 1998), 119, 216.

The Function of the Past

Weil sought to develop a spiritual and aesthetic as well as material critique of working conditions. Medieval Europe, a time during which the Church rather than big industry structured manufacturing, interested her the most. The idea of quasi-independent workshops loosely organized in networks recalls the medieval guilds, while the *Tour de France* (which Weil pictures as a prerequisite for apprentices) is an attested pre-modern practice, and Weil invokes both in her sections on uprootedness in the towns and countryside. Her unreserved admiration for the past has affinities with William Morris' (1834–1896) and John Ruskin's (1819–1900) approach to labor and what John Hughes calls "theo-aesthetic." "Theo-aesthetic" refers to the way English Romantic critiques of capitalism argued that Catholic pre-modern social structures promoted and represented the worker as artisan, with work perceived to be of intrinsic rather than of (merely) utilitarian value.[32] In particular, Weil's envisaging of devolved and decentralized manufacturing bears many striking similarities to William Morris' *News from Nowhere* (1890), a speculative fiction set in a post-industrial future, in which workshops, markets, and independent trade—but also singing, feasting, and ample leisure time—form the decentralized nucleus of the urban economy.[33] Weil took the view that Marx's critique of modern labour had suppressed the spiritual and, moreover, aesthetic aspects of work in favour of "scientific" and utilitarian outlooks, with the result that Marx's socialism ended up affirming the very assumptions of progress and economic growth it was supposed to resist. In Weil's thinking, the recovery of the past is the *only* means of re-establishing the working classes:

> Up to the very beginning of this century, few things in Europe were closer to the Middle Ages than French trade-unionism, sole reflected ray, with us, of the guild spirit. The feeble

---

32. Hughes, *End of Work*, 97–136.

33. William Morris, *News from Nowhere and Other Writings*, Clive Wilmer, ed. (London: Penguin Classics, 1994). As Hughes points out, though Morris labelled himself as socialist, his socialism was distinctly different from mainstream Marxist philosophies; Hughes suggests that we think of it as an "alternative" socialism. This description could also be applied to Weil's philosophy of work, although, for reasons of history and context, I prefer to situate her in the tradition of French classical radicalism, as mentioned above.

remains of this trade-unionism are among the number of
embers upon which it is most urgent that we should blow.
(NR 51)

Trade unions reflect the "guild spirit" of the past; however, they do so
imperfectly and "feebly." Like Morris and the English Romantics, Weil
was suspicious of the extent to which socialist workers' movements
focused on issues of salaries and the increase of material welfare, ne-
glecting the spiritual welfare of its members. The guilds attracted Weil
because they had provided rituals, lore, and sense of belonging, what
Weil calls the ability of workers "to feel themselves at home" (NR 45).
It is this function of the guilds that she chiefly admires. For Weil, the
past thus becomes important not in terms of its historicity but in terms
of its function or quality, i.e., as tradition. The past is not the object of
revival; what needs to be revived is rather the totality of ancestral and
local custom in which a person's sense of belonging is shaped. In this
way, the past is historical but also present, and, in an important way
which she deems lacking from the more popular socialist movements,
the only realistic way in which to build a sustainable alternative to
oppressive regimes of power:

> In this almost desperate situation, all we can look to for en-
> couragement here below is in those historical atolls of the liv-
> ing past left upon the surface of the earth. [...]
>   It would be useless to turn one's back on the past in order
> simply to concentrate on the future. It is a dangerous illusion
> to believe that such a thing is even possible. [...] The future
> brings us nothing, gives us nothing; it is we who in order to
> build it have to give it everything, our very life. But to be able
> to give, one has to possess; and we possess no other life, no
> other living sap, than the treasures stored up from the past and
> digested, assimilated and created afresh by us. Of all the hu-
> man soul's needs, none is more vital than this one of the past.
>   Love of the past has nothing to do with any reactionary
> political attitude. (NR 51)

A present based on the possession of an indeterminate future with no
purchase on reality, and impossible to grasp except as an object of fantasy and escapism, are contrasted here with a present based on the possession of lived memories and ancestral traditions passed down between

generations and, for this reason, subject to renewal in the present day.[34] Two notions of what constitutes the proletariat's "dispossession" are also implicitly contrasted. The first is that one can be robbed of material goods; this is the sense chiefly at play in Weil's understanding of Marxist materialism. The second is that one can be robbed of a sense of personal history, and that this dispossession is comparable to the material category prominent in Marx's definition of the proletariat but, it is for Weil, of infinitely deeper significance because it is constitutive of identity.[35] A dispossession in the second sense is, for example, the destruction of ancestral practices and indigenous lifeways through industrialization, clearances, and the general ravaging of the countryside—but also by colonialism:

> For several centuries now, men of the white race have everywhere destroyed the past, stupidly, blindly, both at home and abroad. If in certain respects there has been, nevertheless, real progress during this period, it is not because of this frenzy, but in spite of it, under the impulse of what little of the past remained alive.
>
> The past once destroyed never returns. The destruction of the past is perhaps the greatest of all crimes. (NR 51–52)

This function of the past might be interpreted as a decolonization of working conditions and a turn to indigeneity, an aspiration not for a nostalgic glorification of history nor for a defence of one or more *specific* traditions (Catholic or French, in the case of Weil), but rather to a reclaiming of those para-utilitarian activities which traditions make possible, and which risk being neglected in a purely production-oriented economy.[36]

---

34. On the notion of lived versus projected time operating in *NR*, see the illuminating essay by Casey Ford, "Captured Time: Simone Weil's Vital Temporality Against the State," in Sophie Bourgault and Julie Daigle, eds. *Simone Weil: Beyond Ideology* (Cham: Palgrave Macmillan, 2020), 161–184.

35. Gustave Thibon, at whose house Weil was staying while employed as a casual worker in the Ardèche, took a similar view of tradition, emphasizing the role of the past as the worker's inalienable possession. See for instance, *What Ails Mankind?: An Essay on Social Physiology*, Willard Hill trans. (New York: Sheed and Ward, 1947), 104, 141.

36. Cf. B. P. Davis, "The Colonial Frame: Judith Butler and Simone Weil on Force and Grief," in Bourgault and Daigle, *Simone Weil: Beyond Ideology*, 123–142.

Weil's critique of working conditions depends on the assumption that the situation is one that cannot be targeted in an isolated manner but must be rebuilt on a system-wide basis. It is no good improving the pay of unskilled laborers if the overall social system dispensing payment continues to support specialization that degrades the worker. Weil opposed the targeted approach of politicians and trade unionists, who claim to be liberating the worker while continuing to ignore the larger picture, to the heroic individuals able to envision and act upon an alternative view of the whole. On the one hand, there are causes (regimes, movements, and political parties) that cast workers' rights as rallying cries and slogans, while failing to attend to the systemic inequalities making those rallying cries necessary. Examples of slogans cited by Weil are "Work, Family, Country" and "Liberty, Equality, Fraternity." Weil argues that what she envisages for workers in *Need for Roots* must not be limited to expressing itself in terms of slogans, nor must it become embodied in a movement or proposition:

> [These words] must not be attached to a cause or a movement, nor even to a régime, nor to a nation either. We must not do them the sort of harm Pétain has done to the words "Work, Family, Country," nor the harm which the Third Republic has done to the words "Liberty, Equality, Fraternity." They must not become a slogan. (NR 97–98, note omitted)[37]

The philosophical meaning of a political slogan and its social function may diverge or contradict one another. For example, it is possible to trumpet the idea that society is suffering from a lack of balance in a way that is, itself, unbalanced with respect to one's audience, who rightly "look upon any slightly elevated proposition as a snare set to trap them" (NR 98). Thus, Weil judges that rhetorical tactics aimed at firing up the workers would be counter-productive in the long run, since such measures always end up serving a collective and robbing the individual of their freedom. "If [these ideas] are presented to the public," she writes,

---

37. Philippe Pétain was Chief of State of Vichy France, 1940–1944, and famously organized propaganda around the concept of work, announcing that the "new France" would be founded on toil. See Peter Davies, *The Extreme Right in France, 1789 to the Present: From de Maistre to Le Pen* (London: Routledge, 2002), 100–120.

it must be solely as the expression of a thought which reaches very far beyond men [*sic*] and the societies of today, and which one proposes in all humility to keep ever before the mind as a guide in all things. If such modesty has less power to carry the masses with it than more ostentatious attitudes have, it cannot be helped. It is better to fail than succeed in doing harm. (NR 98)

These general ideas provide the framework for a brief analysis of what Weil calls "a civilization founded upon the spirituality of work" (NR 97). "Spirituality" must be understood more specifically than the application of the term in sociological studies or philosophy might imply. It is not a matter of uniting workers around universal beliefs, but of determining how the particular beliefs they already have intersect and converge and then cultivating these intersections: "It is a conception that can be propagated without running the risk of promoting the slightest discord. The word spirituality doesn't imply any particular affiliation" (NR 97).

"Spirituality" would provide common ground for persons of different religious, ethnic, political, and cultural affiliation. Weil does not deny that the spirituality of work needs to be communicated, and that *Need for Roots* is one such attempt at communication; in fact, elsewhere in the text she urges writers and intellectuals of all stripes to contribute to this common purpose wherever possible. This notion is odd in light of Weil's criticisms of movements, regimes, and the rhetoric of the collective. The image of "propagation" also stands in stark contrast to the perspective of the individual that Weil otherwise champions. It is as if Weil is falling into the very traps she has outlined painstakingly over the course of the opening chapter of the book, finally presenting *Need for Roots* as yet another rallying cry in which the individual is sacrificed to the collective. That her own text could be misread in this manner is an obvious risk, and one of which Weil is painfully aware:

> But one can only lay hold of such a conception [i.e., a civilization based on the spirituality of work] in fear and trembling. How can we touch it without soiling it, turning it into a lie? Our age is so poisoned by lies that it converts everything it touches into a lie. And we are of our age, and have no reason to consider ourselves better than our age. (NR 97)

Weil thus sought to include the text of *Need for Roots* itself within her concept of a spirituality of work, to show the tendency of not only political rhetoric but also of philosophical texts, such as her own, to become not the exposition of oppressive regimes they were intended but rather utile to new oppressive impulses.

Work as Daily Death

While the main discussion of work in *Need for Roots* is focused in Part II of the book, an important argument is developed in its very last pages. Here Weil pronounces a general theory regarding the spiritual nature of work that is meant to apply to any form of physical labor, even (if not especially) to its most gruelling forms. This theory was predicated on transcribing, mystically, the range of physical and psychological affliction Weil experienced in the factories, including the feeling that one was close to death and little more than a mere cog in the wheel of a machine. The result is some of Weil's most difficult writing on the subject of work, for Weil now appears to valorise precisely the type of dehumanizing experience which, elsewhere in the book, she condemns and exposes. As such, these final pages of *Need for Roots* demand careful parsing unless we are to misread them entirely.

Weil opens the finals pages of *Need for Roots* by arguing, once again, that the core of society's "sickness" lies in its ignorance regarding "what place to give to physical labour and to those engaged in physical labour" (NR 295). We have seen this sentiment already. Over the following pages, Weil's strategy will be to reiterate the claim, elaborated previously in her discussion of uprootedness in the town and countryside, that the place of physical labor is religious and that physical laborers are natural mystics with an innate closeness to divine truth. However, the way in which Weil expounds this claim differs somewhat from her argument in earlier portions of the book, and, indeed, in her earlier writing on labor—especially her "Factory Journal." In the latter, Weil had remarked on the way in which revolt became impossible in the factory (FW 171), arguing that one of the most deplorable aspects of gruelling manual labor was that it left a person with very little spirit for thought and autonomous action. In these final pages, however, it is precisely such experiences that become mystically charged, sketched as forms of ecstatic self-abandonment:

> Physical labour willingly consented to is, after death willingly consented to, the most perfect form of obedience. [...]
> Physical labour is a daily death.
> To labour is to place one's own being, body and soul, in the circuit of inert matter [...]
> Death and labour are things of necessity and not of choice. The world gives itself to Man [*sic*] in the form of food and warmth if Man gives himself to the world in the form of labour. But death and labour can be submitted to either in an attitude of revolt or in one of consent. They can be submitted to either in their naked truth or else wrapped around with lies [...]
> Consent to suffer death [...] constitutes a final, sudden wrenching away from what each one calls "I." (NR 292, 297)

The equation between labor and death, and between both these states and willing "consent" to material inertia, seems jarring and it is different, certainly, from the way Weil describes the spirituality of work elsewhere. Yet, the path Weil takes to these pronouncements is not arbitrary and, moreover, is connected intimately to the objections Weil raises, earlier in the text, against conventional understandings of human agency. Weil's concept of attention as a form of "waiting" (*l'attente*) is a critique of secular portrayals of human agency as the achievement of a self-determined will, that is, of autonomy as vitality and power. Weil defends, instead, a mystical account of autonomy as a "negative effort" based on passiveness, affectability, and receptivity (WG 55). Elsewhere in *Need for Roots*, she thus defends her position from the vitalist tendencies of spiritualists like Bergson, arguing that "[i]n this world of ours life, the élan vital so dear to Bergson, is but a lie; only death is true" (NR 246).[38]

Weil's sense of "death" in *Need for Roots*, however, is critical rather than pessimistic, and remains committed to the spiritualist idea of harmonizing freedom with necessity, or mind with matter. In part, the crit-

---

38. Maurice Schumann, "Henri Bergson et Simone Weil," *Revue des deux mondes* (Novembre 1993): 194–203.

ical sense of death is derived from her reading of John of the Cross, who emphasized the need to let go and "die" to the individual will before uniting with God.[39] This, too, is how Weil understands work in these final pages of *Need for Roots*: as an intense union of mind to body, in which thought yields so completely to matter it seems to "die" in the process. In part, however, the critical sense of death is derived from Weil's understanding of evolutionary biology, which is closer to Lamarck's than it is to either Darwin's or Bergson's, and which sees habit and passiveness—rather than vitality and activity—as the agency creating organic life.[40] Weil held that cells and organisms at base contract rather than exert power over their environments, responding to oxygen, water, carbon, and solar energy by virtue of their radical affectability. One of her favourite analogies is the comparison of the way solar energy is received by the plant (rather than willed by it), to the way grace is received into the soul (rather than willed by it) (SNL 148–152). In this way, Weil believed that, at bottom, agency was fundamentally passive and that therefore "death"—being associated strongly with passiveness and inertia—provided critical concepts that went a long way in illuminating the nature of autonomy. Although Weil admired Immanuel Kant and defended the language of autonomy, she did not perceive autonomy as independency, but rather as interdependency: for Weil, human spirit realized itself not in contradistinction from matter but in recognition of its own, inevitable, submission to materiality.[41] She thus defended her interpretation of agency against what she called "secular morality,"

---

39. *The Collected Works*, 353–460 ("Dark Night"). John speaks of a "spiritual death" undergone by the mystic as they pray continuously to God.

40. On Weil's understanding of matter as perpetual becoming and yet as mechanistic, see IC 151–201 ("The Pythagorean Doctrine"). The idea of creative evolution as passive rather than active is a minor though persistent theme in French philosophy. It has been expounded recently, and brilliantly, by Quentin Meillassoux, who distinguishes between two forms of vitalism, one that equates life with activity, another that equates it with passivity. Against Bergson, Meillassoux argues that concepts of "encounter, of passivity, and even of affect" describe the movement of life prior to organic being. This is very close to Weil's reasoning. See *After Finitude: An Essay on the Necessity of Contingency*, Ray Brassier trans. (London: Continuum, 2008), 101.

41. Lyra Koli has recently demonstrated Weil's reading of Kant to be an inversion of the latter's central concept of autonomy. See "Hungry for Beauty: Simone Weil's Inversion of Kant's Aesthetics," https://www.academia.edu/35344582/Hungry_for_Beauty_Simone _Weil_s_Inversion_of_Kant_s_Aesthetics.

which, for Weil, was distinguished by seeking to dominate and conquer matter (WG 127), a position Weil connects closely with fascist ideals and with Hitler's propaganda.

Weil also defends her position against Catholic humanist versions of Kantianism and the theology of human rights. In the pages leading up to the denouement of *Need for Roots* and the discussion of labor as death Weil cites a recent essay by her contemporary, the French Catholic humanist Jacques Maritain: "God has a sovereign right over his creatures and He [*sic*] has no moral obligations towards them."[42] The problem with the language of sovereign rights, Weil argues, is that, when applied to God, it casts God as a person whom it is necessary to obey but impossible to love (NR 274). Weil then contrasts this argument to her idea of radical affectability, mentioned above. In order for God to be the object of both love and obedience, it is necessary that God should be conceived of as both personal and *impersonal*. Instead of modelling God on a sovereign, Weil suggests modelling God on the natural order, since the natural order is equal for all. Here Weil argues that mysticism follows Greek philosophy in modelling God on providence. Weil argues that providence is not "a personal intervention in the world on the part of God," (NR 276) but rather "[a]ll the events which go to make up the universe in the total stream of time," i.e., material becoming as such (NR 280). What is sovereign in this world, Weil argues, is not will but "determinateness, limit [...] The universe accepts passively. The brute force of matter, which appears to us sovereign, is nothing else in reality but perfect obedience" (NR 282). To imitate God is not to strive to escape the world but rather to immerse oneself more fully into matter. For Weil the most spiritual state is also the most material: "Matter is [...] a perfect model for us" (WG 72). Matter becomes the model also for Christ, who obeys God not by following a command but by imitating the radical affectability of matter (IC 184). This view of matter as spiritual guide, however, depends on a prior understanding of materiality as passive becoming that creates through receptivity to circumstance rather than through imposition of will. In this way, spirituality is the prefiguring of death,

---

42. Jacques Maritain, "The Natural Law: An Inquiry into its Relationship with the Rights of the Human Person," *Commonweal* (May 15, 1942), https://www.commonweal magazine.org/natural-law-0.

albeit also of life, since what Weil defines as death is in fact nothing but the cycle of organic becoming.

Work and Obedience

Returning now to the final pages of *Need for Roots*, we see Weil trying to break free of the idea of autonomy as independent action. In particular, Weil believes this idea is responsible for popularizing a notion we have already seen her attack at length: the notion that physical labor is by nature servile, and that, as a consequence, workers need to be liberated from physical labor. Weil agrees that servile forms of labor in contemporary society should be abolished, but she also maintains that, at bottom, human agency remains servile in relation to the natural order, and that, considered as organisms, humans are indeed dependent on their environments and must submit to them in order to flourish. The tragedy of work in modern society, for Weil, is thus not that workers must submit daily to circumstance but that they are made to do so in an attitude motivated by fear. Weil's task in these final pages will then be to narrate an alternative understanding of what it means to submit to circumstance. Weil begins by taking the reader back to Genesis 3:17–20, where physical labor and death are awarded to the first humans as punishments for disobedience (NR 292). It would seem, Weil comments, that death and physical labor for this reason are impositions on human freedom and autonomy. But Weil argues that a deeper reading of the text suggests otherwise. First, there is the fact that prior to their disobedience, the first humans were instructed to work and presumably did so gladly. Weil argues that ancient mythologies as a rule tended to value rather than dishonour work, and Weil spends some time enumerating the correspondences between human trades and deities in Greek mythology, and reflects once more on the guild spirit of the Middle Ages (NR 292–296). Although labor is a punishment in *Genesis*, Weil argues that it cannot be physical work itself which constitutes the essence of the biblical punishment, but rather the miserable experience of labor which God divines for human beings. This leads Weil onto the question of whether death, too, was not also once viewed more positively in ancient societies and whether Genesis retains memories of this view also. At this point Weil gives a summary form of the argument regarding the mystical meaning of obedience to the natural order that I have sketched out above, joining this to her gloss on labor:

> Man [*sic*] placed himself outside the current of Obedience. God chose as his punishments labour and death. Consequently, labour and death, if Man undergoes them in a spirit of willingness, constitute a transference back into the current of supreme Good, which is obedience to God.
>
> This takes on a luminous clarity if, as in antiquity, one looks upon the passivity of matter as the perfection of obedience to God, and upon the beauty of the world as the radiance of this perfect Obedience.
>
> Whatever, in heaven, may be the mysterious significance of death, on earth it is the transformation of a being composed of palpitating flesh and of mind, of a being who loves and hates, hopes and fears, wants and doesn't want, into a little pile of inert matter.
>
> Man's consent to such a transformation represents his supreme act of total obedience. (NR 296)

The definition of "obedience" depends on a theory of natural order as passive acceptance, "waiting," and receptivity. Labor and death, which are aspects of the natural order, are punishments only insofar as they are actively resisted. If labor and death are consented to, they are no longer punishments but instances of communion with God. For Weil, death is the moment when it becomes impossible for a person to submit in anything but a spirit of consent. However, until the moment of actual death, the experience of death remains "abstract and distant," and so cannot easily become a means—in life—for consent (NR 296). The phrase, "physical labour is a daily death" then follows immediately upon these remarks: "Labour does violence to human nature [...] monotony brings with it disgust, and time hangs with an almost intolerable heaviness. [...] [H]e [*sic*] who labours is subject to time in the same way as inert matter that can only move slowly from one moment to the next" (NR 297). Weil's meaning is that when a person performs the heavy, monotonous physical labor typical of the unskilled factory worker, they must be receptive to the elements in the same unconditional way that a person approaching death must become radically accepting of the natural order that now overwhelms them. Thus, "[t]o labour is to place one's own being, body and soul, in the circuit of inert matter" (NR 297). As a result, work may be seen as a "daily death," that is, as the closest structural homology, in life, to death, or, more specifically, to the radical receptivity with which matter generates organic life.

It goes without saying that such remarks can easily be misread. For example, many critics have argued that Weil's arguments in the final pages of *Need for Roots* reflect a death wish rather than a philosophical argument regarding the nature of physical labor.[43] Weil appeals instead to the surrendering of self-possessed agency and the subsequent participation in—and pure receptivity to—the elements, to matter. Her point is that even when working conditions are dreadful, workers are not without spiritual nourishment, for spiritual nourishment cannot be conditional on property, learning, or individual effort. Weil took seriously the idea that nothing is achieved without grace and that God is present everywhere: in Weil's opinion, the one thing keeping humans from God was not effort but rather the opposite—receptivity.[44] She also took seriously the idea that this truth could not exclude milieux of misery. If God is present everywhere, God must be present in the factory; and if it seemed impossible to perceive God in a factory, this was not the fault of God, but of the society that had excluded affectability, vulnerability, weakness, and suffering from its idea of human agency. For Weil, there is a genuine interplay between knowing the world by means of the physical senses, and knowing the world through spiritual senses. For Weil, to know "spiritually" meant to know how the material relation to the world work, how, at bottom, they are determined not by will but by willing submission to circumstance. Stoicism is a direct comparison, and Weil always held the latter in high regard, viewing it as essentially Christian and mystical.[45] Such spirituality involved deriving the experience of the

---

43. For a critical reading of Weil's preoccupation with death, placing it in the historical context of modern French Catholic spirituality, see Richard D.E. Burton, *Holy Tears, Holy Blood: Women, Catholicism, and the Culture of Suffering in France, 1840–1970* (Ithaca: Cornell University Press, 2004), 133–147.

44. "The plant does not have any control or choice in the matter of its own growth. As for us, we are like plants which have the one choice of being in or out of the light" (WG 82).

45. Weil discusses Stoic concepts both directly and indirectly throughout the final chapter of NR, e.g., 186 (method as *logos*), 225 (Marcus Aurelius), 258ff (the identification of God with the natural order). On Weil and Stoicism, see Gilbert Kahn, "Simone Weil et le stoïcisme grec," *Cahiers Simone Weil*, vol. 5, no. 4 (1982): 270–84, and Kotva, *Effort and Grace*, 151–163.

world from the quality of one's submission to circumstance, and not from the quality of the circumstances themselves.

According to Weil, spiritual knowledge of the world in the latter sense, to know the world as it was and not how it was imagined, was becoming increasingly difficult in European society. The rethinking of work in terms of "death" remains in her writing as a metaphor which intrudes, sometimes dramatically, into her utopian analyses of a civilization founded upon the spirituality of work. Thus, Weil does not accept Marxist ideas about workers' liberation as an *a priori* truth about society but presents rather a liberation of the concept of work: Weil shows that various concepts of freedom, autonomy, and power enslave rather than emancipate the worker, and Weil gives instead an account of agency drawn from realities familiar to workers. Unskilled workers in typical inter-war factories did not choose their occupations but were driven to them by circumstance. Weil sees a structural similarity between unskilled workers' submission to factory work and Christ's submission to death. Yet while this, for Weil, gives spiritual meaning to hard, physical labor in humiliating situations, it does not justify existing working conditions, nor does it glorify workers' suffering. While the question no longer is that of liberating workers from the need to submit to circumstance (for such submission, Weil reasons, is an essential part of what it means to be alive, and in itself nothing to be deplored), the question of liberating the social constructions of submission from their present, oppressive and tyrannical manifestations, looms large. In the final pages of *Need for Roots*, Weil's achievement is to have reconstructed the critique of working conditions at the level of spiritual meaning in a way that avoids either romanticizing or merely lamenting workers' experience, and thus does not reconstruct the "spirituality of work" on a plane that is disconnected from the practices on which it is founded. In other words, Weil maintains that if work is spiritual, it cannot be so in spite of the nature of the direst, most humiliating forms of physical labor, but must be so because of the nature of the latter, and this is the point on which she elaborates in the final pages of *Need for Roots*.

Study for a Declaration of Obligations towards the Human Being[1]

Simone Weil

*Weil's own title on the manuscript of what is now **The Need for Roots** was **Prelude to a Declaration of Duties towards the Human Being**. This was also the final title of the study that she had been preparing in several drafts, and properly the final draft constitutes a preface to the work. What follows is that final draft.*

Profession of Faith

There is a reality that is outside the world, which is to say beyond time and space, beyond the mental universe of human beings, beyond any domain that human faculties can grasp.

---

1. This is the text of Weil's final draft of this study and declaration as printed in OC V.2 96–105, omitting a four line note to herself after the Profession of Faith, which sketches her intentions for the rest of the study, not all of which she followed out in the remaining text. As noted in the introduction to this book, there were several drafts, and a number of sketches of this document, which means that previous printed versions of this Declaration or Study can often differ. In the previous English version, namely at SE 219–227, there are two or three additional paragraphs that are not in this text now in front of the reader. The SE version is reproduced in SWA 201–211.

To this reality corresponds, at the center of the human heart, a need for an absolute good, which always lives there and which can never be satisfied by any object in this world.

This reality is also made evident here below by the absurdities, the insoluble contradictions, which always bring an abrupt end to human thought when it moves solely in this world.

Just as the reality of this world is the sole foundation of facts, so is this other reality the sole foundation of what is good.

It is from this reality alone that all the good capable of existing descends into this world, all beauty, all truth, all justice, all legitimacy, all order, all subordination of human conduct to its obligations.

The sole intermediary by which the good can descend and dwell among human beings is those human beings who have their attention and their love turned towards it.

Although this reality is beyond the grasp of all human faculties, one can turn one's attention and love towards it.

Nothing can justify us from supposing that any human being has lost that power.

This power is something that is only real here below in its exercise. The sole condition for its exercise is consent.

This consent may be expressed. It may also not be, even tacitly, and it may be unclear to one's consciousness, even if it has really a place in the soul. Often, even if it is expressed openly, it has no place in the soul. But expressed or not, its sole and sufficient condition is that it has a place in the soul.

To those who have in fact consented to orient their attention and love outside the world, towards that reality beyond all human faculties, it is given that they will succeed. In this case, sooner or later, a light will descend on them from the good that will shine through them on everything around them.

The need for absolute good that lives at the center of the heart, and the power, however unformed, of orienting one's attention and love outside the world and receiving the good from there, together constitute a link which attaches every human being, without exception, to that other reality.

Those who recognize that other reality also recognize this link. Because of it, they hold all human beings without exception as something sacred to which respect is to be shown.

There is no other possible motive for the universal respect of all human beings. Whatever the formula of belief or unbelief that one might choose, those whose hearts incline them to practice this respect, in fact, recognize a reality other than this world. To those for whom this respect is, in fact, foreign, the other reality is also foreign.

This world's reality is made up of differences. Objects are not equal and they solicit attention unequally. A certain play of circumstances or a certain attraction propose the personality of certain human beings to one's attention. By the effect of different circumstances and by a certain lack of attractiveness, other people remain anonymous. They escape attention, or, if it does happen to be directed towards them, only common, collective things are seen.

The sort of attention that lives entirely in this world is entirely submissive to the effect of these inequalities, and is no less so even if one remains unaware of that effect.

Given all the factual inequalities there can only be an equal respect towards all human beings when attention is brought to bear on something identical in all of them. Human beings are different in all respects in which they are linked to specific things in this world, without exception. There is only something identical in them when there is the presence of a link to that other reality.

All human beings are absolutely identical insofar as they can be conceived as constituted by a core need for good around which is disposed both psychic and fleshly matter.

Only the attention that is actually oriented beyond the world has contact with the essential structure of human nature. It alone possesses a constant faculty of projecting itself on any human being whatsoever.

Those who have this faculty also have their attention actually oriented beyond the world, whether or not they say so.

The link that attaches the human being to that other reality is, like that reality, beyond the grasp of human faculties. The respect that it brings about when it is recognized cannot be shown to them.

This respect cannot find here below any kind of direct expression. If it is not expressed, though, it does not have any existence. There is a possibility, however, of indirect expression.

The respect inspired by the link of the human to that other reality outside this world bears witness to that part of the human that is situated in the reality of this world.

The reality of this world is necessity. The part of the human being which is situated there is the part abandoned to necessity and put under the misery of need.

There is a single possibility of an indirect expression for the respect felt for the human being, and that is given by the needs of human beings in this world, the earthly needs of the soul and of the body.

It is founded on a relation established in human nature between the need for good, which is the essence of the human, and human sensibility. Nothing would ever authorize us to believe of any human being that this relation does not exist.

Because of it, when, due either to acts or omissions by other people, the life of a human being is destroyed or mutilated by a wound or by a deprivation of the soul or body, it is not only the sensibility that suffers the blow, but also the aspiration to the good. There is then a sacrilege committed against what is sacred in every human being.

Sometimes, however, the sensibility may alone be in play if a human being suffers a privation or a wound by the blind mechanism of natural forces, and if the one who is injured takes into account that those who seem to be hurting him do not wish him any evil, but are only obeying a necessity that this one recognizes.

The possibility of an indirect expression of respect towards the human being is the foundation of obligations. Obligations have as their object the earthly needs of the soul and body of human being whoever they may be. To each need corresponds an obligation. To each obligation corresponds a need. There is not any other kind of obligation that is related to human things.

If one thinks that there are other kinds, either they are frauds, or they have been misclassified.

Whoever has one's attention and love actually turned to that otherworldly reality recognizes at the same time that one must, in public and private life, due to the unique and perpetual obligation that is part of one's responsibilities, and to the degree that one can do so, to remedy all the privations of the soul and body that can possibly destroy or mutilate the earthly life of a human being, whoever that human being might be.

One cannot legitimately excuse oneself from doing one's full duty on the basis of inability or not bearing responsibility, unless one has done everything possible to make those who suffer the consequences of that necessity aware of it, doing so without deceit and in such a way that they can accept it consentingly.

No combination of circumstances can ever excuse one from this universal obligation. The circumstances that would seem to dispense someone or some category of people from it, are only all the more imperative.

The thought of this obligation is spread among all peoples in very different forms and with very different degrees of clarity. People are inclined more or less strongly either to consent or refuse to adopt it as ruling their conduct.

Consent to it is often mixed with deception. When it is without deception, its practice is impeccable. Refusal makes one fall into crime.

The proportion of good to evil in a society depends in one part on the proportion of those who consent to those who refuse, in another part on the distribution of power between those who consent and those who refuse.

All power, of whatever kind it may be, if left in the hands of someone who has not given consent totally, clearly, and without deception to this obligation, is power badly placed.

With respect to people who have refused their consent, the exercise of any function, small or big, public or private, that requires them to weigh human destinies between their hands, constitutes in itself a criminal activity. They are all accomplices who, knowing how these people think, still authorize them to exercise the function.

A State whose official doctrine as a whole is an enticement to this crime has placed made itself guilty of this crime. There is no trace of legitimacy left in it.

A State which does not press for a doctrine directed against all forms of this crime does not have full legitimacy.

A legal system where nothing is done to prevent this crime lacks the essence of legality. A system of laws that takes measures to prevent certain forms of this crime, but not others, only has a sort of half legality.

A government whose members commit this crime or authorize it for their subordinates has betrayed its function.

It does not matter what sort of collectivity, institution, or mode of collective life it is, if its normal functioning implicitly lets this crime inhere in it, or leads to it, then it bears the mark of illegitimacy, and is subject to reform or suppression.

Those who have any part, big or small, in setting public opinion, and who fail to blame appropriately each instance of this crime that they are aware of, or that they turn a blind eye to so that they do not have to denounce it, are accomplices of this crime.

A country is not innocent of this crime if public opinion, where there is freedom of opinion, does not denounce this practice, or, in places where freedom of opinion is not allowed, there is not an underground denunciation of it.

The point of public life consists in putting all the forms of power, to the greatest degree possible, into the hands of those who actually consent to be bound by the obligation to all human beings, and that is incumbent on everyone, and those who understand it.

The law is the whole of the permanent provisions that make for this effect.

The awareness of obligations is twofold. In the first place, it involves the knowledge of its principle. In the second place, it is a matter of knowing how to apply it.

Since the domain of application is constituted by human needs in this world, it is incumbent upon the intelligence to conceive what a need is, and to discern, distinguish, and number all the earthly needs of the soul and body, with all the precision that one can.

This study is always capable of being revised.

Statement of Obligations

The fundamental obligation towards the human being can be subdivided into several concrete obligations by enumerating the essential needs of the human creature. Each need is the object of an obligation; each obligation has a need for its object.

It is a question only of earthly needs, for one can only satisfy those. It is a question of the needs of the soul just as much as it is of bodily needs. The soul has needs, and when they are not satisfied, it falls into a state like that of the body when it is starved and beaten.

The needs of the soul can for the most part be ordered into opposite pairs that balance and complement each other.

The human body has above all a need for food, warmth, sleep, hygiene, rest, exercise, and clean air.

The human soul has a need for equality and hierarchy.

Equality is the public recognition, expressed effectively and in morals, of the principle that an equal degree of attention is due to the needs of all human beings. Hierarchy is the scale of responsibilities. As the attention is inclined to bear itself upwards, and to stay there, special provisions are necessary to render equality and hierarchy actually compatible.

The human soul has need for obedience consented to, and for liberty.

Obedience consented to is what one gives to an authority that one esteems as legitimate. It is not possible to give it to a political power that is based on conquest, or by a *coup d'etat*, nor to economic power based on money. Liberty is the power of choice at the interior of the space left open by the direct constraint of natural and accepted legitimate social authority. This space needs to be quite large so that liberty is not a fiction, but it should cover only innocent things, without ever making certain kinds of crimes legal.

The human soul needs truth, and it needs freedom of expression.

The need for truth requires that all have access to intellectual culture without having to be either materially or morally transplanted. It requires that no pressure, material or moral, be exercised on the mind except for an exclusive concern for the truth; this implies an absolute prohibition on any and all propaganda. It requires protection against error and deception, which means that any material avoidable falsity that is argued publicly is to be punished. It requires for reasons of public health protection against any poison in the domain of the intellect.

But the intellect also has a need to be exercised without any authority limiting it. It is therefore necessary that there be a domain of pure intellectual research that is distinct, but accessible to everybody, and where no authority may insert itself.

The human soul has need, on the one hand, for solitude and intimacy, and on the other, for social life.

The human soul has need for private property and for collective property.

Private property is never constituted by a matter of money, but rather is the accumulation of concrete objects, such as a house, a field, furniture, and tools, all of which the soul looks at as an extension of itself and the body. Justice requires that private property be, like liberty, inalienable.

Collective property is not by legal title, but by the sense that the members of a human milieu have that certain material objects are like an extension and crystallization of themselves. This sense is only possible where certain objective conditions obtain.

The existence of a social class defined by the lack of private property and collective property is as shameful as slavery.

The human soul has a need for punishment and honor.

Every human being who has committed a crime that has put that him or her outside the good needs to be reintegrated into the good by means of suffering. That suffering needs to be inflicted in such a way as to lead the soul to freely recognize one day that all has been done justly. This reintegration into the good is what punishment is about. Every innocent human being, whether that one is innocent, or one who has paid the appropriate penalty, needs to have his or her honor recognized, the one as much as the other.

The human soul needs disciplined participation in a useful communal and public project, and it needs to be able to take personal initiative in this participation.

The human soul needs security, and it needs to take risks. The fear of violence, of hunger, or any other extreme evil, makes the soul sick. Boredom caused by the absence of all risk makes it just as sick.

The human being needs above all to be rooted in several natural milieux in order to be in touch with the universe through them.

The uprooting of a human being or the prevention of a human being from taking root is criminal.

The criterion by which one can recognize whether or not human needs have been satisfied is the expansion of fraternity, joy, beauty, and happiness. Where there is a turning in on oneself and sadness and ugliness, there are privations that need healing.

Practical Application

For this Declaration to become the practical inspiration of the life of the country, the first condition is that it be adopted with just this intention by the people.

The second condition is that those who wield, or want to wield, any kind of power—political, administrative, judicial, economic, technical, spiritual, or anything other, should pledge themselves to take it as the practical rule of their conduct.

In this case, the equal and universal character of the obligation is in a certain measure qualified by the particular responsibilities implied by a specific power. This is why it would be necessary to add to the pledge of commitment this formula: "... by paying special attention to the human needs that depend on me."

The violation of such a pledge, whether in word or deed, ought, in principle, always to be subject to punishment. But the appearance of institutions and morals permitting this punishment in most cases is the task of several future generations.

Assent to this Declaration impels one to make a continual effort to raise up as rapidly as possible these institutions and morals.

Translated by Eric O. Springsted

The Legal and Moral Foundations of the Resistance[1]

André Philip

In October 1942, Charles de Gaulle sent André Philip, the head of the Committee of the Interior for the Free French, to the United States to deliver a letter to President Roosevelt. He remained for two months. Towards the end of this time, he was in New York, where he interviewed Simone Weil. He also delivered a lecture there on November 7, 1942. It is believed that Weil attended it, as the next day she wrote to Boris Souvarine about a lecture that she had just heard and was enthusiastic about.

To understand what has happened in France over the course of the last two years, it is first necessary to remember the situation in which we found ourselves the morning after the debacle. At that moment, it appeared that all was laid low. The elites, political, intellectual, economic, and social, had largely abandoned their posts; the administrative ranks had been broken; the people were alone, without anyone who could give them direction, or who could tell them what to do.

It was under these conditions that the Vichy regime was established, and, in the general confusion, it was accepted for a moment by the great majority of the public.

---

1. A lecture given in New York on November 7, 1942. See the Introduction to this book for a description of the lecture, and its relation to Weil and footnote 2 there for a description of the Free French. This lecture is translated from the French text, ENR 425–437.

Vichy

The chief intellectual characteristic of this regime has been what one might call its political realism. This is to say, that it was not just happy with submitting to the defeat which had been imposed on us by the brutal force of the enemy, the regime rapidly gave to it an internal adherence, too. All the propaganda of the press the day after the armistice tried to show that France was responsible not only for the defeat, but for the war itself, and this responsibility belonged not to particular men, but to our whole system, our ideology, and the educational methods of the Third Republic, which is to say, the whole intellectual orientation that characterized the previous years. The men of Vichy proclaimed above all their admiration for German methods. They bowed before Hitlerian principles, ceaselessly arguing that France had to accept its defeat and to consider it as the supreme reality in whose light all our values had to be reformed.

At the same time, as it is always impossible to impose on the French people a pure and simple material realism, they attempted a process of psychological compensation by which they tried to remedy the concrete disappearance of certain realities by arguing for them in the abstract.

The army was in ruins, so they gave all its power to a Marshal. It was no longer armed, so they increased the military reviews. They realized the moral and material disarmament of the nation; they then made saluting the flag obligatory as well as singing *La Marseillaise*. At the moment when, by a total abdication, they denied the honor of a country, they argued for the necessity of a spiritual and moral renewal. The supreme crime of Vichy is not only, by its political realism, having turned facts into law, and present facts into values: it is also that they wove an ideological veil by which they prostituted all moral realities, for, at the same time that they affirmed them as being right for the moment, they, in fact, violated them.

The Spiritual Resistance

The French resistance appeared right away in the declarations of our greatest writers and in the sermons of preachers. It consisted above all in their affirmations that certain principles exist that need to be proclaimed and followed at any cost, no matter what the consequences. It is interesting to note that this resistance began very soon after the debacle, soon after the call from General DeGaulle, while most people were convinced of the inevitable defeat of England and of Germany's triumph in Europe. Even in this case, even against all hope, the spiritual resistance appeared necessary to us because it was a matter of saving the honor of our people and the traditions of our civilization. For us, ten tons of reality did not make for one ounce of truth and having ten thousand tanks could not transform a lie into something sincere.

Our position was, therefore, from the outset, that the armistice was not only a mistake but a crime, and that there existed values that were both French and universal and that we needed to stand on, no matter what the circumstances. I use the word "values" here and not "ideals." We used to have a lot of ideals before the war, which is to say, intellectual constructions built by a rational calculus. The unfortunate thing was that most often this idealism was strictly a matter of words and that by force of having gotten used to it, we had stopped taking this idealism with enough seriousness. In every case, most people were not ready to put themselves in its service and to run the necessary risks it involved. The tragedy of France before the war was, for many years, the weakness of its character, and the progressive disappearance of the idea of risk, as well as those of engagement and responsibility to which risk is linked. This was seen in the military belief that we could simply remain in the shade of the Maginot Line and wait for things to happen. It was expressed in our politics which were characterized by the desperate search for a security that demanded something from others but was not ready to make the necessary sacrifices ourselves that would guarantee them something in return. It appeared ultimately in economic life where the notions of adventure and enterprise were attenuated and replaced by the ideal of the *petit rentier*,[2] with its eagerness to hold on to one's small fortune, making the savings passbook the symbol of the moral ideal.

---

2. *Rentier*: someone who lives a financially self-contained private life; a person of private means, including somebody living on an annuity. *Ed.*

The Sense of Risk

Today the men of the French resistance have acquired a sense of risk and responsibility. When one of them speaks, it is not just some general ideas that he is expressing, some proposals that he is waving in the air; there is a value that he believes, an engagement that he has taken on and that can mean for him the loss of his liberty and even his life; thus, his beliefs have real meaning; thus is produced, by the value believed and lived, the incarnation of an ideal in concrete reality; thus is realized in each individual by the engagement of all his being, an indissoluble unity of the future and the present.

Universal Values

So, what are these spiritual values whose affirmation has been the origin of the French resistance? Some of them are universal values, others are specifically French. The universal values are entirely centered on the fundamental idea of the sacred character of the human person. This notion is truly what characterizes our Western, Christian civilization. It was unknown in Antiquity where the value of a man was measured only by the degree of his participation in the group; it is denied in today's totalitarian systems, in which race, nation, or blood now appear as the new barbaric deity to which human persons are sacrificed. For us, on the contrary, man is not just a bit of matter or an animal. There is something more in him, something which constitutes a whole, a universe in which the world can be contained by thought and love, something which rules over time and death. This man is not an isolated individual; he is not a self-enclosed whole, but he is, on the contrary, open to other persons, participating in social life by a series of communities: local, familial, and professional, all of which are personally based. Society is, therefore, a whole of wholes, a whole made up of liberties; it needs to exercise a positive function. It is not a question only of creating an open order in which individual initiatives can be launched, while leaving the strong to impose themselves on the weak, according to the old formula of *laisser faire*, of letting be, or of the free fox in the free henhouse. Society has a concrete goal, a particular vocation to fulfill, which is not a defense of I-know-not-what general interest, for there has never been anything but particular interests; rather, its goal is the coordination and the ranking of all particular interests, even collective ones, in the service of a value of the whole.

Man is therefore subordinate to society, but, at the same time, he exceeds it because it is subordinate to him in political and economic matters. He exceeds it by all that is in him that makes him part of religious, intellectual, and artistic life. A man is in the service of the group, yet, the group only reaches its end by serving men and knowing that, according to Maritain's admirable formula, each man has secrets kept from the group and vocations that the group does not have. Such are, for us, for all those who are at the heart of the interior resistance, the fundamental principles of our Western and Christian civilization that we use to guide our actions.

The Role of France

Besides these universal values, there are also certain properly French values that serve to define our nation; more precisely, what characterizes France is not its affirmation of certain different and autonomous values, which are actually common to all Western civilization, it is, rather, a certain way of expressing and realizing these universal values. Let us insist on this point because it is essential. France has always defined herself; she has always appeared to the world as the bearer of a general idea. Sometimes she was the elder daughter of the Church; other times she was the herald of revolution: in both cases, and in the selfsame spirit, France has carried a value to the world for everybody, proclaiming herself both its origin and its servant. In this sense, we are obliged to say that French nationalism, ancient and modern, is an unthinkable, contradictory reality because it is two things at once.

One France in part believed itself the supreme value, putting the nation up as a value in itself, breaking with its past, with all its tradition. French patriotism did not always consist in believing the nation to be an end in itself, but in serving through the nation a reality which is superior; but what is specifically French is the way it serves universal values. Whereas some other nations are particularly given to express them sentimentally, and others to realize them technically, and still others to balance them with everyday reality in a compromise that is forever unstable, the role of France is always to think them. France, in the eyes of the world, is above all the country of frank men, the country of the open mind, the place where the intellect, even when trampled underfoot, still seeks to express itself because, no matter what the circumstances, the truth always needs to be sought out and always to be spoken. The role of France is also to think about the world clearly, with precise and constructive logic. Besides our indomitable intellectual independence, clarity of thought and precision of the mind are still what characterize us in the eyes of the world. Today, ruined and dishonored by treason, France will end the war weakened, perhaps less capable than in the past of playing a major military and economic role. It also appears more indispensable than ever that it takes heed of the cultural function that is above all and essentially its function in the chaos and the contradictions of the modern world. Even in the midst of the present sufferings, the role of France is to think out a synthesis of the diverse national and social forces that are actually engaged in the conflict. This ought to be its role in tomorrow's Europe, it ought to be its role now, and French thought ought to be present in all the studies of and research into the problem of reconstruction after the war.

A New Declaration of the Rights of Man

I have just shown that the French resistance has affirmed above all the primacy of certain spiritual values in the face of a brutal reality. I have indicated that these values are sometimes universal ones centered on respect for the human person, and sometimes they are French ones, expressing under a particular form, namely, a clear and lucid intellect, this respect for the person. From these two sets of values emerge, from a practical point of view, the principle that there exist a certain number of rules of law transposing these values onto the economic and juridical plane, rules of law superior to the will of any leader and which alone found the authority of the State and at the same time limit it. These rules are not derived either from the State or from the individual, but from the values that we have just affirmed. The State is the guardian and not the creator of law. It is, therefore, necessary in all civilized societies that certain fundamental juridical principles should be affirmed that define the state of civilization that the national community has come to at any given moment. This is what the declarations of the rights of man did in the past. This, we believe, needs to be done anew in our work for tomorrow. The France that comes out of the war ought to be defined by a new declaration of rights adapted to current sociological insights and developed in its economic and social consequences. This declaration of rights will be a true confession of faith; it will serve to define the national community. It will be necessary to adhere to it, if not to be a citizen, at least in order to play a role in it as someone who helps direct the life of the country, for the Republic can no longer tolerate the highest administrative, economic, or military posts being held in the hands of men who only think about undermining its principles and institutions. These fundamental rights whose negation can no longer be tolerated in France, are the rights of every man with respect to his physical existence, with respect to the integrity of his person, and his thoughts, it is the right to come and go freely in the country, the right to gather and associate, the right of each to freely choose his destiny, his place of work, of establishing his family home, it is the right of the worker to trade union freedoms and to an ever increasing participation in the administration of the country's economic life. It is, finally, the principle of juridical equality for all. In the eyes of the law, there does not exist any race, or any who are the elect, or any who have been forgotten; if they are not equal with respect to their talents, or different because of their jobs, still all men remain equal in their right to have access to the law, no matter what their aptitudes, their positions, or their jobs.

Democracy

How are we to realize these fundamental legal principles? There is, actually, only one way, namely, democracy. Every regime based on personal power, as long experience has shown and has been abundantly proven by our current submission to one, quickly succeeds in negating the value of the person, and destroying all fundamental rights. There exist, moreover, only two ways of governing: persuading men that one is right, or breaking their heads. The second, without doubt, is easier and faster, but also in the long run it is the less durable and the less effective. If one believes that political authority has the function of giving direction to free men, it belongs to these free men and to them alone to choose who will give them direction. Universal suffrage, as with respect for the person, and as with the affirmation of fundamental rights, is, therefore, a given necessity for our modern civilization. The France of tomorrow, the Fourth Republic, will be a democracy based on universal suffrage, and this time it will be general, including both men and women.

Here an observation is necessary because we have lost sight of it in the past: it is that universal suffrage is the only means of letting the general will be known. The general will is not expressed just by the majority, but at the same time by the majority and the minority, by the government, and by the opposition. There have to be heretics; the opposition has a salutary function that is necessary and creative; such is the great lesson that we have learned from our Anglo-Saxon friends and, in particular, from British democracy. The opposition needs to be recognized. It always has the right to exist, to frankly express its criticisms from the interior of the nation or through a movement, and to seek by persuasion to bring its point of view to prevail and one day to become the majority. On the other hand, the majority has the right to govern, to make decisions, and to enforce them without the opposition ever seeking to hinder them, either by changing their needed, constructive criticisms that are part of internal debate, into personal attacks against individuals or by actions that come from ulterior motives. I insist on this point because it is very clearly there that we have sinned in the past. We have often tried to bring together political democracy and an authoritative morality. One cannot have a democracy in doing that, and one only will fatally succeed in bringing about absolutism of a single leader or a party if one believes oneself capable of reaching the total truth and then imposing it on others. We have too often oscillated between a totalitarian fanaticism of the truth and skepticism that has been disabused of that possibility and that then cynically manages to have the same attitude. A democracy can only go forward if it is founded on a vocational morality. Each side needs to understand that no one ever possesses the truth, but if one seeks it with a lot of perseverance, love, and humility, then, sometimes, one can be possessed by the truth. It is a question therefore of each individual or group making itself aware of its particular calling, while being obstinately faithful in respecting the callings of other men which are obviously different than our own.

The Present Situation

In sum, where is France now? Abandoned by its ruling classes, betrayed by the phony government of Vichy, the people of France are recovering on their own, and now find themselves in a new situation. The past has been blown apart. The former parties have for the most part disappeared. The former organizations are destroyed. One can no longer discuss political or economic problems in the same terms or on the same bases as before. Certain of those who used to deny liberty in the old days have become faithful to it when they have argued concretely what it means to live in slavery; others who used to have the word "democracy" in their mouths all the time have proved that they did not mean it because they were not ready to die for it.

It is necessary that our American friends and our compatriots who left the country soon after the armistice understand this. It is not now a question of continuing the past, nor of returning to an epoch before the deluge. France is a dead nation, killed by an assassin. It has descended into hell, yet in the third year of the war, the dead have begun to come to life. This resurrection, which pools together in the breast of the Free French the unanimity of our people, comes about by a number of clear and elementary ideas. That is the sole intention for France re-entering the war, of liberating its territory, of reconquering ourselves, by our efforts and our sacrifices, our lost liberties; it is the will to restore a democracy of integrity, yet one renewed.

It is on these bases that the internal resistance has been raised. It is on these bases that the concord has been realized between captive France and free France, in the unity of action by the Free French under the inspiration and direction of General de Gaulle.

What is therefore actually the function of the Free French and its National Committee which directs its deliberations?

The Function of the Free French

1. It is above all and before all the liberation of the French territory and its re-entry into the war. The Free French need to be present everywhere where the struggle goes on. The Free French need to be present everywhere where a colonial or metropolitan territory has been liber-

ated in order to assure it right away of an administration, realizing there a general mobilization, and assuring its re-entry into the struggle with all its forces, both military and economic. Let us clear up a common suspicion by saying that the Free French is not a volunteer army; it is the reuniting of all those who, inside and outside France, consider the armistice null and void and, who, recognized the authority of the laws of the Republic, carry out in that army the order for a general mobilization which is always in force.

2. But the Free French is not only a military movement or an administrative organization. It is the depository of these essential values of French civilization, denied by Hitler, prostituted by Vichy, of which all of us have today acquired a profound understanding, no matter what our former social and political ideas might have been.

The role of the Free French is to express these values, to make the voice of our country heard from now on among the nations, to participate everywhere in the discussion of the post-war organizational issues, to begin from here on, side by side with our allies, to think about the future.

3. At the moment of the definitive liberation of French territory, the role of the Free French will be to assure the provisory administration of the country so that all the liberties that have been denied to us; having been, during this sad and difficult time, the trustee of the materials and spiritual values of the nation, it will then hand back intact this patrimony into the hands of the Constitutional National Assembly that the people of France will have elected as sovereign.

What will happen after that, we do not know. Perhaps those who up to now have found themselves united will go their own ways, according to their political and social affinities, defending the form which appears to each of them the most desirable for realizing national values. Perhaps we will see then that the present problems are entirely different than those of the past, that unthought-of groupings can come about, that old adversaries might find themselves neighbors, and that we will, at least for a certain time, agree on a common agenda. In any case, whether we remain united or whether we go our own ways, what is to be hoped is that what we struggled for in common, that all the risks that we ran, all the sufferings we consented to together, elbow to elbow, will have served to create among all the combatants, whether of the Free French or those in captive France, a friendship capable of purifying the political atmo-

sphere, and of truly creating the necessary spiritual bases for the functioning of a renewed democracy.

Translated by Eric O. Springsted

Contributors

Robert Chenavier is the president of l'Association pour l'étude de la pensée de Simone Weil, and editor of *Cahiers Simone Weil* as well as serving as the editor of the *Oeuvres complètes* of Simone Weil being published by Gallimard. A much in demand speaker on matters relating to Simone Weil, he is the author and editor of five books, including *Simone Weil: Une philosophie de travail* (Paris, éd. du Cerf, 2001), *Simone Weil, l'attention au réel* (Paris, éd. Michalon, 2009) translated as *Simone Weil: Attention to the Real* (Notre Dame, IN: University of Notre Dame Press, 2012), and most recently *Simone Weil, une Juive antisémite? Éteindre les polémiques* (Paris, éd. Gallimard, 2021).

Ronald Collins is the editor of *Attention*, an online journal on the life and legacy of Simone Weil. He is the Lewes Public Library's Distinguished Lecturer and formerly the Harold S. Shefelman Scholar at the University of Washington School of Law. His writings on Weil have appeared in *Simone Weil's Philosophy of Culture: Readings Toward a Divine Humanity* (R. Bell, ed., Cambridge University Press, 1993), *Cahiers Simone Weil*, the *Washington Post*, *Epoché Magazine*, and in the *Los Angeles Review of Books*. He is the author of *The Death of Discourse* (3rd ed., 2022). His next book is *Tragedy on Trial* (2023), a book on the 1955 Emmett Till murder trial and its aftermath.

Julie Daigle received a Ph.D. in political science, with a specialization in political thought, from the University of Ottawa. She is currently a post-doctoral fellow at Concordia University's Department of Political Science. She is the co-editor (with Sophie Bourgault) of *Simone Weil, Beyond Ideology?* (2020).

Emmanuel Gabellieri is Professor Agrégé, HDR at the Faculty of Philosophy of the Catholic University of Lyon, where he was Dean from 2005 to 2014 and Vice-Rector for Research from 2016 to 2021. He is a member of the UR Confluence Sciences & Humanités (EA 1598) and of the Académie catholique de France. He edited the *Cahier de L'Herne* «Simone Weil» (with Fr. L'Yvonnet) (Paris, Ed. de l'Herne, 2014). He is the author of *Etre et Don. S.Weil et la philosophie* («Bibliothèque philosophique de Louvain» n°57, Peeters, 2003); *Blondel et la philosophie française. 1880–1950* (with P. de Cointet) (Parole et Silence, 2007); *Penser le travail avec Simone Weil* (Paris, Nouvelle Cité, 2017); and, most recently, *Le phénomène et l'entre-deux. Essai pour une metaxologie*, (Paris Hermann, 2019). He is currently preparing *Etre et Grace. Simone Weil et le christianisme* (Paris: Cerf, 2022).

Simone Kotva is Research Fellow at the Faculty of Theology, University of Oslo, and an Affiliated Lecturer at the Faculty of Divinity, University of Cambridge. She is the author of *Effort and Grace: On the Spiritual Exercise of Philosophy* (London: Bloomsbury, 2020), the first book in English to situate Weil's thought within the history of French reflexive or spiritualist philosophy, from Maine de Biran to Henri Bergson and Alain (Émile Chartier). Simone has published widely on philosophy as a spiritual exercise and way of life, and her work is a critical intervention seeking to rethink the legacy of Pierre Hadot and Michel Foucault by engaging feminist, decolonial, and ecological theologies of practice. She is currently completing a book on agency and passiveness, *Ecologies of Ecstasy: Practicing Philosophy through Mystical and Vegetal Being*.

Lissa McCullough is the author of *The Religious Philosophy of Simone Weil* (London: I.B. Tauris/Bloomsbury, 2014) and editor of the *Bloomsbury Handbook of Simone Weil* (forthcoming in 2024). She is a lecturer in the Philosophy Department at California State University, Dominguez Hills, Los Angeles.

Lawrence E. Schmidt is professor emeritus in the Center for the Study of Religion at the University of Toronto. He was the editor of *George Grant in Process* (1978), and his interest in the thought of Grant led him to become active in the American Weil Society. He has published many articles on Simone Weil: "Simone Weil on Religion: A Voegelinian Critique," "George Grant on Simone Weil: The Saint and the Thinker," and "Simone Weil's Analysis of Modern Science as the Basis of Her Critique of the Technological Society." His 2008 monograph, *The End of Ethics in the Technological Society* (written with Scott Marratto), explains the ethical background as to the recent environmental and economic crises. He is married to Brigitte Hutter Schmidt and has four adult children and four grandchildren.

Eric O. Springsted has spent a career as a scholar, teacher, and pastor. Co-founder of the American Weil Society, he was its president for thirty-three years. He is the author, editor, and translator of thirteen books, including several on Simone Weil. Most recently, these include *Simone Weil for the Twenty-First Century* (Notre Dame: University of Notre Dame Press, 2021) and, as editor and translator, *Simone Weil: Late Philosophical Works* (Notre Dame: University of Notre Dame Press, 2015). He is on the board of the online journal *Attention* and writes frequently for it, and an associate editor of *Philosophical Investigations*. He is currently working on a book, *Having an Inner Life*. He lives in Santa Fe, New Mexico.

Mario von der Ruhr is *Honorary Senior Lecturer in Philosophy* at Swansea University (UK), Editor of the journal *Philosophical Investigations*, honorary member of the *British Wittgenstein Society*, and advisory board member of the (online) Weil journal *Attention*. He has research interests in Simone Weil, Ludwig Wittgenstein, moral philosophy, philosophical anthropology, and philosophy and literature. His books include *Simone Weil: An Apprenticeship in Attention* (London: Continuum, 2006).

Bibliography

The works of Simone Weil are listed under "Abbreviations" at the front of this volume.

Cited Works and Select Bibliography

Allen, Diogenes. "The Concept of Reading and the Book of Nature." In *Simone Weil's Philosophy of Culture: Reading Toward a Divine Humanity*. Edited by Richard H. Bell. New York: Cambridge University Press, 1993.

Allen, Diogenes, and Springsted, Eric O. *Spirit, Nature, and Community: Issues in the Thought of Simone Weil*. Albany, NY: State University of New York Press, 1994.

Andrew, Edward. "Simone Weil on the Injustice of Rights-Based Doctrines." *Review of Politics* 48, no. 1 (Winter 1986): 60–91.

Avery, Desmond. *Beyond Power: Simone Weil and the Notion of Authority*. Lanham, MD: Lexington Books, 2008.

Bauman, Zygmunt. *Modernity and the Holocaust*. Ithaca, NY: Cornell University Press, 1991.

_____. *Postmodern Ethics*. Oxford: Blackwell, 1993.

Bell, Richard H., ed. *Simone Weil's Philosophy of Culture: Readings Toward a Divine Humanity*. New York: Cambridge University Press, 1993.

Bell, Richard H. *Simone Weil: The Way of Justice as Compassion*. Lanham, MD: Rowman & Littlefield Publishers, 1998.

_____. "Simone Weil on Rights, Justice, and Love." In *Simone Weil's Philosophy of Culture: Readings Toward a Divine Humanity*. Edited by Richard H. Bell. New York: Cambridge University Press, 1993.

Benedict XVI. *Saved in Hope*. San Francisco: Ignatius Press, 2008.

Bergson, Henri. *Matter and Memory*. Translated by N. M. Paul and W. S. Palmer. New York: Zone Books, 1990. First published in 1896.

Blondel, Maurice. *Action: Essay on a Critique of Life and a Science of Practice*. Translated by Oliva Blanchette. Notre Dame, IN: Notre Dame University Press, 1984. First published in 1893.

Blum, Lawrence A., and Victor J. Seidler. *A Truer Liberty: Simone Weil and Marxism*. New York: Routledge, 1989.

Bourgault, Sophie, and Julie Daigle, eds. *Simone Weil, Beyond Ideology?* Cham: Palgrave MacMillan, 2020.

Burns, Steven. "Justice and Impersonality: Simone Weil on Rights and Obligations." *Laval théologique et philosophique* 49, no. 3 (1993): 477–86.

Burton, Richard. *Holy Blood, Holy Tears: Women, Catholicism and the Culture of Suffering in France, 1840–1970*, 133–47. Ithaca: Cornell University Press, 2004.

Calder, James. *Labour and Thought in the Philosophy of Simone Weil: Preface to a Philosophy of Education*, 157. Ph.D. thesis, Dalhousie University, 1985.

Casey, Edward. *The Fate of Place: A Philosophical History*. Berkeley: University of California Press, 1997.

Chenavier, Robert. *Une philosophie du travail*. Paris: Cerf, 2001.

_____. *Simone Weil, une Juive antisémite?: Eteindre les Polémiques*. Paris: Gallimard, 2021.

_____. "*Se Mettre dans la troisiéme Dimension: Une théorie du transfert chez Simone Weil*." In *Simone Weil: Réception et transposition*. Edited by Robert Chenavier and Thomas Pavel. Paris: Classiques Garnier, 2019.

Collins, Ronald K. L. "A Detailed Listing of Topics Contained in Parts II and III of *The Need for Roots*." *Attention* (August 2021). https://attentions.org/a-detailed-listing-of-topics-contained-in-parts-ii-and-iii-of-the-need-for-roots/.

Collins, Ronald K. L., and Finn Nielsen. "The Spirit of Simone Weil's Law." In *Simone Weil's Philosophy of Culture: Readings Toward a Di-*

vine Humanity. Edited by Richard H. Bell, 235–59. New York: Cambridge University Press, 1993.

Courtois, Stéphane. "Les intellectuels et l'antifascisme." In *Le Front populaire.* Edited by Jean-Pierre Rioux. Paris: Tallandier, 2006.

Daigle, Julie. "Thoughts on a Weilian Republicanism." In *Simone Weil, Beyond Ideology?* Edited by Sophie Bourgault and Julie Daigle, 227–52. Cham: Palgrave MacMillan, 2020.

David, Pascal. *Simone Weil, Luttons-nous pour la justice? Manuel d'action politique.* Lyon: Peuple Libre, 2017.

_____. *Un art de vivre par temps de catastrophe.* Valence: Peuple Libre, 2020.

Davis, Benjamin P. "The Colonial Frame: Judith Butler and Simone Weil on Force and Grief." In *Simone Weil, Beyond Ideology?* Edited by Sophie Bourgault and Julie Daigle, 125–42. Cham: Palgrave MacMillan, 2020.

Delsol, Chantal, ed. *Simone Weil, Les Cahiers d'Histoire de la Philosophie.* Paris: Cerf, 2009.

Devaux, André-A. "Présence de Descartes dans la vie et dans l'œuvre de Simone Weil." *Cahiers Simone Weil* 18, no. 1 (1995): 1–23.

Diamond, Cora. *The Realistic Spirit.* London: MIT Press, 1991.

_____. "Martha Nussbaum and the Need for Novels." In *Philosophical Investigations* 16, no. 2 (1993): 141.

Dietz, Mary G. *Between the Human and the Divine: The Political Thought of Simone Weil,* 149–95. Totowa, NJ: Rowman & Littlefield, 1988.

Doering, E. Jane. *Simone Weil and the Specter of Self-Perpetuating Force.* Notre Dame, IN: University of Notre Dame Press, 2010.

Dujardin, Philippe. *Idéologie et politique.* Grenoble: Presses Universitaires Grenoble, 1975.

Dunaway, John M. "Estrangement and the *Need for Roots*: Prophetic Visions of the Human Condition in Albert Camus and Simone Weil." *Religion & Literature* 17, no. 2 (Summer 1985): 35–42.

Eliot, T. S. "Preface." In *The Need for Roots,* by Simone Weil. Translated by Arthur Wills, vii–xiv. New York: Routledge, 2002.

Evans, Christine. *The French Historical Narrative and the Fall of France: Simone Weil and Her Contemporaries Face the Debacle.* Lanham, MD: Lexington Books, 2022.

_____. "The Nature of Narrative in Simone Weil's Vision of History: The Need for New Historical Roots." In *The Beauty that Saves: Essays* on *Aesthetics and Language in Simone Weil*. Edited by John M. Dunaway and Eric O. Springsted, 55–68. Macon, GA: Mercer University Press, 1996.

―――――. "La débâcle vue pas Simone Weil et ses contemporains." *Cahiers Simone Weil* 34, no. 2 (juin 2011): 167–82.

Farron-Landry, Béatrice-Clémentine. "Lecture et non-lecture chez Simone Weil." *Cahiers Simone Weil* 3, no. 4 (1980): 225–44.

Fiori, Gabriella. *Simone Weil: An Intellectual Biography*. Translated by Joseph R. Berrigan, 255–99. Athens, GA: University of Georgia Press, 1989.

Ford, Casey. "Captured Time: Simone Weil's Vital Temporality Against the State." In *Simone Weil: Beyond Ideology?* Edited by Sophie Bourgault and Julie Daigle, 161–84. Cham: Palgrave MacMillan, 2020.

Foucault, Michel. *Dits et Écrits II*. Paris: Gallimard, 2001.

―――――. *Sécurité, Territoire, Population*. Paris: Seuil-Gallimard, 2004.

Fraisse, Simone. "Simone Weil, la personne et les droits de l'homme." *Cahiers Simone Weil* 7, no. 2 (juin 1984): 120–32.

Gabellieri, Emmanuel. *Etre et Don: Simone.Weil et la philosophie*. Louvain, Paris: Bibliothèque philosophique de Louvain, Peeters, 2003.

―――――. *Le phénoméne et l'entre-deux: Pour une metaxologie*. Paris: Hermann, 2019.

―――――. "Simone Weil Between Paganism and the Bible: A Hermeneutic Dialogue with Ricoeur, Lévinas, Schelling and Pascal." In *Between the Human and the Divine, Philosophical and Theological Hermeneutics*. Edited by Andrzej Wiercinski, 456–70. Toronto: Hermeneutic Press, 2002.

―――――. "Judaïsme et querelle des Alliances." *Cahier de L'Herne Simone Weil*, 358–69. Paris: L'Herne, 2014.

―――――. "Vie publique et *vita activa*: S.Weil et H.Arendt." *Cahiers Simone Weil* 22, no. 2 (1999): 135–52.

―――――. "'Action' et 'Inspiration' un double fondement du politique ?" in "Amor mundi, Amor Dei. Simone Weil et Hannah Arendt." *Théophilyon*, 9, no. 2, (2004), 559–79.

―――――. "La double 'profession de foi' de Londres de Simone Weil á J.J. Rousseau et retour." *Cahiers Simone Weil* 44, no. 4 (décembre 2021): 435–64.

Gaita, Raimond. *Good and Evil: An Absolute Conception*. London: Macmillan, 1991.

Garnsey, Peter. *Ideas of Slavery from Aristotle to Augustine*. Cambridge: Cambridge University Press, 1996.

Gilbert, Bennet. "Simone Weil's Philosophy of History." *Journal of the Philosophy of History* 13 (2019).

Harle, Vilho. *Ideas of Social Order in the Ancient World*. Westport, CT: Greenwood Press, 1998.

Hauerwas, Stanley. "How to Think Theologically About Rights." In *Journal of Law and Religion* 30, no. 3 (Oct 2015): 402. Reprinted in Stanley Hauerwas, *The Work of Theology*, 191–207. Grand Rapids: Wm. B. Eerdmans, 2015.

Howell, Ronald. "The Philosopher Alain and French Classical Radicalism." *The Western Political Quarterly* 18, no. 3 (1965): 594–614.

Hughes, John. *End of Work: Theological Critique of Capitalism*. Oxford: Blackwell, 2007.

Irwin, Alexander. *Saints of the Impossible: Bataille, Weil, and the Politics of the Sacred*. Minneapolis: MN: University of Minnesota Press, 2002.

John of the Cross. *Collected Works*. Edited and translated by Kieran Kavanaugh and Otilio Rodriguez. Washington, DC: Institute of Carmelite Studies, 1991.

Kahn, Gilbert. "Simone Weil et Alain." *Cahiers Simone Weil* 14, no. 3 (1991): 206–12.

_____. "Simone Weil et le stoïcisme grec." *Cahier Simone Weil* 5, no. 4 (1982): 270–84.

Kant, Immanuel. *Groundwork for the Metaphysics of Morals*. 3rd ed. Translated by James W. Ellington. Indianapolis, IN: Hackett Publishing, 1993.

_____. *The Critique of Judgment*. Translated by James Creed Meredith. Oxford: Oxford University Press, 1952.

Kershaw, Ian. *Hitler, 1989–1936: Hubris*. London: Allen Lane, Penguin Press, 1998.

King, J. H. "Simone Weil and the Identity of France." *Journal of European Thought* 6 (1976): 125–48.

Koli, Lyra. "Hungry for Beauty: Simone Weil's Inversion of Kant's Aesthetics." https://www.academia.edu/35344582/Hungry_for_Beauty_Simone_Weils_Inversion_of_Kants_Aesthetics.

Kotva, Simone. *Effort and Grace: On the Spiritual Exercise of Philosophy*. London: Bloomsbury, 2020.

Kühn, Rolf. "Le monde comme texte." *Revue des sciences philosophiques et théologiques* (October 1980).

Kuhn, Thomas. *The Structure of Scientific Revolutions*. 2nd ed. Chicago: University of Chicago Press, 1986.

La Boétie, Etienne de. *The Politics of Obedience: The Discourse of Voluntary Servitude*. Introduction by Murray N. Rothbard. Translated by Harry Kurz. Auburn, Alabama: The Mises Institute, 1975.

Lagneau, Jules. Écrits de Jules Lagneau réunis par soins de ses disciples. Paris: Sandre, 2006.

Leibniz, Gottfried Wilhelm. *Theodicy*. Edited by Diogenes Allen. Translated by E. M. Huggard. Indianapolis, IN: Library of Liberal Arts, 1966.

Little, J. P. *Simone Weil: Waiting for Truth*. New York: Berg, 1988.

————. "Weil's Single-Minded Commitment to Truth: A Q & A Interview with J. P. Little." *Attention*, no. 2. https://attentionsw.org/weils-single-minded-commitment-to-truth-a-q-a-interview-with-j-p-little/.

————. "Society as Mediator in Simone Weil's 'Venise Sauvée.'" *The Modern Language Review* 65, no. 2 (1970).

Lukacs, John. *The Hitler of History*. New York: Alfred A. Knopf, 1997.

Macdonald, Dwight. "A Formula to Give a War-Torn Society Fresh Roots." *New York Review of Books* (July 6, 1952), 6.

Maritain, Jacques. *Les Droits de l'homme et la loi naturelle*. New York: Maison Française, 1942.

————. "The Natural Law: An Inquiry into Its Relationship with the Rights of the Human Person." *Commonweal* (May 15, 1942). https://www.commonwealmagazine.org/natural-law-0.

Martins, Alexandre. "Simone Weil's Radical Ontology of Rootedness: Natural and Supernatural Justices." *Praxis: An Interdisciplinary Journal of Faith and Justice* 2, no. 1 (2019): 23–35.

McCullough, Lissa. *The Religious Philosophy of Simone Weil: An Introduction*. London: I. B. Tauris, 2014.

————. "Simone Weil's Phenomenology of the Body." *Comparative and Continental Philosophy* 4, no. 2 (November 2012): 195–218.

McLellan, David. *Utopian Pessimist: The Life and Thought of Simone Weil*. New York: Poseidon Press, 1990.

McNally, David. *Blood and Money: War, Slavery, Finance, and Empire*. Chicago: Haymarket, 2020.

Meilassoux, Quentin. *After Finitude: An Essay on the Necessity of Contingency*. Translated by Ray Brassier. London: Continuum, 2008.

Miegge, Mario. *Vocation et travail: Essai sur l'éthique puritaine*. Geneva: Labor et Fides, 1989.

Montesquieu, Charles de. *Considerations on the Causes of the Greatness of the Romans and Their Decline*. Edited and translated by David Lowenthal. Indianapolis, IN: Hackett Publishing Co., 1999.

Morgan, Vance G. *Weaving the World: Simone Weil on Science, Mathematics, and Love*. Notre Dame, IN: University of Notre Dame Press, 2005.

Moulakis, Athanasios. *Simone Weil and the Politics of Self-Denial*. Translated by Ruth Hein. Columbia, MO: University of Missouri Press, 1998.

Mumford, Lewis. *The Transformations of Man*. New York: Harper and Row, 1956.

————. *Technics and Civilization*. New York: Harcourt, Brace, and World, 1934; reprint, 1963.

O'Brien, Conor Cruise. "Patriotism and *The Need for Roots*: The Anti-Politics of Simone Weil." *The New York Review of Books* 24, no. 8 (1997): 23–28. Reprinted in *Simone Weil: Interpretations of a Life*. Edited by George White, 95–110. Amherst, MA: University of Massachusetts Press.

Pascal, Blaise. *Pensées*, in Œuvres complètes. Paris: Seuil, 1963.

Peer, Shanny. *France on Display: Peasants, Provincials and Folklore in the 1937 Paris World's Fair*. Albany, NY: State University of New York Press, 1998.

Pétrement, Simone. *Simone Weil*. Translated by Raymond Rosenthal. New York: Schocken Books, 1976.

Pierce, Roy. "Sociology and Utopia: The Early Writings of Simone Weil." *Political Science Quarterly* 77, no. 4 (1962): 505–25.

Plant, Stephen. "Nationhood and Roots: Dostoyevsky and Weil on National Culture and Europe." *Religion, State & Society* 26, nos. 3/4, (1998): 279–89.

————. *Simone Weil: A Brief Introduction*. Maryknoll, NY: Orbis Books, 1996/2007.

Plato. *The Collected Works of Plato*. Edited by Huntington Cairns and Edith Hamilton. Princeton, NJ: Princeton University Press, 1961.

Quintana, Oriel. "The Politics of Rootedness: On Simone Weil and George Orwell." In *Simone Weil, Beyond Ideology?* Edited by Sophie Bourgault and Julie Daigle, 103–24. Cham, NY: Palgrave/Macmillan, 2020.

Radzins, Inese. "Simone Weil's 'Need for Roots.'" In *Empire and Christian Tradition: New Readings of Classical Theologians.* Edited by Pui-lan Kwok, Don H. Compier, and Joerg Rieger, chapter 28. Minneapolis, MN: Fortress Press, 2007.

Ravaisson, Félix. *Rapport sur la philosophie en France au XIXème siècle.* Paris: Fayard, 1984. First published in 1867.

Remer, Scott. "A Radical Cure: Hannah Arendt & Simone Weil on the *Need for Roots.*" *Philosophy Now* 127 (Aug./Sept. 2018): 16–19.

Restall, Matthew. *When Montezuma Met Cortés: The True Story of the Meeting that Changed History.* New York: Ecco, 2018.

Rhees, Rush. *Discussions of Simone Weil.* Edited by D. Z. Phillips. Assisted by Mario von der Ruhr. New York: SUNY Press, 2000.

Rioux, Jean-Pierre. "Repères chronologiques." In *Le Front populaire.* Paris: Tallandier, 2006.

Ritner, Scott. "The Training of the Soul." In *Simone Weil and Continental Philosophy.* Edited by A. Rebecca Rozelle-Stone, 198–99. Lanham, MD: Rowman & Littlefield, 2017.

Rolland, Patrice. "Avant Propos" à L'Enracinement. *Oeuvres completes.* V.2 11–45. Paris: Gallimard, 2013.

Rozelle-Stone, Rebecca. "Simone Weil, Sara Ahmed, and a Politics of Hap." In *Simone Weil, Beyond Ideology?* Edited by Sophie Bourgault and Julie Daigle, 61–81. Cham: Palgrave MacMillan, 2020.

Rozelle-Stone, A. Rebecca, & Benjamin P. Davis. "Simone Weil: Social-Political Philosophy." *The Stanford Encyclopedia of Philosophy* (Summer 2022 ed.). https://plato.stanford.edu/cgi-bin/encyclopedia /archinfo.cgi?entry=simone-weil.

Schmidt, Lawrence. "The Language of Limitation as the Key to Simone Weil's Understanding of Beauty and Justice." *Attention,* no. 2 (April 18, 2021). https://attentionsw.org/the-language-of-limitation-as-the-key-to-simone-weils-understanding-of-beauty-and-justice/.

Schramm, Percy Ernst. *Hitler: The Man and Military Leader.* Chicago: Quadrangle Books.

Schumann, Maurice. "Henri Bergson et Simone Weil." *Revue des deux mondes* (November 1993): 194–203.

Seaford, Richard. *Money and the Early Greek Mind: Homer, Philosophy, Tragedy*. Cambridge: Cambridge University Press, 2004.

Searle, John. *Making the Social World: The Structure of Human Civilization*. Oxford: Oxford University Press.

Simeoni, Francesca. "Qu'en est-il de Platon à Londres? Traces platoniciennes dans la psychagogie politique de l'impersonnel." *Cahiers Simone Weil* 44, no. 2 (juin 2021): 129–55.

Simms, Luma. "Immigration and the Desire for Rootedness." *Public Discourse* (July 22, 2019).

————. "Rootedness and National Identity in the Twenty-First Century." In *Polis, Nation, Global Community: The Philosophic Foundations of Citizenship*. New York: Routledge, 2022.

Sontag, Susan. "Simone Weil." *The New York Review of Books* (February 1, 1963).

Springsted, Eric O. *Simone Weil for the Twenty-First Century*. Notre Dame, IN: University of Notre Dame Press, 2021.

————. "Rootedness: Culture and Value." In *Simone Weil's Philosophy of Culture: Readings Toward a Divine Humanity*. Edited by Richard H. Bell, 161–88. New York: Cambridge University Press, 1993. Reprinted in *Spirit, Nature and Community*. Diogenes Allen and Eric O. Springsted, 171–96. New York: SUNY Press, 1994.

————. "The Challenges of Translating Simone Weil's Philosophical Works with an Eye on *The Need for Roots*." *Attention* (May 2022). https://attentionsw.org/the-challenges-of-translating-simone-weils-philosophical-works-with-an-eye-on-the-need-for-roots%EF%BF%BC/.

————. "The Need for Order and the Need for Roots: To Being Through History." In *Simone Weil for the Twenty-First Century*. Edited by Eric O. Springsted, 159–74. Notre Dame, IN: University of Notre Dame Press, 2021.

————. "The Religious Basis of Culture: T. S. Eliot and Simone Weil." *Religious Studies* 25, no. 1 (March 1989): 105–16.

————. "Divine Necessity: Weilian and Platonic Conceptions." In *Spirit, Nature, and Community: Issues in the Thought of Simone Weil*. Edited by Diogenes Allen and Eric O. Springsted, 33–52. Albany, NY: State University of New York Press, 1994.

Steffens, Martin. "*Les Besoins de l'âme—extrait de l'Enracinement*". Barcelona: Folioplus—philosophie, 2007.

Stonebridge, Lyndsey. "Simone Weil's Uprooted." In *Placeless People: Writings, Rights and Refugees*. Edited by Stonebridge, 96–118. New York: Oxford University Press, 2018.

Taylor, Charles. "Why We Need a Radical Redefinition of Secularism." In *The Power of Religion in the Public Sphere*. Edited by E. Mendieta and J. van Antwerpen. New York: Columbia University Press, 2011.

Thibon, Gustav. *What Ails Mankind?: An Essay on Social Physiology*. Translated by Willard Sherman Hill. London: Sheed and Ward, 1949.

Tocqueville, Alexis de. *The Old Regime and the French Revolution*. 1856. Translated by Stuart Gilbert. New York: Doubleday, 1955.

Torigian, Michael. "The Occupation of the Factories: Paris 1936, Flint 1937." *Comparative Studies in Society and History* 41, no. 2 (1999): 324–47.

Vetö, Miklos. *The Religious Metaphysics of Simone Weil*. Translated Joan Dargan. Albany, NY: State University of New York Press, 1994.

————. "Uprootedness and Alienation in Simone Weil." *Blackfriars* 43, no. 507 (Sept. 1962): 383–95.

Vieillard-Baron, Jean-Louis. *Le spiritualisme français*. Paris: Cerf, 2021.

Vlassopoulos, Kostas. *Historicizing Ancient Slavery*. Edinburgh: Edinburgh University Press, 2021.

Von der Ruhr, Mario. *Simone Weil—An Apprenticeship in Attention*. London: Continuum, 2006.

————."Kant and the Language of Reason." In *Commonality and Particularity in Ethics*. Edited by Lilli Alanen, Sarah Heinämaa, and Thomas Wallgren, 384–400. Berlin: Springer, 1997.

Wampole, Christy. *Rootedness: The Ramifications of a Metaphor*. Chicago: University of Chicago Press, 2016.

White, George Abbot. "Simone Weil's Work Experiences: From Wigan Pier to Chrystie Street." *CrossCurrents* 31, no. 2 (1981): 129–62. Reprinted in *Simone Weil: Interpretations of a Life*. Edited by George Abbot White, 137–80. Amherst, MA: University of Massachusetts Press, 1981.

Winch, Peter. *Simone Weil: "The Just Balance."* Cambridge: Cambridge University Press, 1989.

Index of Subjects

Index of Names